Jeff,
I look forward
to changing the world
together!
Melissa Hull

MW00768213

Lessons from Neverland

By Melissa Hull Gallemore

Editor: Vivien Cooper

*Certain names and locations have been changed to protect the innocent from the guilty.

First published by Dog Ear Publishing
4011 Vincennes Rd
Indianapolis, IN 46268
www.dogearpublishing.net

ISBN: 978-1-4575-5238-0

This book is printed on acid-free paper.

This book is a work of fiction. Places, events, and situations in this book are purely fictional and any resemblance to actual persons, living or dead, is coincidental.

Printed in the United States of America

Foreword

Mama knows I'm right here, over the fence. She calls this place Neverland because they are all here too—Peter Pan, Captain Hook and Tinkerbell. Peter Pan always was my favorite.

Mama really wishes she could hug me but she can't anymore. At least I can hug her when she's sad. No one on Mama's side of the fence can come over here to visit me but I'm allowed to visit them. Sometimes I go over there and put my arms around her and it makes her stop crying. Sometimes she hugs a pillow and pretends it's me. I don't mind. I always loved to pretend. Whenever I talk to Mama, I know she can hear me. I talk to her all the time and she talks to me too.

They say I drowned but it wasn't like drowning at all. It wasn't dark and bottomless like being underwater. It was more like flying a kite. Now I'm the kite and it's really fun. Someday Mama and Daddy and Devin and Hopey will come here too but there's no way to tell time over here so I don't know when they will get here. Anyway, there's lots for me to do. And until everyone gets here to see me, I know I can keep visiting them and talking to them.

It's kind of funny how, on their side of the fence, there are so many rules. Mama used to let me break the rules and have ice cream and Bif Raviolays for breakfast. But the rules are still there. They're always there. Don't go outside without your clothes or your shoes. No TV when everyone is sleeping. Never wander too close to the water. But it's okay, Mama. I'm right here. And it wasn't like drowning, at all.

1

*C*hildhood taught me many conflicting things about life—things I found impossible to reconcile.

On the one hand, I recall my mother's gentle, nurturing, loving presence as we baked together in the kitchen of my childhood home, our hands in the cookie dough. I can still see myself at seven years old, wearing an apron that matched hers, and I can see my mom, Cheryl, like it was yesterday—tall, slender, beautiful and fair skinned with green eyes. She was the picture of elegance and grace and a true lady.

Being beside her in the kitchen, baking, made me very happy and contented and, in those special moments, I felt loved and nurtured. I also have memories of my mom brushing and curling my hair. She always took her time and was very tender with me.

In my favorite childhood memories of me and my dad, I was very little. I loved it when he would let me stand on his feet and hold on as he walked. Or sometimes he would lie on his back and I would stand on his hands and then he would put his feet up and I would transition to his feet. And I loved the times when he was driving with me on his lap, allowing me to help steer the car.

I also have a very fond memory of going fishing with my dad when I was about five years old. We were fishing in a big canal that ran through the center of town. (There were many canals in our town.) It was just the two of us in Daddy's little boat and I made a misstep and ended up falling into the water. He quickly jumped in after me, fished me out of the water and got me back up onto the banks of the canal.

After making sure I was okay, he said, "Let's pack up and go home now. And next time we go fishing, you'll have to be more careful!"

I could sense that my fall into the water had scared my father. Knowing I had this kind of impact on him was gratifying and made me feel loved. I thought to myself, *Okay, Daddy does love me.*

The fact that Daddy was worried about me was endearing. I didn't even mind that I was cold and wet as we drove home. I knew that my dad wasn't really angry with me. It was the first time I noticed the difference between him being truly angry with me and scolding me out of concern and I thought about that all the way home. My dad's hair-trigger temper always left me feeling uncertain and afraid. It was vaguely threatening and that undercurrent pervaded the entire household.

I grew up in a small rural town in the desert of the Southwest. My dad, Larry, grew up in the tiny town of Pinkney, Michigan as one of four children. There was his older sister, Claudia, his fraternal twin, Gary, and his younger sister, Judy. His home life was not particularly harmonious, given his mother's depression and his dad's heavy-handed, harsh punishments which tended to be disproportionate to the offense committed. Daddy had a difficult and strained relationship with his father and was closer to his mother. I only met Grandpa a handful of times before he passed away.

Daddy owned a plumbing contracting company and would spend long hours outside. In the heat of the day in the summertime, the temperatures would routinely climb to 118 or 120 degrees and the need to be finished working before the arrival of the scorching noonday heat would drive Daddy out of bed sometimes as early as three o'clock in the morning. He would creep through the house in the dark, getting dressed, and slip out the door long before the sun came up. While the rest of us slept, he would be getting his trucks and piping ready for the job site.

I rarely awoke in time to hear my dad getting ready for work. Usually, I got up in the morning knowing that he had already left for work. When I would hear him coming home around three o'clock in the afternoon, my ears would perk up. I could hardly contain my excitement to see him and I couldn't wait to give him a hug. I would jump up on him, shouting, "Daddy! Daddy!"

To have this little girl bubbling over with exuberance was too much for my dad, who was always tired, sweaty and hot from a long day on the job. He would push me off of him with the command, "Goddammit! Get off of me!" He never returned my embrace.

Why won't Daddy hug me? I wondered. I needed to be close to my dad and his constant rejection hurt me deeply. As an adult, I understand that he was always exhausted from work but all I knew as a child was that my dad didn't seem to want to be around me, a fact which I found profoundly confusing, disturbing and heartbreaking.

I always knew that I could approach my mom. She was the soft one. "Daddy's being mean to me!" I would cry.

Any time I went to her for an explanation of my dad's behavior, she would encourage and comfort me. "Sweetheart," she would say, "Daddy's very tired! He's been up since three in the morning. Be patient and give Daddy time to unwind from his day and he will come find you when he is ready."

I clung to the belief that Daddy just needed a cigarette and a cup of tea before he was ready to interact with me but my patience didn't change anything. Time after time, even after my dad had finished a smoke and had his tea, the most we would share would be a brief conversation. I never did get my hug. I adored my father and was starved for his affection but he was simply not going to hug me or show me any affection.

When my initial attempts to get my dad's attention would fail, I believed that maybe if I just tried harder, I would get a different result. So I pushed the envelope. Whenever my dad needed his space and I wouldn't back off, I would get rewarded for my efforts with a spanking that left me asking myself, *Why is Daddy always trying to get away from me? What is wrong with me?*

It was very difficult for me to understand him. The one constant I could always count on was his temper.

2

$\mathcal{M}$y sister Jennifer was two and a half years younger and had inherited Mom's calm, quiet personality and demeanor. Jennifer was more of an observer and not inclined to ask for affection from our dad. She would stand back a bit and watch things unfold. Later in life, she would share with me that she had vivid memories of watching my attempts to try to get close to our dad. She took note of how harsh Daddy was with me any time I tried to get him to talk to me or play with me or hold me. By watching Daddy react to me, Jennifer learned to back off. She didn't want to risk making an overture toward him, knowing she would likely receive the same chilly reception.

I never understood how she could be stoic when I couldn't seem to let Daddy go. He was my dad and I loved him and I didn't know how I was supposed to live without his attention and affection. At least Jennifer and I had each other. We spent a lot of time together, making mud pies in the outdoor kitchen Daddy built for us and picking corn or tomatoes for Mom from our garden.

When I was six years old and it was time for our little brother to be brought home from the hospital, Jennifer and I dressed up to meet him. We put ribbons in our hair and wore our best church dresses and waited breathlessly for him to be brought to his new home. We were so excited to have a little brother, we hardly knew what to do with ourselves.

I will never forget my mom placing him in my arms as I sat on the sofa. "This is your little brother," she said. "His name is Scott Brian Hull."

"No, Mommy," I said. "Not Scott. *Scottie!*" Those in my close, close family always called me Missy instead of Melissa, and it always made me feel special. I wanted Scott to have his own special name, too. To this day, I still call him Scottie.

Right away, Scottie was my dad's whole world. Every time Daddy would scoop up Scottie and hold him, I would wonder to myself, *Why does Daddy want to be close to my brother but not me? What's wrong with me?*

Thankfully, the start of kindergarten brought Mr. Culvert into my life and he quickly became the object of all the unwanted adoration and affection I was unable to lavish on my own dad. Thanks to Mr. Culvert, I fell instantly in love with school. He was nice, funny, warm and caring and I looked forward to going to school each day just to see him.

I would say that he took a real interest in me but the truth is that he had very little choice in the matter. I was very demanding of his time and attention, often bringing him flowers or cookies that Mom and I had baked together. Or I would make him something or draw him a picture and then bring it to school with me.

Mr. Culvert told me that I was smart and encouraged me to learn how to read. I would rush home with my kindergarten workbooks and put everything I had into completing my assignments. I knew that if I got an "A" on the assignment, Mr. Culvert would give me a sticker, an acknowledgment that gave me the best feeling in the world.

I looked to poor Mr. Culvert for everything I wasn't getting at home. He was a tall, thin man with brown hair and gray eyes. My dad was a tall, thin man with dark brown hair and intensely blue eyes—like Elvis Presley. Daddy was extremely handsome but he wasn't as kind or as warm as Mr. Culvert.

When I was six years old and seven, Jennifer and I shared a room. At bedtime, Mom used to put us in the same bed, snuggle up with us and read us a story. They were usually Disney stories like Cinderella or Snow White. She would be reading along, following the words on the page, and then she would take the story in a funny direction. "Cinderella was doing laundry but then a delivery man came and delivered some pipes—large plumbing pipes. So, after Cinderella was finished milking the goats, she put the pipes on the truck..." It was a nonsensical mishmash.

She had a habit of nodding off while reading to us and, as she started to drift, she would become very cute and silly. I would ask her, "Mom, how many fingers am I holding up?" And she would say something like, "I don't know. I stopped counting after a hundred."

Whenever Mom fell asleep next to us, she would awaken later and go back to her own bedroom. I loved having her in bed next to us and, when I would awaken to discover that she'd returned to her own room, I wandered into her room and tried to join her in bed. I was always trying to get close to my mom.

She never minded when I showed up in their room but Daddy was not a fan of this practice. I thought I might be out of the way if I just lay down on the floor of their room instead of trying to get into bed with them but that didn't make Daddy any happier. He wanted us girls to stay in our own room. He didn't want his children in bed with him and his wife or even in the same bedroom.

Any time I was sent back to my own bed, I always tried to crawl into bed with Jennifer, with whom I shared a room. She was so comforting to me and I liked being close to her and talking and giggling together. Sometimes she just wanted to sleep in her own bed by herself and she would try to wriggle away from me.

"No," I would say. "I have to sleep next to you!" I wouldn't let her go.

3

*A*s I was growing up, Mom regularly took us kids to church with her. Mom was a practicing Mormon and Daddy converted to Mormonism but wasn't a practicing church member and didn't regularly accompany us on Sundays.

Having a dad who wasn't active in the church made me different and people would say the oddest things to me. Out of the blue, someone would come up to me and say, "We're praying for you and your dad and your whole family!" I took that to mean that something was wrong with us, and we weren't quite "there" yet, whatever that was supposed to mean.

In the Mormon Church, eight years old is the age of accountability. We were taught that God understands that children under the age of eight are still learning to find their conscience and learning to listen to the still, small voice of the Holy Ghost. I knew the Holy Ghost and I knew the difference between good and bad, wrong and right. I knew how to listen to that still, small voice to know for certain whether I was making good choices.

When I came of age, I was interviewed by the Bishop. "Tell me, Melissa. Are you ready to be accountable for your life?"

"Yes! I'm ready!" I was filled with enthusiasm over my baptism.

Typically the father is the one to baptize the child and I loved the idea that Daddy and I would be sharing something so monumental. When I found out that he wouldn't be permitted to baptize me because he wasn't a practicing member of the church, I was so disappointed. I was one of the only girls at church whose father didn't follow the faith. My maternal uncle, Duane, would be doing the honors and I would have to content myself with the fact that my dad was present on this special occasion.

Wearing a long, flowing white dress, I entered the baptismal pool and waded to the center where Uncle Duane awaited me. He said a few words and asked me whether I was ready to take on this baptism and receive the Holy Ghost. I was filled with humility and I had the sense that my obedience was pleasing to God.

I responded with an enthusiastic "YES!"

After I emerged from the baptismal pool, dripping water, I was sent into a changing room and, when I came out wearing dry clothes, my family and I went into a private room. It thrilled me to have my entire family there along with the bishop—my parents and siblings as well as my aunt, uncle, cousins and grandparents.

A group of church elders, joined by my dad, surrounded me and began to pray. "Dear God, please bless Melissa with the ability to live a life of service, of compassion, and of love and to always rely upon this gift of baptism and your Holy Spirit which are now and forever a part of her life. Let her always seek the good and the righteous from this day forward..."

After the prayer, we gathered for some refreshments. Then we returned home for a special dinner prepared by Mom with the help of Grandma, a very petite, Irish-Scandinavian redhead with light green eyes. Having all this fuss made over me made me feel very special and deeply loved. It was the first time in my brief life that I had ever felt like a princess.

After dinner, Grandma presented me with a baptism gift—a CTR ring. The initials stood for "choose the right" and receiving this CTR ring was a rite of passage and my reminder to always remember the Holy Ghost and choose the right. The phrase hearkens from church song lyrics, "Choose the right when the right is there before you..."

I cherished my CTR ring and especially because it was a gift from Grandma. It was not a compass guiding me in the direction of right choices as much as it was a reflection of my true nature. I seemed to have been born seeking what is right in all things. I have an innate guidance system that is always prompting me with the question, *How do I make sure I am on the right side of decisions?* I have always endeavored to choose the right or moral option, the decent option, even if it invites the scorn or contempt of others. I would rather pay whatever price, including the disapproval of others, than live with the awareness that I failed to choose the right.

For my baptism, I also received my very first journal from my mother. Inside, she had attached a picture of herself and written a little testimony on the importance of choosing the right, living a righteous life and being kind. I treasured that journal and still have it to this day. Everything about my baptism was special and memorable and brought to me expressions of love from my family that I was desperately craving.

4

On December 5th, 1981, ten years after my own birth, Carrie was born. I was getting a little sister this time. When she made her debut at home, I asked my mom, "Can I really hold her?" Looking into her face, I thought she was the most beautiful, perfect baby I had ever seen. With her peaches and cream complexion, she was a little doll—and that's exactly how I treated her. She was my own personal baby doll.

The arrival of our brand new baby sister made for the most wonderful Christmas ever. Naturally, we had homemade Christmas cookies and fudge—a family tradition. All of us were very happy until the spring of 1982 when melanoma moved into our house with us.

It all started when Mom needed to see a doctor to have a mole removed. When Mom went to the doctor, the biopsy of the mole revealed that it was malignant and the cancer had migrated to the lymph nodes in her leg. The diagnosis was explained to us kids in this way, so as not to frighten us: "The mole on Mommy's leg was sick so the doctors took it off. Now, the doctors need to take off more of the sick skin so Mommy's leg will be all better."

The mole removal surgery was done locally but, after the biopsy, Mom was referred to doctors in California for a second surgery. She stayed there for a few weeks and then returned home. When she came home, I could see that her leg looked different—weird somehow. Unfortunately, even the drastic step of removing part of her calf had failed to keep the cancer from spreading. So it was back to California for more surgery.

It was summertime and, while Mom and Daddy awaited the lab work from the second surgery, I headed off to 4-H camp. While I was away, I didn't give Mom's health situation much thought until the day the camp director pulled me into the office. "Melissa, your dad is on his way to pick you up. You need to get your things together. Your mother isn't well."

I was pulled out of camp by my dad and taken to my grandparents' home in California. Up until then, I had no inkling that my mom's medical situation might be serious. Obviously, for my parents to pull me out of camp, something was seriously off.

Mom's second surgery had been scheduled and she wanted to see all of us kids and spend some time with us beforehand. So, while we were all in California, we visited the zoo and, for a special treat, stopped by Thrifty Drugstore for ice cream cones. (Thrifty's was known for their ice cream counter.) After we finished our ice cream cones, we went back to my grandparents' house and played cards.

Every effort was made to distract us kids from worry and ensure an enjoyable visit. None of us had any idea what was going on inside the mind or heart of our mother, as she faced the knife once again and tried to put on a pleasant face. For the most part, she managed to hide her anguish but I did see her get teary from time to time.

At one point over those few days, she pulled me aside and said, "Honey, I'm going to have another surgery and I am going to have to stay here with Grandma while I get better. I need you to go home with Daddy and help him take care of Scottie and Jennifer. Carrie is too little to go home with you, so she will stay here where Grandma and Grandpa can look after her."

I tried to reassure my mom, promising that I would help Daddy, but her distress frightened me and made me uneasy. So, even as I was trying to console her, I was crying. I didn't want to leave her behind at Grandma and Grandpa's. I couldn't help but think, *What if I never see her again?*

Grandpa called the Mormon bishop and had him come to their house to give mom a patriarchal blessing. I was very reassured by the presence of the bishop. As I stood back and watched him anoint Mom with oil, I silently prayed, *Dear God, please take care of my mom!* I had complete trust that the oil anointing combined with the Bishop's blessing would protect my mom's body, and I thought, *Okay, good. Mom's going to be okay now.*

As Mom went through her surgery, we all waited on pins and needles at Grandma and Grandpa's house. Afterwards, Daddy took us to the hospital to see Mom. Then it was time to say goodbye. I didn't want to say goodbye. Sure, I was deeply comforted and reassured by the bishop's blessing but Mom was the only one Jennifer and I could turn to with our problems. She mitigated Daddy's hurtfulness.

Daddy could be scary and both Jennifer and I were fearful of going to him when we needed someone. We loved him and always wanted him to love us back but we definitely feared his temper. Mom always acted as the buffer between us and Daddy's fury and now she was going to be all the way in California, recuperating. Not surprisingly, my sister was terrified over leaving Mom behind and I had an anxiety attack pretty much all the way home.

I kept asking myself, *How are we supposed to get by without her? And how are we supposed to live with only Daddy?*

5

*A*s Daddy drove us home, I was sitting in the backseat of our Volvo with Jennifer, who was very upset over leaving Mom. Leaning over to me in the backseat, she said softly so Daddy wouldn't hear, "Mommy could die, you know!"

I was startled by this proclamation but unfazed. "No," I calmly explained. "She had that blessing. She'll be okay."

"But I think Aunt Joyce said that Mommy could die!" My sister had the uncanny ability to enter a room almost soundlessly and become invisible and, in that way, she became privy to all sorts of things adults would not normally discuss in the presence of a child. No wonder she was scared.

I kept trying to comfort her, saying, "Mom will be fine. You'll see. She'll come home and she'll be okay." But there was no consoling her.

I tried to get Daddy to reassure Jennifer and me that Mom wasn't really going to die. All he said was, "We're not going to worry about that. We don't know what's going to happen." And then he suggested that we color or do something else on the drive home to take our minds off our mom's situation.

When we got home, I tried to approach my dad again to ask him whether there was any truth to what Jennifer thought she overheard about Mom. He was brusque and impatient but did try to tell me not to worry about things. He said, "The sun will come up tomorrow. Now, let's just take this a day a time. I'm sure your mom will be fine."

Despite my best efforts to remain calm, Jennifer's fear that Mom might die started to rub off on me. I wondered, *Could I be wrong? Is it possible that the blessing from the bishop might not protect Mom, after all? Does cancer mean certain death?*

Overnight I went from being comforted by the blessing I had witnessed to being very scared that we could lose our mom. Not only did I have this uneasy feeling gnawing away at my insides, I now had to cope with the realities of living with an inaccessible, irritable dad. This was tricky and required all the ingenuity I could muster.

The minute we returned home from California, Daddy started laying down the law: it was our job to help him keep everything up and running in Mom's absence. For starters, he wanted to make it clear that he expected a clean house and my help with the younger kids. Even though I was only ten years old, I needed to "Step up, grow up and be responsible!" As usual, his delivery was short and to the point.

Having my dad count on me in this way made me feel both important and lost. I liked knowing that he was counting on me but I didn't have any reference point for the things he was asking me to do and I didn't have any idea whether I was capable of coming through for him.

Daddy made his expectations of us known in a way that didn't leave a lot of room for questions and closed the door on any discussion of our feelings or fears. Despite our fears and confusion and, despite not really knowing how to cook, clean or raise children, we had to look after things in our mom's absence.

He never asked us, "Are you okay with this?" In fact, he wouldn't allow us *not* to be okay—being fine with whatever he expected of us was a foregone conclusion. This was in keeping with his usual modus operandi. Efficiency was a mainstay and a staple of my home life.

Dad said things like, "You just have to put one foot in front of the other." And, "This is how it's going to work, and this is who's in charge of it." That was pretty much it—he was not a conversationalist.

When I started to cry, he said in a matter-of-fact tone, "No tears! Your mom will be okay. And when she's feeling better, we can go visit her. Then when she gets all better, she will come home. For now, you can talk to her on the phone. But you need to buck up and just get through this!"

I was profoundly in need of comforting and persisted in trying to get my dad to hug me. But even when he would relent and accept my embrace, he always let go almost immediately and sent me off to do my chores or something. At any given moment, those chores might include laundry, dusting, vacuuming, making the beds, cooking and anything else that would have been handled by Mom.

Jennifer and I had only each other when we wanted to talk about our fears over our mom's illness and absence. As for Scottie, he was only four years old when Mom went away to Grandma's house and, while he might have been confused, he wasn't scared. He seemed content with reassurances such as, "We'll see Mommy in just a little bit." As long as he had his toys, his food, his blanket and us, he was happy.

Before we left California, Daddy had made it clear that I would be expected to stay home after school and take care of my little brother.

"Stay home? All the time? What about visiting my friends?"

"They can come to the house and visit you."

The way things worked out, Daddy often ended up taking Scottie with him to work. Being his own boss, Daddy was free to do as he pleased. I could hardly get him to spend any time with me but he seemed to enjoy having Scottie with him as he drove to the job site and checked on his crews in the field.

Having a sick wife who was beyond his reach and having to carry the full responsibility of us kids seemed to evoke in my dad some deep emotions but what he was feeling beneath his gruff demeanor was a mystery to me. In retrospect, I expect that he might have been dealing with a combination of sadness and concern over my mother and frustration over having to single-handedly juggle all of us kids.

The extensive medical care Mom was receiving also put a tremendous burden on my dad's shoulders. This wasn't good because financial pressure was a big stressor in his life and he did not handle the stress well at all.

I was hypervigilant when it came to Daddy's changes in mood and, any time I would sense him becoming upset, I grew concerned.

By now, the equation was black and white—Daddy being stressed and upset equaled a difficult and much less rosy life for me.

"You don't appreciate how hard I have to work to put food on the table and pay the bills!" he would say if I had forgotten to unplug the iron or had inadvertently left a light on when I walked out of the room.

Daddy's every emotion was telegraphed as anger. I recently came across my baptism journal—the one I began keeping when I was about ten years old. As I thumbed through it, I was struck by one recurring thread: "Daddy is very tired," which translated to, "Daddy is grumpy and upset."

"Leave me alone—I'm tired." This was his mantra.

"But, Daddy, we don't have any bread in the house!" I would say.

"Remind me later. I don't have time to deal with it right now!"

"But, I'm hungry!" I said.

He would put a stop to the conversation by saying, "Then eat something else!"

Between my absentee mom and my undemonstrative dad, I was starving for human warmth and connection. So you won't be too surprised when I tell you that my friends became extremely important to me. In fact, they became my whole world.

6

*D*own the street from us in a household straight out of the classic TV show, *The Adventures of Ozzie & Harriet,* lived a girl named Julie who was lucky enough to have both her mom and dad at home. Her family went everywhere together, ate meals together, played games together and in every way imaginable, shone a spotlight on what I was missing. Julie's life was my perfect world and she quickly became my best friend. She seemed to be the luckiest girl in the world.

I loved going over to her house because it felt like a real home. Julie's mom helped to fill the vacuum created by my mom's absence. When a teacher at school told me that the time had come for me to start wearing deodorant and a bra, for example, it was Julie's mom I turned to. She explained what the teacher was talking about and then said, "You need to tell your dad to take you shopping for these." She even offered to talk to him for me if I was uncomfortable or embarrassed to do so myself.

When I talked to my dad, he said, "Okay, put deodorant on the grocery list."

I still needed a bra and, when I talked to him about that, he teased me about my "little mosquito bites" and joked that I could simply put Band-Aids on them. I didn't understand what was happening to my body and his teasing made me very uncomfortable. When he took me bra shopping at a Mervyn's store, he made it a very embarrassing experience by loudly asking the salespeople, "Where do you keep the bras for mosquito bites?"

His teasing invited a type of attention I didn't like and wounded me in a way I couldn't understand or articulate to myself. I'm sure that, in my dad's mind, he was just having fun with me. But I wondered, *Doesn't he understand that he's humiliating me?*

I whispered, "Dad! Please don't say that! You're embarrassing me."

That just seemed to provoke him to further teasing. "Okay, then," he joked, "where are the little trainer bras?"

I laughed nervously, thinking, *Gosh, I wish he wouldn't say that!*

Once I got the bra home, I realized it needed adjusting but I was still stinging from the scene Dad had caused at the store and I wasn't about to ask for his help. Instead, I turned to one of Julie's older sisters for help.

That was the first time I ever felt embarrassed by—and of—my dad. *I can't turn to him for things anymore,* I realized. From that day forward, I relied on Dad for only so much and shared with him only so much. On some fundamental level, I no longer completely trusted him and, as I felt myself make the necessary internal adjustment, I sensed that it was permanent and irrevocable.

What my dad failed to understand was this: I was hypersensitive to embarrassment because I already felt different. I wasn't like the other girls at school. I was the girl with the sick mom. I also had a secret—something no one knew about me. I could see someone and empathically pick up on their unexpressed emotions. I could read when someone was sad or afraid, for example. Along with my intuitive sense about people's hidden feelings would come associated colors. The colors I would see when I looked at a person guided me to what they were feeling.

One day, I made a comment about a little girl's grandmother who had just passed. "Your grandmother is right there!" I said. "You don't see that white circle?"

"No," she said. "My grandmother's dead!"

"I know she's dead but she's *here*. Don't you see the white globe?"

Clearly the girl couldn't see anything I was seeing. This was the first time I became aware that other people couldn't see the same things I saw.

When I was around eight years old, I would try to discuss this with the bishop and his reaction made me feel like this was not a special gift I possessed but that I needed to shut down that part of myself because it was coming from an evil spirit that was trying to gain dominion over me.

I was now at an age when boys were becoming a topic of conversation so it was all the more important to me to blend in and not embarrass myself. I worried that, when people found out I didn't have a mom at home, I would stand out in a negative way.

Since my mom was absent, there was no one to teach me etiquette and social graces. For example, I had no idea how to determine when it was time to excuse myself from my friends' houses and go home. So I sometimes managed to wear out my welcome. I wasn't trying to overstay my welcome but, without the luxury of the kind of attention a young girl needs to thrive and, without ever having been taught appropriate boundaries, I clung to my friends and their families. All of these things conspired to make me stand out and feel different.

Julie lived three doors down from me and, once I had finished my chores at home, my dad would let me go over to her house—as long as I took Jennifer and Scottie with me. Julie and her family understood that having me over was a package deal. I couldn't always come by myself. Thankfully, the Wallaces lived next door to the Greers (Julie's family) and they had a little boy named Robbie who was Scottie's age so we went back and forth between the two households.

Whenever I would overstay my welcome, my friends or their parents would have to say, "Missy, it's time to go home now."

They felt like family to me so this was hard for me to hear. At the time, my own home was a very sterile and lonely place for me. I would say, "But, *why* do I have to go home?"

Whenever I would catch someone looking at me with an expression that told me I had inadvertently crossed some sort of line, I would suffer profound embarrassment. I struggled with social awkwardness and became very reliant on validation from my friends. I needed them to tell me whether my outfit or my hair looked good and I became anxious when a friend wasn't available to spend time with me or failed to return my call right away.

I was still too young to realize that the feelings I was sensing from others had nothing to do with me. I would always attribute other people's negative feelings to something I was doing or some deficiency in me. This caused a low-grade anxiety in me that would last most of my life. It wouldn't be until much later in life that I learned to detach from the feelings of others and realize that their emotions had little or nothing to do with me.

Outward confirmation of our bond took on an unbalanced sense of importance and somebody smiling at me—or not smiling—could make or break my entire day. As I said, this extreme imbalance arose from the fact that there was no parent at home addressing my most basic emotional needs.

My mom's absence and illness and my dad's continual rejection of me had eroded my sense of self. I leaned heavily on my friendships to make me feel like I was loved and cared about and to make me feel good about myself. I spent as much time with my friends as I could, either at their house or mine.

7

*M*any of my friends were Mormon and we LDS girls stuck together. Being as dependent for my sanity and emotional support as I was upon my friends, it was natural for me to go with them to church. The neighbor girls' families would give me rides to church rather than my dad. Neither Jennifer nor Scottie would go but I needed the social interaction.

When I was about twelve years old, I had a Mormon friend who was also named Missy and she became very sick. And, just like my mother, Missy received a blessing from the Mormon Church who brought in the Priesthood to administer the blessing. (Not all men in the church were worthy of holding the Priesthood—those are privileges that must be granted.)

The mere fact that the Priesthood had gathered to bless Missy was an indication to me of the seriousness of her illness. A group of Missy's friends congregated at her house, including me. I went into her room and held her hand, saying, "Missy, I really want you to be okay!"

Suddenly, her eyes flew open and, as clear as day, she whispered to me, "Come closer…"

I bent my head down so I could hear her and she said, "Missy, I love you."

When she said that, I felt like she was saying goodbye to me. I had already been sobbing but now I started to wail. I said to myself, *Oh, my God! She's gonna die! She's gonna die!*

Missy was a really important friend in my life and I was afraid I was going to lose her. In my anguish, I started to become short of breath and dizzy. Then I noticed my hearing had changed and I was experiencing a buzzing in my head. Everything took on a slow motion quality and I found myself in what seemed to be a tunnel. I was still holding Missy's hand as waves of panic washed over me and I was powerless to stop them. I became fixated on a point on the wall. Everything else fell away and the room became elongated. I was cold, sweaty and clammy—and hot, all at the same time.

I was crying and shaking almost uncontrollably and was afraid I might faint or vomit. I could feel myself losing control. Nothing like that had ever happened to me before and it really terrified me. I was having my very first panic attack.

All the other girls gathered around me, trying to calm me down. Even poor Missy was saying, "I love you and it's okay…please calm down…please calm down." All this attention on me tripped me into a state of embarrassment as I realized I was making a spectacle of myself. I did not like that kind of attention.

When I left Missy's house that day, an older friend of mine named Stephanie took me to her house where she could look after me. She let me stay in her room with her and we talked about Missy. As we sat there talking, I was quite distraught, partially due to my fears about Missy and partially due to the overwhelming realization that the one thing I thought could never happen had just happened. I didn't know I could lose control of my emotions in that way.

As it turned out, my friend Missy was seriously ill for some time but she eventually recovered. It was my reaction to her illness that had a profound and lingering effect on me. I knew that my reaction was abnormal. I was shaken up and worried that I might have inherited some sort of mental illness from my paternal grandmother who had killed herself. I thought to myself, *I must be crazy! I'm just like Grandma.*

Grandma killed herself before I was even born so I knew her only through stories and photos, none of which ever depicted her smiling. It was very disturbing to think I might be headed down the same road and the thought terrified me. *Who am I going to talk to about this?* I wondered. *I can't very well go to Dad for reassurance.*

Dad's usual reticence to engage in meaningful conversation was exacerbated by his reluctance to speak about his mother. And the possibility that he might embarrass me over my fears, as he had in the bra department of Mervyn's, made talking to him completely out of the question.

There was no doubt about it—I was a difficult child for my dad to handle. I was very happy go lucky and very friendly but I had big reactions to everything. It was much easier for him to be around my quieter siblings. He didn't really have any problem being around Jennifer. He didn't love on her or hold her any more than he did with me but at least he could stand to be in the same room with her. With me, it was always, "I'm tired and I need some peace and quiet! You're too loud! Go in the other room."

I was so mad at my dad over his inability to show me love, I began to do things to get in trouble just so he would pay attention to me. I didn't have to search for ways to anger him or invent elaborate schemes—all I had to do to get his attention was fail to do my chores. I would "forget" to vacuum or make the beds or do the dishes. Or I would leave the milk on the counter instead of putting it back in the fridge. Or I would fail to pick up after Scottie.

One day, Dad threw a half-smoked cigarette on the ground and I picked it up and put the wet filter to my lips. As I inhaled, there was a loud thunk across the side of my head and I literally saw stars—like a cartoon character.

"Don't you ever do that again!" he yelled.

He smacked me in the head so hard, I couldn't hear out of that ear for days. I was hurt in a way that made me want to fold up inside myself and disappear. What I felt in my heart at that moment was a wound so deep that the only way for me to live with it was to disassociate from it. So, I boxed it up, spiritually separating this deep pain and keeping my distance from it. As long as it wasn't a part of me, I didn't have to feel the pain and hurt. I could wipe my tears and go about my life.

"You know," I said, "little girls should have daddies who love them!"

"Well, little girls should be worthy of their daddy's love!"

In that moment, I decided, *He's the meanest person I know and I hate him!*

"I hate you!" I shouted at him.

"That's fine," he said, and walked into the house. I followed him into the house and put ice on my face where his handprint was turning into a swollen red welt. I was startled and frightened by my dad's capacity for abuse. That was the first time I ever wondered if he might one day completely lose control and hurt me.

8

*A*s I entered middle school and started eighth grade, I was lucky enough to have a wonderful set of school friends, separate and apart from my neighborhood friends. My school friends were the really popular girls—the ones all the other girls admired, tried to emulate in their fashion style, and sought out as friends. Being friends with not one but several of these popular girls made me feel very good about myself.

My social life on campus made going to school a joy. School became a safe haven to which I could escape from all that was going on at home. Then one day, I got off the school bus and headed toward the area in front of the school where different groups of kids would hang out before school and where I always met my popular group of friends. When I walked up to the group of popular girls, they all turned their backs on me and walked away as if I were a leper. Every single one of them froze me out and, without a word of explanation, stopped speaking to me.

I was incredulous and devastated and I couldn't believe that such a thing could happen overnight. I decided that they must have been playing a joke on me. I went to class and, around lunchtime, a boy who was friends with both me and the popular girls came up to me and said, "Hey, these girls don't want to be your friends anymore. You're no longer one of us."

Despite what this boy had told me, I approached the popular girls' lunch table and tried to sit with them anyway.

When I went to sit down, they stopped me, saying, "You can't sit here."

I dropped my tray of food and ran to the bathroom, sobbing. As I ran off, I could hear them laughing at me. I felt abandoned, lonely and sad and I became hysterical. I was in such a state of emotional upheaval, I feared I might be on the verge of another panic attack so I went to the nurse's office.

The school nurse explained these girls' behavior toward me like this: "Unfortunately, honey, this is something girls do sometimes. You're just going to have to find a way to be okay, whether or not they are still your friends."

"I don't want to go to school anymore if they're not going to be my friends!" I said.

"But you can't just stop coming to school!"

For days on end, I suffered over this rejection, crying and barely getting any sleep. I was completely and utterly traumatized and it caused me to withdraw in a way that continues to reverberate inside me, even to this day.

In class, I passed notes to my former friends, asking them to please tell me what I had done to make them reject me. I couldn't accept that they had just stopped talking to me without any explanation. I begged them to resume our friendship and clawed at them for any small kindness they might show me. I tried everything to get them to be nice and talk to me again.

At one point while I was still pleading with them to let me be their friend again, one of them said, "You're not good enough to be our friend. You don't even have a mom!"

I was devastated by her cruel words and felt an overwhelming ball of rage rise up from the center of me. "How could you talk to me like that?" I completely unleashed on her to the extent that she and her snotty friends now had all the ammunition they needed to declare, "You're out of your mind!"

Great, I thought. *Now they feel justified in shunning me.* I was too distraught to eat and I lost about ten pounds. I remember thinking to myself, *I want to die...*

I had been carrying as much as I could, between Mom being sick with cancer and constantly absent from home and Dad being emotionally unavailable, grumpy and downright mean. This rejection by my school friends was the proverbial straw that broke the camel's back and it was more than I could handle. I felt totally and completely abandoned. I once again separated myself from my pain and folded myself up a little more to protect my fragile heart.

I walked around asking myself, *What's wrong with me? Why doesn't my dad love me? Why do my friends hate me?* I felt very unsure of myself.

In this sorrowful state, I turned to the neighborhood friends I had neglected a little bit while I was wrapped up in being friends with the popular girls. They welcomed me back into the fold with open arms at a time when I was in deep emotional pain. My neighborhood friends loved me like they always had and, in the process, taught me the difference between true friends and acquaintances.

9

I was ten years old when my mom first went to live with Grandma and Grandpa in California. She would stay there for a week or so at a time and return home intermittently. Even when she was home, her presence hardly registered with me. She was off limits to us kids when she wasn't feeling up to interacting with us and that uncertainty always filled me with apprehension.

Over the next couple of years as I turned eleven and twelve and Mom continued her intermittent travel to and from California, Dad got into the dairy goat business. Actually it started out as more of a hobby.

Despite their reputation for being hard-headed, the goats were playful and fun and loved to prance around. They all had names and one particular goat stands out in memory—Ruby, my dad's prize goat. When she gave birth, her kids were the cutest things I'd ever seen. I used to bring them into the house in blankets and let them fall asleep beside my siblings and me as we watched cartoons. I would bottle-feed the kids like human infants. I enjoyed loving on these cute little creatures and feeling like they loved me back.

Dad taught me how to milk the goats and then bring in the milk and separate out the whey so we could make butter from the cream. Goat milk definitely has a singular taste, which can range from mild to strong, depending on whether the goats are grass fed, which gives the milk a strong taste, or grain fed with molasses, which gives the milk a milder taste.

Dad gave the goat milk to Mom because the doctors had recommended she drink it. (I am not sure whether it actually had therapeutic properties or was simply hormone free.) I never cared for the goat milk but the butter was really delicious. Dad also got into making goat cheese, which I hated.

Dad began traveling around to regional dairy goat shows and bringing me with him. Jennifer and Scottie came too and we would stay at hotels near the fairgrounds. I was amazed and happy that Dad and I were doing something together. Not only was I getting to spend some much needed time with my dad but being around the animals proved to be therapeutic, as well. As a side benefit, I was having a positive experience rather than pining away for my so-called friends and envisioning all the things they were doing without me.

We traveled with Mr. Shwaggart, a close friend of my dad's. He was very encouraging and comfortable showing me fatherly affection and became a father figure to me. He never thought twice about putting his arm around my shoulder and saying, "Good job, kid!"

My dad was encouraging as well, and would say, "Good job, Missy!" but, as you know by now, he wasn't touchy-feely so there was no affection that went along with his verbal encouragement.

The goats stayed in our lives for a long time and every year I did a dairy goat project for my 4-H after school program. I would continue 4-H until my junior year of high school.

By this point in my life, Mom was home for longer periods of time. She was no longer leaving multiple times each month. Now, she would leave for California about once a month for appointments with oncologists and researchers at institutions like UCLA and John Hopkins. She was also going to appointments with her dermatologist.

Mom resumed her role as homemaker as best she could, doing the grocery shopping and some of the cooking. And she tried to make things special for us, baking cookies and decorating for the holidays. But she still spent an awful lot of time lying down, resting. She did her best to be there for us but she was not nearly as active as other moms. Given that Scott and Carrie were younger, any little bit of energy and attention Mom could muster usually went to them.

When I imagined finally having Mom around more, I couldn't have imagined that her presence would usher in a negative change in the family dynamic, but that's exactly what happened. Now that she was home more regularly, the relationship between my dad and me grew more contentious. He made me the one responsible for ensuring that Mom got the rest she needed. If she was lying down, I had to keep my brother and sisters occupied. And I had to make sure I got my homework done and they did too. I resented this responsibility because it limited the amount of time I was able to spend with my friends.

10

My neighborhood friends were always there for me and, as I said, they became my soft place to fall after the devastating rejection by my school friends. And when Renee moved into our neighborhood, I had a best friend nearby. I felt really good about having a best friend and spending time with her.

Renee lived with her father and stepmother and the arrangement was hard on her. She did a lot of the cooking and cleaning and she looked after her stepfather. We were both carrying a heavy load and it became a point of bonding for us. We both felt like we had been thrust into motherhood prematurely rather than getting to be carefree teenagers. We would commiserate, saying, "Why are we the ones that get stuck doing this?"

We were both struggling to get any sign from our dads that we were important to them and that they appreciated us. Over time, my desire to please my dad was replaced by anger, annoyance and resentment.

Dad wasn't the only source of my resentment. I also resented my mom for not doing more to keep me from being in trouble with my dad. When it came to Dad and me, "trouble" had come to mean some pretty ugly verbal exchanges. Those verbal sparring matches were wounding enough, but it didn't always stop there.

Dad was a hitter and often resorted to using the belt. When our shouting matches escalated, he would grab the belt and start wildly swinging it. He aimed for my rear end but, in his wild frenzy, he often ended up hitting my back and legs. I don't have a single memory of Mom hitting me.

I have to admit that I started to provoke Dad's anger. I was sick and tired of being responsible for things that shouldn't have been my responsibility and I became manipulative as a means of survival.

For example, whenever I wanted to stay at a friend's house to avoid having to go home, I would make up stories like, "My mom and dad have to be in California for my mom's doctor's appointments, and they want to know if I can spend the weekend here."

Then I would go home and, if Mom was in California, I'd tell Dad, "I'm going to stay down at the Wallace's house for the weekend." Or, "I'm going to stay down at the Greer's. Is that okay?" Occasionally he would say yes.

I didn't think it through real well and inevitably I'd get caught and be in trouble on both ends. My friends' parents would be upset with me for misleading them and I started being labeled as a liar and somebody you couldn't trust. I even started lying about inconsequential things just to avoid conflict.

The verbal fights between Dad and me often began with me misbehaving in some way and him retorting, "You don't want to listen? I'll make you listen!" Or, "You want something to complain about? I'll give you something to complain about!" Or, "You're a little bitch and I need to teach you to have some respect!" He thought nothing of saying ugly, ugly things to me.

Dad would let his own barbed words fly but he wouldn't listen to a word I said. He didn't care how I felt or what I said. He flat out didn't want to hear it. Having him ignore me like that infuriated me and there were times that I just hated him. He never even attempted to understand what I was saying or feeling. He expected me to do as I was told, period, and get busy doing it. He had no patience with me.

I figured out pretty early on that only the first few poison word-darts he threw at me hurt my heart. After that I went numb. I started giving back as good as I got, saying things like, "You're an abusive asshole. I'm going to call Child Protective Services on you and they'll throw your ass in jail!"

He certainly did not like me at this point in my life and I didn't like him either. There was an icy distance between us which was painful but preferable to being hit by him.

When my dad would physically hurt me, my mom would say to me, "Come over here, Missy, and show me where you're hurt."

"Why do you care? You sit there and let him do it!" I was pretty angry with her for failing to protect me from my dad.

One time, I was being belligerent and my dad came at me and pinned me against a wall by my neck. Dad had his hands so firmly around my neck, my feet weren't even touching the ground.

Jennifer witnessed this but was immobilized by fear. Mom was out of the room when it started but came running in when she heard arguing. She started begging Dad to stop. She tried to pull him backwards by his shoulders—but she never put herself between my dad and me.

I don't know which came first—whether I passed out and Dad dropped me because he could see that I'd passed out, or he dropped me and then I passed out. As this was happening, Jennifer was frozen in place in the corner, crying.

When I came to, I was still on the floor and Mom was sobbing and holding me. Mom yelled at Dad, "Get OUT!"

This was one of the most devastating run-ins with my dad. Had Mom placed herself between Dad and me, she might have been able to stop him before things escalated to the point where I passed out. Instead, Dad's temper got completely out of hand. If my dad was capable of treating a child that way, I can only imagine what he might have done to Mom. So, perhaps she was afraid of his temper.

I was the only one in the family who would tell Dad, "You're being mean!" or "You're being an asshole!"

Mom would say to me, "Missy, you need to learn how to just not say anything to him! Stop arguing with him!"

My feeling was, *Screw this! I'm going to say it. Dad already hates me so I've got nothing to lose.*

I learned that, if I didn't need my dad to love me, it didn't hurt as badly. So, I started to detach from him.

Occasionally, he would actually make an effort to talk to me and want to know, "How do you feel about this?"

Instead of being happy that he was putting himself out there, I mistrusted the gesture, thinking to myself, *What's the point? This is not going to result in anything good for me!* I had no interest in talking to him. As the years had gone by, he had managed to completely extinguish my desire for his attention. I was just plain over it.

And the constant worry that my mom might die wore me down to the point where I began to detach from her, as well. I learned that it was easier to function if I didn't need them or want their love. I wrote in my journal about my decision to unburden my heart by teaching myself not to need those relationships.

In retrospect, I can see that this was a horrible way to approach the situation but, back then, I had no one to turn to, no counselor and no real tools or resources for dealing with my difficult life. And I knew that Mom was never going to protect me from Dad. It just wasn't going to happen. So, I tried to alleviate my anger in the only way I knew how—by not caring. While this was misguided, it was also effective to some extent, as it did bring about a decrease in the frequency of the confrontation and punishment I suffered at the hands of my dad.

I stuffed my feelings down as far as they would go but, of course, such powerful emotions don't stay put for long. My repressed anger and resentment began to show up in my life in the form of reckless and impulsive decisions as well as underage drinking to help numb the pain. I never drank with daily frequency but when I did drink, I drank to get drunk. I never felt good about having gotten drunk and always suffered remorse afterwards but, in those moments when the alcohol was doing its job and numbing the pain, I was happy for the momentary relief.

Thankfully I never developed a drinking problem or substance abuse problem. Instead, I tried to escape through writing in my journal. So much of the turmoil I was experiencing internally seemed beyond my ability to express verbally to another soul so I wrote about it instead.

Even if I had been able and inclined to speak about what was going on at home, I was reticent to do so because I feared it would reinforce my sense of being different. With the exception of my new best friend, Renee, all the other girls I knew had great dads and wonderful relationships with them. I envied those girls but I also had a strong instinct that told me I needed to guard what I disclosed to them.

My repressed emotional turmoil also expressed itself as a negative and damaging internal critic. Any time I failed at even the smallest task, I saw it as a monumental failure and further proof of my inadequacy. I was constantly feeling badly about myself and having thoughts like: *Oh, you're so stupid! I can't believe you'd be so stupid as to do that! Of course you're a disappointment to Mom and Dad...you can't even do this right!*

I was depressed, anxious, nervous and overwhelmed. I lived with the pervasive and prevalent fear of not being perfect—or normal. Fears and questions about my inherited tendency toward suicide continued to plague me. I was terrified that I would get labeled with mental illness just like my grandmother. Labels hurt.

11

I knew that there was no point in trying to tell an authority figure at school about the way I was being treated at home. I knew that no good would come of it. Even if they wanted to remove me from my home, where would I go? So I kept my mouth shut around outsiders.

As I was busy trying to survive my disastrous home life, I began to notice that something was terribly off with my little sister, Carrie. From the time she was very little, she was prone to extreme reactions and strange behaviors. She threw tantrums and had emotional meltdowns, especially in the presence of our mom. She was constantly being bounced back and forth between our house and Grandma and Grandpa's house in California and perhaps that instability contributed to her issues.

When Carrie was five years old and getting ready to go into kindergarten, she decided that she didn't want to wear underwear to school. When my mother insisted on it, Carrie completely lost her mind—and not for a day or an hour, but for months. Every time the subject of wearing undies to school came up, she flipped out. Finally, out of desperation, Mom decided to let Carrie wear sweatpants to school. Even then, the sweatpants had to be very loose fitting and baggy because Carrie would get agitated if the fabric was touching her skin.

I remember asking my little sister one day, "Why are you acting like this?"

"I don't want anything touching me!" she said.

"But why not? Did something touch you in a bad way?"

She said no but I'm not sure I ever believed her. I had been touched inappropriately by someone in the family and thought it might have happened to her too. It happened the first time when I was eleven and then again when I was thirteen.

Here's what happened. During those times when Mom was in California, I sometimes went to visit her at Grandma and Grandpa's house. Aunt Joyce, my mother's older sister, was a little bit behind the curve in terms of her mental development and was living with my grandparents. She had been married and was now divorced from her husband, Ken, but she still spent time with him and we still considered him Uncle Ken.

Aunt Joyce was in her thirties at that time, and Uncle Ken was a few years older. My grandparents forbade her from seeing Uncle Ken. They were protective of Aunt Joyce and a little bit controlling due to her special needs status. So, when Aunt Joyce needed an excuse to get out of the house and I happened to be there visiting my mom, she would say to my grandparents, "I am taking Missy to the movies." She used me as her cover story.

Grandma and Grandpa liked to see Aunt Joyce and me doing things together and encouraged it. They knew that I was a smart girl and they seemed to feel that I'd keep my aunt from getting into trouble. Aunt Joyce and I really would go to the movies—and Uncle Ken would meet us there. When we got to the movies, Aunt Joyce and Uncle Ken would sit in one row, kissing and making out, and I would sit in the row in front of them. I knew what was happening between them but I didn't mention it to anyone because Aunt Joyce had begged me to keep her secret.

Altogether, there were probably ten occasions where I spent time around Uncle Ken and, on each occasion, he made me feel very uneasy. I didn't appreciate his attention and I instinctively knew I wasn't safe around him. On two of those occasions, he touched me inappropriately. The first time, he started by rubbing my feet and then began inching his way up my legs—moving to my calves and then my knees.

This led me to tell him, "I don't want you to rub my feet any-more."

The next encounter occurred when Aunt Joyce took me to see *Porky's* at a drive-in movie theater. (This movie was completely inappropriate for a girl of my age!) Once again, she and Uncle Ken sat in the backseat and I sat in the front. During intermission, Aunt Joyce left Uncle Ken and me alone while she went to the snack bar and restroom.

As soon as my aunt was out of sight, Uncle Ken climbed into the front seat with me and began touching me inappropriately. He started grabbing at my undies and trying to remove them.

I started yelling and screaming and managed to stop him and move away from him. There was no penetration, just touching. I was extremely upset.

He warned me, "If you tell her, she will never believe you and she will hate you for the rest of your life! And I'll tell her you came on to me."

Uncle Ken's attempts to intimidate me flipped a switch inside me that caused me to go from being scared to angry. I never reacted well to being threatened or manipulated and, any time someone tried to shut me up, it triggered memories of me trying to express my feelings toward my dad and him shutting me down, either with words or with actions. He would always let me know that what I felt didn't matter and he didn't want to hear it.

For the moment, I kept my mouth shut about what Uncle Ken had done but I thought to myself, *How dare you try to threaten and intimidate me to keep this information concealed? You're the one who did something wrong!*

When Aunt Joyce returned to the car, the three of us sat there and finished watching the movie. I didn't say a word until we got home and then I immediately started telling on Uncle Ken. I wanted to show him that I couldn't be intimidated and I figured the best way to do that was by telling the truth. I also needed to make sure that what he had done to me was out in the open so that it would never happen again.

When I told Grandma, Grandpa and Mom what had happened, all hell broke loose. Grandma and Grandpa stopped Aunt Joyce from seeing Uncle Ken. My aunt misunderstood what I had disclosed about Uncle Ken, thinking I had told my grandparents merely that she was seeing him. So she was very upset with me, saying, "I'm so disappointed in you!"

Once I explained to her what Uncle Ken had done and she had time to process the situation, she cried and said she was sorry. She felt really badly about getting upset with me, especially when she realized that I had kept her secret up until the point where Uncle Ken tried to molest me.

Aunt Joyce got in trouble with my grandparents and was out of favor with them for a little while as a result of this information about Uncle Ken coming forth. I didn't like seeing my aunt upset and I felt badly but I knew that, if I didn't say something, Uncle Ken would try again. Somehow, even at that young age, I instinctively understood that he was grooming me for sexual encounters.

Meanwhile, Uncle Ken had our home phone number and called for two or three weeks, saying, "I still know how to find you!" He was mentally torturing me as retribution for telling on him. Dad had to get the police involved before Uncle Ken finally left me alone.

Anyway, that's what made me wonder whether Uncle Ken might have been responsible for Carrie's insistence that nothing touch her. I knew she had spent a lot of time at Grandma and Grandpa's during the periods of time that Mom was there and, knowing what Uncle Ken had done to me, it was feasible to me that the same thing could have happened to her.

Carrie never said anything to that effect but, knowing what Uncle Ken did to try to silence me, I figured he could have also threatened her. Then again, my sister's odd behaviors were not confined to the insistence that she not be touched. She was prone to meltdowns and was ritualistic and compulsive about all sorts of things.

Mom begged Dad to let her take Carrie to see a psychiatrist but my sister's condition went undiagnosed. Dad's feeling was, "It's just a stage. She will grow out of it." He had that "It's just a stage" approach to all sorts of things, including me being afraid of the dark and having recurring nightmares. It was his stock answer for many things.

Knowing that Dad was unlikely to want to spend any money, my mom adopted that same approach with me, only taking me to the doctor when I was very sick. For lesser maladies, I was expected to grin and bear it.

12

*A*round this time, I developed an innocent preoccupation with boys and fantasized about having a boyfriend. There was one boy from church who had caught my eye. Matt was different than the good, Mormon boys I was used to seeing at church. He didn't try to fit into the Mormons' cookie cutter mold.

I didn't fit in with the other kids at school and I was always painfully aware of that fact. So, I really appreciated and admired Matt, who seemed indifferent to the fact that he was an outsider. All the way around, I thought he was the coolest, cutest boy I'd ever seen.

I had a big crush on Matt and he liked me too but he also liked kissing—French kissing. French kissing was more than I was ready for at that point in time. For me, a kiss was a little peck and I didn't know what to do when he tried to French kiss me. His attempts just made me wonder, *What is he doing?*

As for Matt, he thought I was a really good, sweet girl but he lost interest in me.

Even though I knew I wasn't ready to take our relationship to a physical level, I started to second guess my decision when he started to pull away from me. I asked myself, *Did I make a mistake by refusing to make out with him?*

Then I remembered the words of my grandmother, who always told me, "You need to be protective of your purity, Missy. There will always be people who will encourage you to part with it, but once you've parted with it, you can never get it back. Be careful and make sure you're ready. And, when that day comes, make sure it's your choice because, from that point onward, you'll be forever changed!"

Since Mom was gone so much of the time as I was growing up, we never did have the talk about the birds and the bees. My only insights into sex came from what I'd gleaned from the health video shown to us girls in school. That video tipped me off as to the changes I could expect my body to go through. Watching it, I was uncomfortable and grossed out and thinking to myself, *Eww! No! Does this really have to happen?*

I probably could have discussed the video with my mom but I really didn't want to. By this point in my life, I was conditioned to avoid talking to my parents. Given a choice, I preferred to talk to my girlfriends. Other than my girlfriends and my sister, Jennifer, the only other person I'd ever really been able to fully confide in was Sister Gideon.

I met Sister Gideon when I was twelve or thirteen and still heavily involved in the Mormon Church. At that age, it was customary to attend a sacrament type of service where all the families assembled together, and then afterwards, we youth would break off into Sunday school groups. That was something I really enjoyed. I especially enjoyed being around the teachers and Sister Gideon in particular. She was familiar with my mom's health history and really took me under her wing.

Sister Gideon was a special person in my life. She was in her forties and was sweet, loving and encouraging. I really enjoyed being around her. I liked being in any environment where someone took an interest in me. I also enjoyed the church activities, whether we were studying Bible scriptures, learning about the church's prophet, Joseph Smith, and church doctrine and covenants, or discussing the true meaning of virtue and the importance of being virtuous.

The things Sister Gideon would talk with me about filled with me hope. "I know you may not always feel loved, Missy, but I want you to know that God does love you!"

I appreciated that I was able to open up and talk to her about my feelings toward my dad and the changes in my relationship with my mom. I was going through so much at that time. For starters, my body was going through profound hormonal changes.

With Sister Gideon, I was able to emotionally let my guard down. She was there for me in a way that the teachers never were. I would always get frustrated any time I went to my teachers for help. I would say, "I am having trouble with my homework, and my mom doesn't live with us and my dad's too busy to help me. Can't you get some help for me?"

They did make an effort, sometimes staying in at recess to try to help me understand whatever seemed to be confusing me, but they couldn't offer the kind of help I really needed. The reality was that I needed more than answers—there was a certain amount of attention I was in need of, and when I couldn't get it from my teachers, I stopped trying.

Sister Gideon had a way of making me feel very safe and completely loved. She was one of the most kind, nurturing women I had ever been around at that point in my life. Sadly, she was only in my life for a little while. She and her family moved and we lost touch.

13

*A*s I entered my freshman year of high school, I was preoccupied, fearful and overwhelmed. It was a big transition from my small elementary school to my larger high school. I really wanted to put my best foot forward and I was obsessed and worried over whether or not I would fit in. For one thing, I wanted to make sure I was wearing the right clothes. It was important to me to look good and not stand out as different.

I could still vividly recall that fateful day when my so-called friends abruptly stopped speaking to me. That experience left me feeling apprehensive and concerned as I entered my new school. I made a journal entry around that time about how I felt that the best strategy was to try to make friends with everyone. I decided that I would be friendly and kind to everyone, no matter what, and not limit myself to a small clique of girls who might later turn on me.

This seemed to be the obvious takeaway from that painful experience: I hadn't taken the time to get to know enough people so I was left stranded when my small clique of friends shunned me. As I said earlier, my neighborhood friends welcomed me back into the fold— but they were a little bit offended that I'd put so much of my attention on my popular-girl friends. I realized I'd made some mistakes and I wanted to do a better job this time.

There were two high schools in my area but due to a re-drawing of the school boundaries, I ended up attending the one furthest from my home. Had I gone to the school closer to me, I would have known more of the students. On the first day of school, I felt very awkward as I struggled to find the buildings where my classes were being held and I ended up arriving late to most of my classes. I had to stop several times and say, "I'm so sorry, but can you help me figure out where to go?"

Everyone was nicer than I expected, which was a relief. I did not suffer from the debilitating panic attacks of the past and I felt more at ease. Little by little, I began to recover from the self-doubt and self-destructive mantras that had plagued me for so long. I was happy for the first time in ages.

One thing I really liked about high school was the fact that every hour, we got to get up and walk to a different class. It gave me a chance to socialize with the other kids and to make friends. Since everyone was in the same boat and none of us were familiar with high school or knew where we were going, it was an even playing field.

At my old school, everyone knew about my situation with my sick, absentee mom. So I had been stuck wearing the label of "different" from that point forward. I didn't have the feeling of being an outsider at my new high school. I found it easy to assimilate into this new group of students and to make new friends. Since I didn't know hardly anyone and hardly anyone knew me, I didn't feel like I was at a disadvantage and trying to fit into already established cliques.

Some of the girls who had shunned me happened to also be students at my new school but they were humbler, nicer and not as cocky or mean to me. Since they no longer had the strength of the popular girls' clique behind them, their power to influence the way others responded to me was gone.

I felt like they had been dethroned and no longer had a hold over me. Being only human, I derived a certain sense of satisfaction from seeing them have to struggle along with the rest of us who were trying to adapt to our new environment.

As I said, I feared that limiting myself to one best friend or a small group of friends could backfire on me, as it had before, and so I wasn't looking for one best friend. I found that I was easily able to talk to most everyone in all my classes and, before I knew it, I had friends everywhere. There was a variety of people I could call if I wanted to go to the movies or make social plans.

Now that I was in high school, boys became more important to me than ever. Whenever I would see one particular boy named Mark, I would get anxious and get butterflies in my stomach. In fact, just the sight of him could almost make me nauseous from nervous excitement. I had a crush on him and he liked me back, which was the best feeling in the world.

Whenever he would call me, my response to hearing his voice was almost euphoric. Even the awkward teen silences that naturally come with such phone calls did not detract from the thrill of finding out it was him on the phone. He was calling just to say hi and ask me about my day and we would have very surface level conversations. But, I would read into every little thing that was said and assign it deeper meaning in my mind.

Then I would torture myself with questions like, *Am I reading into this or is he really being nice?* I struggled with whether or not I could trust him.

Mark was five-foot-seven and skinny with shaggy light brown hair and big, bright, sparkling blue eyes. I am five-foot-six so we were close in height. Mark came from an intact family, with two parents, an older brother, Dana, and a robust family dynamic. The family ate dinner together and engaged in various family activities, and his aunt often came over to visit. I was as attracted to Mark's wonderful family situation as I was to Mark himself. I found his family to be very grounding.

Mark had many friends, was very social, and was warm and affectionate with me. Being with someone who was well received by others made me feel safe and, before long, Mark became my best friend—and then my whole world. I enjoyed having him as my sole focus and didn't even seek out other friends.

It was as if I'd completely forgotten my resolve not to focus all my attention on one friend. Maybe the fact that Mark was a guy, rather than one of the popular girls, made the situation seem different. In reality, I was doing it again—putting all my eggs in one basket. He was the first guy with whom I ever fell in love.

When we were dating, I was only a freshman in high school but Mark was a senior. So, by the end of our first year of dating, he was already preparing to leave for college. As he entered this new stage of life, I had a difficult time adjusting to the changes. At the thought of him moving away and leaving me, I became very panicky and nervous. Intellectually I knew that he was going away to school but, emotionally, I felt like he was abandoning me.

Sadly, as the relationship changed, it brought out the very worst in me. My overwhelming fears made me suspicious of everything he did and I even tried to catch him cheating. I became very intense and clingy. I knew I was making things worse between us and sabotaging the relationship but I couldn't seem to stop myself.

The relationship ultimately went from being very good to extremely unhealthy as we argued constantly and hurled ugly accusations at each other. When we weren't arguing, I would spend as much time as I could with him as a way to stave off my fears and try to recapture a feeling of safety. This was a confusing time of life for me.

When Mark and I had been dating and all was well, it boosted my self-esteem. When the relationship started to unravel and he started to pull away from me as he prepared to leave for college, my lifelong struggle with feelings of inadequacy returned. My feeling was, *Well, if Mark doesn't love me and my dad doesn't love me, there must be something inherently wrong with me.*

There were periods where I spiraled into a dark depression and picked at my skin with a tweezers until I bled. As I was hurting myself with the tweezers, I noticed something strange—my ability to feel physical pain seemed to be muted. I could pick at my skin endlessly, never feel any pain, and never have the conscious thought that I was harming myself. It wasn't until I drew blood that the thought would occur to me, *Okay, I'm bleeding so I'd better stop this now.*

I was aware that something about the way I was reacting to Mark pulling away was not quite right. My need for him to love me was all-consuming and, when I doubted his love, I experienced moments of sheer panic. When Mark and I finally officially broke up, I was almost sixteen years old. Things had seemed so promising while we were together but now they took a definite turn for the worse.

Growing up with my mom often gone and seriously ill, I had an extreme fear of loss. This fear returned now, loomed larger than ever, and became limiting. I had started high school with an openness and willingness to make friends with everyone. That openness now turned into a disinclination to form authentic relationships. I remained outwardly friendly and social and I still walked the walk and talked the talk—but I was no longer fully myself. I didn't want to subject myself to rejection.

When I first started high school, I quickly discovered that I seemed to possess natural leadership qualities but I never embraced a leadership role. I would be voted class president or secretary for this club or that, but I would decline the nomination because I couldn't push through my fear of being scrutinized or judged.

14

$\mathcal{W}$hile I was in my junior year of high school, a notice was posted in the local paper stating that the cast of a performance organization known as Up with People (UWP) would be spending three or four days in our town, performing, and host families were needed. The notice stated that hosting would entail integrating cast member(s) into your family while they were in town, and providing room and board as well as rides to rehearsals or other UWP community events.

Up with People is defined on their website as, "A global education and arts organization whose goal is to bridge cultural barriers and create global understanding through service and music." The cast of UWP is comprised of international students who travel the world and promote understanding on philanthropic themes like cultural and religious acceptance.

Much to my surprise, my parents decided that being a host family sounded like fun. We hosted two females—Helga from Sweden and Karen from Australia. When the girls arrived, they told us a little bit about themselves and their backgrounds. Each cast member carried with them a little book which served as an introduction of themselves to their host family.

Karen told us that she had broken her back, had to spend a long time in a back brace and struggled to regain her health and learn to walk again. She also told us about the depression and emotional struggles that went along with her physical injury.

The emotional aspect of what Karen had gone through really spoke to me. One day, we were talking about life and she asked me what I was planning to do with my future. I decided to share with her my own struggles with Dad. I told her that I was in a lot of emotional pain and explained that Dad and I had a cold, abrasive, unfeeling relationship. I talked about conditioning myself to live with it, figuring that, if I got accustomed to the way he treated me and even expected it from him, it might not hurt as badly. I also told Karen that Dad was not supportive of my desire to get a university education once I finished high school.

"You know, you should audition for Up with People!" she said. "It could be a really good thing for you to do after graduation." She described how each performance was a live two-hour song-and-dance performance, "Like a mini Broadway show!"

I liked the idea and, without mentioning anything to my parents yet, I auditioned to become an international student and part of the UWP cast. My audition was actually an interview rather than a singing or dancing audition. It was similar to the interview segment of a beauty pageant in the sense that I was asked questions related to my worldview on culture, humanity and religion and asked to share about my interests.

After my interview, I spent a few weeks on pins and needles while I waited to find out whether or not I would be accepted. Finally, about a month after my interview, I received a letter in the mail congratulating me and welcoming me into the 1989—1990 UWP cast!

I had previously taken ballet classes and been a cheerleader so UWP knew that I had enough experience to feel comfortable performing in front of large crowds of people. Once I was accepted into the cast, I went through a traditional audition where I sang and danced for the director so they would know where to place me in the cast. I did really well on the microphone for certain songs and was a featured dancer in certain numbers.

The logistics worked like this: In advance of the actual performance, certain members of the cast traveled to the city where the next performance would be held. They promoted the show and took care of set-up so that when the rest of the cast arrived, there would be a buzz in the community and everyone would be looking forward to the show. It was a communal cast and everyone put up the stage together, tore it down, and loaded up the truck. And for the performances themselves, everyone played a part, whether a cast member was right up front as a featured singer or dancer in the performance, in the chorus singing background or vamping behind the other performers.

When I was accepted into the cast, I wrote to Karen but she was traveling and it took a long time for her to get the letter and reply to me. Naturally, she was very excited for me and encouraged me to go for it. Her letter read: "Seize this opportunity and don't limit yourself to what you're being told you should do. Do what you want to do with your life. Go for your dreams!"

At that point in time, traveling with UWP and being part of the cast was definitely my dream. As I said earlier, my dad did not support my desire to go to college and my parents didn't have any money to contribute to my tuition so I would have had to pay for college entirely on my own. Before UWP came along, I had resigned myself to going to the local junior college but that wasn't something I really wanted to do. Going to junior college would have doomed me to living at home while I got my degree. If I was going to attend college, I desperately wanted to do so away from my parents. I particularly needed to escape the contentious and adversarial relationship between Dad and me.

With my UWP acceptance letter in hand, I went to my parents and told them how badly I wanted to go. My mother was excited for me but had a lot of questions about the logistics of the situation and the fact that I would be required to travel out of the country. My father's feeling was, "Well, good job. But that's a lot of money to come up with, and you're going to have to find a way to come up with it on your own!"

I hadn't expected my parents to outright forbid it and I hadn't expected hearty congratulations, either. So I wasn't surprised when they said yes with conditions, and I wasn't surprised when my dad wasn't overly supportive or encouraging. I had also figured that any obstacles would be financial so I wasn't surprised when Dad said I had to figure out how to pay for it myself.

Acceptance into the UWP cast came with a one-year commitment and the acceptance letter spelled out where I would be spending that year. I would be starting my tour in the Southeastern United States and traveling from there to Europe, where I would spend nine months. It just so happened that the year of my acceptance was also the year that they would have an expanded European tour, including more countries than ever before.

Now all I had to do was raise ten thousand dollars! That money would cover everything but spending money for souvenirs. I wrote letters to every single Rotary Club and Optimist Club in town, as well as every local business that came to mind. With my dad's permission, I sold my pick-up truck. And my maternal grandparents also contributed some money. (My paternal grandparents were not a part of my life at all. My father rarely ever saw them and I had only met them three or four times.)

It took me about a year but somehow I managed to cobble together enough money. My dream was becoming a reality.

15

I graduated from high school and, four weeks later, I was in Tucson at the University of Arizona, learning the show and meeting other cast members. In Tucson, I was being hosted by a young couple, Doug and Lisa, who were working professionals who had not yet started a family. Funny enough, Helga was also staying with them, which was great for me. Doug and Lisa opened their home and their hearts to me and we spent a lot of time together.

To my amazement, I found that I was actually homesick. This was a novel feeling for me. It was my brother and sisters that I missed, of course, and my mom. I also missed my friends. Thankfully, my mom was well enough to travel to see our final stateside performance before the cast was set to leave for Europe. My dad even came to the show and loved it. Imagine my surprise when he hugged me, smiled and let me know that he was proud of me.

The show was two hours of high-energy song and dance (mostly contemporary dance), and the theme of every number was acceptance, unity and brotherly love. It was similar to *We Are the World* in terms of the unity theme and the fact that I was traveling with cast mates from all over the globe—places like China, Japan, Norway and Morocco. We were a little microcosm of the world's population.

I was featured in four dances and two songs. There were many opportunities for enjoyable interactions between cast members, as we were paired up together for the song and dance numbers and would sing to each other.

I had just turned eighteen as I boarded the plane to Florida, which marked the first leg of our journey toward Europe. There was only one cast mate younger than I—Sophie—and our oldest member was twenty-nine years old. During the flight, I was acutely aware that I wouldn't see my family or friends for an entire year. I was a little bit nervous but mostly I was excited that something I really wanted was actually coming to pass.

Right away, it became obvious to me that functioning in this large group was going to require me to pay close attention in order to adapt to the protocols that everyone observed. It was a whole new way of living for me. I had to quickly identify those behaviors of mine which I considered normal but the group considered unacceptable, or else risk getting called out and embarrassed.

I learned to be aware of others, look people in the eye and be mindful of my tone of voice. Due to my difficult home life and in particular the dynamic between my father and me, I had learned to keep to myself and keep quiet. My propensity to isolate rather than engage and contribute to a conversation was seen as offensive and no one hesitated to let me know.

Someone would ask me a question and my knee-jerk response would be, "I don't know…whatever you guys want is fine."

And someone in the group would reply, "No! We are asking you a question—what do *you* want?"

My home was not an environment where I was encouraged or even allowed to voice my feelings, ideas or concerns. My father always told me to shut up and do as I was told. Speaking my mind was a huge adjustment for me and it made me very uncomfortable and forced me to stretch and grow emotionally.

I embraced the opportunity to grow instead of giving in to my impulse to flee. The fact that I felt genuinely cared for and heard gave me the emotional courage I needed to make the adjustments necessary to stay and grow.

Around this same time, the Berlin Wall was coming down and this led to some interesting discussions about world politics, especially considering that there were Germans in the cast. They asked me questions and appreciated my thoughts and contributions during our discussions. They truly seemed to value my opinions and I was surprised and delighted by their level of interest.

As we toured the Southeast before leaving for Europe, I entered the home of a new host family every two or three days. I had to learn how to live out of a suitcase—and how to be mature enough to resist the temptation to isolate in my room when I was tired from rehearsing and performing. After all, these families were kind enough to take us in and it was important to engage with them and interact. I learned about hospitality, developed great communication skills and learned to ask questions in order to get to know people.

We were finally on our way to Europe and, during the plane trip overseas, all my cast mates and I talked about our upcoming tour. Our European cast mates were excited to introduce us to the European way of living and looked forward to showing us how it differed from the American lifestyle. And those of us from the States were excited and curious about how different life would be over in Europe.

I had no idea what to expect. I had only been on a plane two other times in my life up to that point. The first time was when I was six or seven years old and my father took me on a surprise father-daughter trip to visit his family in Michigan. My brother Scottie was still a baby and my sister Jennifer was still too young so it was just Dad and me on the trip, which was very special.

It was funny because the entire family went to the airport to see Dad off on his trip. When we got to the airport, my dad turned to me and said, "Hey, Miss, you want to go with me?" My parents had planned this little surprise for me.

"Really?" I said, "Are you serious?" I was completely shocked and wasn't sure what to believe. Mom started snapping photos of my surprised reaction.

When Dad and I got to Michigan, we visited his sisters and his brother. Dad didn't really consider them close family since they did not grow up together. It was my first time meeting my cousins and my aunts and uncle. It was also the first time I'd ever met my paternal grandfather and his wife Mary. Dad's father married Mary after Dad was already grown and out of the house. Dad was not very accepting of my grandfather's marriage to Mary. He believed that his father and Mary had been having an affair and that's what caused my grandmother to commit suicide.

Despite the dramatic back story of this side of the family, I enjoyed meeting them all. I had an especially good time with my cousin Chandra who was seventeen and in high school. We spent a lot of time together on that trip as she drove us around and we sang together to the radio. I never saw her again after that trip but we spoke on the phone and she sent me birthday cards for about five years. When I think of her, I often find myself singing this one song we sang together—a song that went something like this: *It's not that far to paradise, at least it's not for me. When the wind is right, you can sail away and find serenity.*

My second plane flight occurred when I was thirteen. I went on a family trip to Mexico during the summer between my freshman and sophomore year of high school. We were staying at Club Med in Ixtapa. The resort had everything we could have needed or wanted, so once we got there, we pretty much stayed put. We spent a week there, and being as young as I was, that felt like an especially long time.

Now I was on my way to Europe. As our plane prepared to make its descent into Denmark, I began to see the land below the plane.

I thought, *Wow! It looks like a picture. Like something out of a movie scene...or a postcard...or the illustrations in the classic books Grandma used to read to us when we were little.*

16

$\mathcal{U}$p with People performed in Denmark, Norway, Luxembourg, France, Germany, Sweden, the Netherlands, Belgium, Portugal and Spain. During the tour, we had personal days away from the cast where we could spend time with our host families. Or, sometimes they would drop us off at a point of interest and return for us later. Everywhere we went, the architecture and the churches were the high point for me.

Every family that hosted me had the same request: Would I make them a traditional American cheeseburger and French fries? And what did *Hostess Twinkies* taste like—or *Wonder Bread?* Everyone seemed to be filled with a combination of repulsion and fascination over our curious American eating habits.

Making an American cheeseburger in Europe was harder than it sounds, considering that cheese was sold in blocks in tiny little shops, not in plastic packages hanging on metal racks at the supermarket. And there was no *Heinz Ketchup* or dill pickles. And iceberg lettuce? No one had ever even heard of it. I asked my parents to send me a bottle of ketchup and I took it with me everywhere I went.

In Norway, I had my first experience with seasickness. When we landed, we had to take a ferry and the water was so choppy that, by the time I set foot on land, I was green with nausea. Having to contend with my luggage while being nauseous was not easy but I had to put my feelings aside. The host family was waiting for us at the designated meeting spot so, as we exited the ferry building, I put a smile on my face and went to greet them.

While in Norway, I was struck by the interactive and communal nature of the lifestyle. Everyone was joyful and happy and everyone gathered together around food, conversation and music. There was none of the American tendency to interact for a few minutes with others and then retreat to your own room. I embraced this togetherness wholeheartedly and found it incredibly healing. It was an antidote to the isolation with which I'd lived for so long at home.

The entire tour became an awakening for me in a way I would not have thought possible. I would return to America with a deep longing to incorporate some of the European customs into my own life back home. I would also return home with a deep appreciation for craftsmanship of the type that surrounded me in Europe. The architecture was awe inspiring, especially the church buildings, and all the more so when I considered the fact that these churches were created without the benefit of advanced technology.

One of the most profound ways that this tour would change me had to do with the interaction with the rest of the cast. After a while, we all got into a routine with our performances but, inevitably, at each show, someone would say the wrong line or sing the wrong lyric. My dancing was never an issue but my biggest fear was that I would sing off key on the microphone. One day, the worst did happen and my voice cracked while I was singing.

After the show, Tom, the casting director said to me, "Boy, I bet you wish you could sing that note again!"

"You're not mad at me?"

"Why would I be mad at you?" he said. "It has happened to every single person here and, believe me, it's going to happen again! You're too hard on yourself. You need to learn to let go and just relax and enjoy yourself!"

I was thinking, *You mean it's okay to be human?* I had never before heard this message from a person in a position of authority

Tom was sensitive to the fact that I was the second youngest in the cast and he was very good to me and took me under his wing. I think he could tell that I had come from a home where affection was a real problem. Whenever anyone tried to hug me, I bristled. I wanted the affection but it was a hard adjustment to make after having to constantly sublimate my need for affection at home. The entire cast really worked with me to help me break down my personal barriers and become more open to everyone and everything around me.

We even had group sessions to air our grievances with each other. Naturally, being in such close quarters for an extended period of time, we got on each other's nerves and this was our chance to get it out in the open. Someone in the cast shared that they were really upset with me because I seemed aloof. That was the first time I had ever heard that word.

"I don't even know what that means!" I said.

"You're standoffish and quiet," they explained. "You keep to yourself."

When they said this, something inside me crumbled and I felt overwhelmed and panicky. "My mom was gone and didn't live at home during most of my childhood. And my dad was a very hard person to get affection from, and the truth is, I don't even think he liked me. I'm just figuring this out...I don't know how to do this! I'm asking myself how I fit in here and if I do fit in here!"

Then I told them about how I went to school one day and was rejected by my entire group of friends. "I trust and believe that you guys really do like me but sometimes people say nice things and then one day they're not your friend anymore."

Once I had finished talking and looked around, I saw blank looks on everyone's faces. I was afraid they were going to reject me.

Someone finally spoke up. "We had no idea!"

"Well, no, you wouldn't," I said. "I don't talk about it."

Then, every single person in the cast came up and hugged me and thanked me for being so open. The collective feeling seemed to be, "We really understand you now!"

A weight had been taken off my shoulders and I felt a great sense of relief. Finally, I could breathe a little deeper. It was a beautiful thing to feel like I didn't have to hide anymore and I truly began to love my cast mates.

One day, I was sitting in a church somewhere in Europe, looking at a beautiful altar, and I realized, *I am so different from the girl who left home five months ago!*

I reflected on how my life had changed the moment my family decided to host Helga and Karen in our home. I had been so unaware of so many things about myself. I remembered Helga telling me while she was staying with our family, "You will find a new depth of personal awareness and growth and learn to love yourself and everyone around you. You'll start to see how we're all connected." At the time she said those words to me, I thought they sounded great but it was only while sitting in that church that her words really started to register.

I was experiencing so many changes and, when I looked around, I could see that the world was changing right along with me. I started journaling about all the changes I was experiencing. Surprisingly, even my views about my dad were migrating. I started to realize that I had him to thank for my resilience. Others in the cast had a harder time handling all the stress of what we were going through—the fast pace and the constant change.

I had adopted my dad's attitude of, "This isn't the worst thing that could happen, so pull yourself together! The sun's going to come up tomorrow. Let's just get through today."

He didn't teach me these lessons in a loving way but he definitely got his point across. I was now using this very same wisdom to motivate my cast mates.

17

$\mathcal{W}$hile I was in Holland with a fellow cast mate named Andrea, working on setting up the city for the entire cast's arrival, we were using an office provided to us by our sponsor when Andrea got a call. I was on another call with a newspaper at the time.

Andrea turned to me and whispered, "I need you to wrap up your call!"

I could see in her eyes that something was wrong and my first thought was that my mother had died. I concluded my call and hung up the phone, trembling with fear—but then I found out that it wasn't my mother who had died but my friend, Shannon, the trumpet player for our cast.

Andrea explained, "That was Tom calling to tell us that Shannon died yesterday and his body is being flown home."

Apparently, Shannon was at the beach with his host family, and he and the son in the host family swam out to a rock in the ocean and stood atop it so that the family could take a photo of them. A huge wave came and knocked them off the rock and swept them under. In a freak accident, they both drowned. Perhaps they hit their heads when they were swept under and were knocked unconscious. In any case, Shannon's body was recovered but not that of the other boy.

The rest of the cast was planning to gather on the beach where Shannon lost his life to remember him and say their goodbyes. As the saying goes, the show must go on, so Andrea and I were not going to be able to stop what we were doing and join them. We had to remain in Holland and continue preparing for the upcoming performance. We were asked to write a letter that could be read at the memorial service.

As we wrote our letter to Shannon, I felt a mixture of sadness over the loss of my friend and relief that it wasn't my mother. Experiencing that relief made me feel badly about myself and I wondered, *How can I be so selfish?*

I still had such high expectations of myself and I was extremely hard on myself when I failed to live up to them. Even though I had undergone a tremendous period of personal growth while in Europe, there was still that part of me that was relentless in my judgment of myself and unwilling to forgive and excuse my flawed humanness. No one could make me feel worse about myself than I did.

When the rest of the cast joined us in Holland, Andrea and I momentarily felt like outsiders. They had all bonded over the death of Shannon, and Andrea and I weren't there to participate in the memorial. It took a little time to get past the feeling of having become an outsider.

Meanwhile I was visiting shops in the area and handing out flyers to promote the show when I met a Dutch boy who became a very important part of my European experience. Patrick was twenty years old and lived on his own, which was a novelty to me because I wanted to be independent more than anything. Although I was steadily gaining confidence, standing on my own two feet was still a scary and daunting proposition.

Patrick was a model and he was handsome and charismatic. He had fair skin, hazel eyes and brown hair, cut in a European style I'd never seen before. I was attracted to him on many levels. I loved his independence and strength and found those qualities inspiring. And he had the warmest smile. I loved it when he spoke to me in broken English.

We began to date, or as much as my schedule would allow, anyway. We were only in town for a few weeks and, between rehearsals and performances, I didn't have that much spare time. Whenever I could break free to meet him, we went to cafes and ordered coffee and sat and talked about all sorts of things and nothing at all. We listened to music. And, thanks to a powerful attraction between us, we engaged in plenty of kissing and making out. Our make-out sessions were rated PG and it was always sweet torture to tear ourselves apart so I could return to the home of my host family.

Patrick ignited in me a beautiful awareness of what love could feel like. Our connection had more depth and spirituality than the bonds I had experienced with high school boyfriends. We would stare at each other endlessly, smiling, do some kissing, some talking, and then find ourselves staring at each other again.

When it was time for the cast to leave Holland, I was heartbroken. I wasn't nearly ready to leave Patrick. But what could I do? I couldn't have quit the show. UWP would not have refunded my money to me and I would have found myself alone in Europe with no means of support. I wouldn't have been able to find a job because I didn't have a work visa. Both Patrick and I understood that I couldn't stay in Holland with him, so we said goodbye and I continued with the cast.

18

One day about three and a half months before my yearlong commitment in the cast had run its course, our casting director got a phone call from my dad, who told him that my mom was very sick. I was told that "my mom wasn't going to be with us for very long," and my dad needed me to return home. Mom was about to undergo some very aggressive treatment, including another surgery, radiation and chemotherapy.

I was heartbroken over having to leave the tour early. I was finally finding myself and now that was being taken away from me. I had already given up so much of my childhood in order to take care of my mom and younger siblings. Once again, I had to devote myself to taking care of my family and, as much as I loved them, I didn't want to go home early.

I was worried about my mom and dreading living at home with my dad again. I knew it wasn't going to be easy. I was beginning to feel like I would never truly have a life of my own and the thought of it made me feel depressed and hopeless. Thankfully, the despondency didn't derail me. Having been abroad for the first time in my life, I had truly become my own person and grown more and more independent in my thinking.

I had spent my life plagued and paralyzed by fears of ridicule, scrutiny and criticism. Over time, I had become less and less inclined to allow the input of others to outweigh my own opinions. Little by little, thanks to my time as part of the cast of Up with People, I acquired confidence and autonomy.

I had been calling home from time to time (using a calling card) and I noticed that, whenever I spoke to my dad, it was less problematic. His words no longer wounded or rattled me or destroyed my confidence in myself and my future. I had developed enough of a belief in myself that his hurtful comments and the limitations he tried to place on my future had less of an impact. Now his words fueled my motivation.

During one phone call home, I'd said, "Oh, Dad, I really like this country! Part of me thinks I could live here."

He said, "Oh, that's never going to happen!"

I took it in stride. I knew I could have a wonderful life, even if Dad didn't. I felt happy and grateful that I had evolved into a more confident and independent version of myself and I felt certain that when I got home from Europe, I would be free of the constant fear that I was going to stumble and disappoint. I didn't feel like I needed to be perfect anymore.

I possessed a new compass to guide me through life, and the tools to approach my life with understanding and compassion for others. I came to realize that, during all those years that I had lived at home in such emotional deprivation, I was focused primarily on myself. With the maturity I'd gained in Europe, I now viewed that self-centered approach to life as immature.

I returned home and my mother went into surgery. Seeing her in the hospital looking sick and fragile brought back all my old fears and I realized that she really might die. This time, she had cancer in her abdomen.

After her surgery, it was hard for Mom to get around due to the fact that the surgeons had snipped her abdominal muscles. I had to help her in and out of bed and the bathroom. During radiation and chemotherapy, she went to live with my grandparents in California. She would stay there for three or four days at a time before returning home. While Mom was away, I helped Dad with my brother and sisters, which was pretty arduous.

When I had been home for about six months, I had an interesting conversation with Grandma. She had just brought Mom home from California and I had just returned from picking up my siblings from school. In her usual candor, Grandma said, "You're just sitting here rotting!"

Ninety percent of the time, I loved Grandma's candor—but when I was wrong, she was the first one to tell me. She never, ever minced words and she would not let you hide from your accountability. At those moments when you weren't at your best, Grandma wasn't likely to let it slide.

From the time I was a little girl, Grandma had told me, "You have choices in this world. You have choices in what you say and what you do. No one can take those two choices from you, so do your best with both."

She had also given me a lifetime of guidance on how to best deal with my dad. As you know by now, I had a bit of a temper and living with my dad was not easy.

"You have a mouth on you and you say too much!" Grandma would tell me. "Sometimes you have to learn when to walk away. That way, you don't give him anything to come back at you with."

"I know, Grandma, but I get so mad!"

"I absolutely understand, Missy. But nobody can make you say those ugly, hateful things and nobody can make you stand there and fight with him. Just walk away!"

Grandma never advocated for me becoming passive with Dad. Whenever Grandma witnessed the cold, harsh way Dad talked to me, she talked to him about it, and she also talked to me about it. "Don't ever let a man talk to you like that! Don't ever think you need to accept that kind of treatment!"

"Well, I don't really have a choice, Grandma! I can't exactly leave."

Now, she was letting me know that, while I had returned from Europe in many ways a more mature and confident version of myself, my life was going nowhere. She always did shoot straight from the hip.

Grandma was right, of course. Since my return from Europe, my life consisted of taking care of my siblings and working at the part-time secretarial job I had gotten to help me fill the time while they were at school. Grandma could see that I was just spinning my wheels.

"Believe me—I don't want to be here!" I told her. "I want to go to college but Dad is not in support of me doing that." I went on to say that I felt that I had taken on an awful lot of responsibility at home at the expense of my own dreams.

I said, "Honestly, I'm a little resentful, Grandma!"

Dad didn't seem to see me as anything more than a burden to be married off to the first guy who would have me. I was very angry and resented him for it. My time spent living in Europe as an independent adult made it all the more difficult to listen to him tell me what to do with my life.

"We both know that your dad's never going to support you in getting higher education," Grandma said. "He just wants you to get married!"

She was referring to the time Dad had said to her, "Well, what's the point of putting twenty, thirty, forty thousand dollars into Missy's education when she's just going to end up getting married and having kids? She'll never use her degree and it will be a waste of money."

"Let's not be negative, Missy," Grandma continued. "You're a smart girl and you can figure this out. And I can give you a hand—but I'm not going to hand this to you. You're going to have to work for it!"

Grandma offered to pay for the first semester of my education. She also told me I could stay in the Phoenix home that she and Grandpa owned but didn't occupy while they were in California. I was elated.

"Now, remember, you're going to have to maintain your grades," Grandma said. "And I expect you to keep the house in order and act like a lady. No boys and no booze!"

"Okay, Grandma," I said. "I can do that...but I don't even know if Dad will give me the gas money to drive up there! I will need to leave quickly in order to arrive in time for enrollment."

"Here you go, honey," Grandma said, handing me a hundred dollar bill. "Problem solved. Now, what?"

She was letting me know that I needed to ask myself whether I was serious or looking for one excuse after another to keep from committing to college.

I took the hundred-dollar bill from her and said, "I am going to start packing!"

"That's my girl," she said. Grandma was a strong, no-nonsense, no-excuses woman. That could be hard for me to handle, not because it was hurtful but because it forced me to face the fact that I could be my own worst enemy. She helped me realize that I wasn't moving toward my goals—I was standing still—and it was time to take action.

About fifteen minutes after this conversation with Grandma, I went to talk to my dad. "Grandma is going to let me live at her house in Phoenix while I go to college and she is going to pay for my first semester's tuition!"

"Well, the next thing you need to figure out is how to pay for your food," he said, without missing a beat, "because I'm not supporting you!"

"Okay," I said. "I'll figure it out."

He later relented somewhat, agreeing to contribute a certain amount of money toward my expenses while making it clear that I needed to be careful managing my money. Even so, it would be a stretch to say that he was supportive of me going to college.

When I told my mom that I was going to live at Grandma and Grandpa's place and go to college, she was excited for me and also a little bit sad to think of me leaving home. My brother and sisters felt the same way—excited for me but sad to see me leaving home so soon after returning from Europe.

Jennifer and I had a close relationship and, when she heard that I was going away to college in Phoenix, she let me know she was going to miss me. We spent a lot of time together, going out on the weekends in my car that we loaded up with our friends. We drove around town, laughing and having fun and talking about life. Sometimes we met up with friends at our local Burger King hotspot.

Since we went to parties and did a lot of social things together, her friends became my friends despite our thirty-month age difference. When Jennifer had friends over, I would go into her room and see if they'd let me hang out with them. It was harder to make friends after returning from Europe. All my high school friends had moved away to attend college, so being able to hang out with Jennifer and her friends grounded me.

Jennifer was also a bit envious. I was getting to escape our home life and she wished she could join me.

Scottie, meanwhile, was going to miss having me at his football games where I was his biggest fan, always encouraging him and telling him that he was special. My brother was a naturally gifted athlete and had a great disposition and a wonderful sense of humor. We loved to be silly together and he got a kick out of playing practical jokes on me.

My relationship with my sister Carrie wasn't as close as the relationship between me and my other siblings. She was still dealing with some sort of internal imbalance and was prone to outbursts, temper tantrums and meltdowns. She needed everything to be a certain way and any deviation from that could cause her to unravel and explode.

We all suspected some sort of underlying issue, be it neurological, psychological or emotional but, as I said earlier, my parents never pursued a diagnosis for Carrie. It was a shame because the situation put a great strain on the family and must have caused a lot of suffering for Carrie, herself. Not surprisingly, her unaddressed issues led her to self-medicate. This is all to say that I could have lived at home or on the moon and it would have all been the same to Carrie.

19

I enrolled in community college with the intention to later transfer to Arizona State, and began taking general courses with an emphasis on art history and psychology. It was easy to settle in at my grandparents' house since it already felt like home. I immediately started looking for part-time work, which triggered all my insecurities and anxiety.

I applied at retail stores, figuring the work would be easy and the schedule flexible and got hired at Broadway Department Store in the children's clothing department. I was enjoying a sense of freedom I hadn't experienced since I was in Europe, and it felt good to be able to do as I pleased and not have to answer to anyone but myself.

I met Trevor, my first college boyfriend, and we dated for a couple of years but the relationship was ultimately sunk by the fact that he had a drinking problem and became volatile when he was drunk. I had so anesthetized myself to emotional abuse while living at home with my dad that it wasn't until my boyfriend put me in the emergency room that I finally came to my senses and broke things off with him.

Even though I knew I needed to get away from Trevor for my own safety and well being, there was a part of me that still wanted to rescue him. Strangely enough, it was Trevor's own mother who warned me against getting back together with him.

"No, Melissa! This is too dangerous for you!" she said. "You can't fix him or love him through this. You need to let him face this, come to terms with it and fix it on his own. If you don't leave him, he will continue to do this for the rest of his life."

Within a few months of breaking things off with Trevor, I met a guy named George who lived in Rhode Island but was visiting his brother who went to Arizona State. We met at a nightclub and hit it off immediately. George was studying architecture in Rhode Island. He was very well read and well-spoken and, best of all, when I met him at the nightclub, he was drinking water rather than alcohol. (I was determined to be careful this time around and watch out for red flags.)

This was a different type of relationship for me—one based on an intellectual exchange. George introduced me, for example, to a whole range of classic literature to which I'd never been exposed. I also found him very attractive, with his long, curly black hair and his olive skin and dark eyes. He was tall and slender with a big warm smile and an artistic temperament.

George and I dated for six months, long distance, and then right before Christmas of 1992, he came out to the Southwest to visit me. He proposed marriage and I accepted. Right after the proposal, we drove to my parents' house so that we could tell them our big news and they could meet George. Even though he'd already proposed to me, George went through the formality of asking Dad for my hand in marriage.

Dad said "Sure!" Both my parents liked George. I had expected that my dad, especially, would be very happy and eager to see me go from a young adult to a full grown adult who was ready to get married and raise a family of my own. Now that marriage was actually on the horizon, I found that I didn't resent my dad's enthusiasm over my engagement. I was happy that he was happy for me. I felt like I was finally getting something right.

Two months later in the dead of winter, I moved to Bristol, Rhode Island to be with my fiancé. I certainly could not make such a long drive on my own so my dad drove back east with me. This cross country drive at that time of year was tricky. We alternately ran into patches of complete darkness where we couldn't see and heavy downpours where the windshield was so pelted with rain, all visibility was gone and we found ourselves sliding off the road.

Dad set his mind on covering as many miles a day as he could and absolutely refused to stop for bathroom breaks. It was kind of a difficult trip as there were times I was sure I was going to pee in my pants. Somehow we managed to arrive at our destination in one piece and even had some laughs along the way. Things were better between us than they had been in a very long time.

At a roadside diner somewhere between Phoenix and Rhode Island, Dad and I sat at the counter. Between the waitress who wore a typical pink frock with a white apron and the fact that customers were flocking to the diner because it was famous for its cherry pie, Dad and I had the strange feeling that we were in a movie. While we were there, I thought to myself, *This is probably one of the best moments I've ever had with Dad!*

When we finally reached Rhode Island, we stayed at the home of George's parents who were wonderful hosts. Wanting us to have the quintessential New England dining experience, they served crab and we ate at picnic tables. Around George's parents, Dad was funny, lighthearted and pleasant. This was Dad at his very best. My dad and George's dad immediately took to each other and became instant friends. Everything was going very smoothly and the future looked bright. Dad stayed for about three days and then returned home.

George was living on campus. I rented an apartment and found a job working at a Rhode Island department store called Filene's, first in the children's department and then in cosmetics. I had worked at various cosmetic counters back home before meeting George so this was right up my alley. I made friends easily at my new job and everyone seemed to get a kick out of seeing a fair-skinned blonde. Nearly everyone who lived in the region was Italian, with dark hair and olive skin.

As George and I transitioned from having a long distance relationship to living in the same town, we got to know each other at a deeper level and soon discovered we were profoundly incompatible.

George was a great student and very committed to his studies but he was in no hurry to get a job. In fact, he didn't seem to understand the financial responsibilities associated with having a family and didn't have much ambition at all in terms of his long term goals.

When George started pressuring me to move to a communal farm owned by the parents of a female friend of his, the fundamental differences in our natures, outlooks and goals came into stark relief.

This was his ideal mode of living—living in a commune with a bunch of friends who shared expenses. He was already spending his weekends at the farm. While I was busy working, he would drive to the farm in a car filled with gas paid for by me. When he wasn't at the farm, he stayed over at my apartment and ate food paid for by me. In the evenings, he liked to go to poetry readings or open mic nights at bars where musicians would get up and play. That was fun for me too but my enthusiasm was dampened by the fact that I had to get up in the mornings and go to work.

I could not escape the fact that I was engaged to a man who was unwilling to grow up. Before long, he would graduate with his architecture degree and be compelled to take his degree out into the workplace and earn a living but, in the meantime, he seemed determine to relive his youth—at my expense, literally.

Everything came to a head one day when, exasperated, I called George's dad and said, "I just can't afford George!"

He was horrified that I would consider breaking things off with his son. He didn't seem to grasp the fact that George had managed to drain my entire nest egg and every penny I'd earned at Filene's.

"This is part of being married." he said. "You need to open a dialogue with George and you both need to be committed to working this out!"

"That's great and everything but I can't support him!" I said. I was over it—completely fed up and done with the engagement. I had only spent five months in Rhode Island but the relationship had already run its course. It was time to go home.

George and I had to admit that we wanted totally different ways of life and were never going to be a great fit. It was a sad realization because we really cared for each other and I also loved his parents.

They loved me as well and were heartbroken to hear that their son and I were dissolving our relationship.

It was a very mutual decision and our ending was harmonious. Thank goodness, the relationship between George and me never devolved to the point where we were fighting all the time and hated each other. George and I were better friends than anything else and should I run into him some day, I know that I would enjoy sitting and listening to him share with me the details of his life. He was a great guy and I have very fond memories of him.

20

J moved back home right after the Fourth of July. I was twenty-one years old and couldn't imagine living at home again with my parents. I got lucky and was able to move into a condo they owned for investment purposes. I loved my new home and found the ideal roommate—Sheryl, a girl I'd known since childhood, as we attended the same school and church. Dad helped me find a job at a construction company so I was able to pay monthly rent to my parents. I loved my new home, which was the perfect size to share with a roommate.

Sheryl and I often went out together and had fun. When Sheryl's best friend, Stephanie, wanted to set her up on a blind date, she felt obligated to agree. Her blind date was Joey, a dentist who was one of the roommates of Stephanie's boyfriend, Sam. Sheryl didn't want to go alone and asked me to come along. "Please! This guy's old! He even has *kids.* And if you're with me and the date's horrible, you can get me out of there."

By "old," Sheryl meant that her blind date was twenty-nine. We were only twenty-one, so twenty-nine with children sounded ancient to us.

Joey planned to cook dinner for Sheryl. So I drove Sheryl to the house and we knocked on the door and stood there in matching sundresses, with our exit strategy carefully rehearsed. It was August and it was a warm evening. As we stepped inside the house, the first thing I noticed was a large wolf with piercing eyes, named, appropriately,

Lobos. I have always been afraid of wolves but this one was very sweet and gentle. The animal was the pet of Kevin, another roommate.

Kevin stood beside his wolf and urged me to be careful. Meanwhile, Sheryl went inside to meet Joey and say hi to Sam. After a few moments, Kevin, Lobos and I joined the others, and when Sheryl saw the wolf, she started screaming, "Get him out of here! Get him out of here!"

As Kevin was leading Lobos toward his room, Joey—a good looking man with an olive complexion—came around the corner and said to me, "Oh, you're not afraid of the dog?"

"No," I said. "I think he's gorgeous! It's not every day you see a wolf."

"So true. By the way, I didn't know you were coming but I made dinner and we have plenty," he said. "Pasta and salad. And I made the sauce myself."

It made sense that Joey would know how to make delicious pasta sauce—he was Italian. He happened to be friendly and charismatic, as well, and made an effort to pay attention to his date, Sheryl. He needn't have bothered—she wanted absolutely nothing to do with him. I felt badly that she was giving Joey the cold shoulder so I jumped in and started talking to him, myself.

After dinner, Joey said, "Well, I guess I'd better iron my scrubs for tomorrow. I'm so bad at it!"

"No problem," I said. "I'll do it."

Joey pulled out the ironing board and plugged in the iron, not believing that I really planned to do his ironing for him.

"Here, I'll do it." I said. When I saw the bright color of his scrubs, we had a laugh together. Apparently at Joey's dental office (owned by Kevin, the roommate with the wolf) they wore different brightly colored scrubs for each day of the week.

While I ironed, we talked and laughed. Joey was larger than life and very funny, the type of guy who could enter a roomful of strangers and turn them all into his biggest fans by the end of the evening.

Suddenly, Sheryl was giving me our prearranged, "Hey, I need to go!" signal. It was so obvious and awkward.

Joey could clearly see what was happening and said to Sheryl, "I'm not interested in you either but I'm talking to your friend, if that's okay." Joey wasn't trying to embarrass us—he was just letting us know that he knew what was going on and had no problem with it.

Sheryl and I were embarrassed and exchanged knowing glances, acknowledging that we'd just been caught in our obvious deception. "Oh, okay, sure…" Sheryl said. "I'm just going to hang out over here…"

We stayed for a while longer and, as we were leaving, Joey said to me, "Hey, I'd really like to take you to dinner sometime."

I had no issue with our age difference. We seemed to have a great rapport and, in fact, I had laughed so much with him that night, my face hurt as Sheryl and I prepared to leave.

"Let me check with Sheryl," I said, "and make sure she's really okay with it."

Sheryl let me know that she had absolutely zero interest in Joey, so I accepted his invitation to dinner.

21

A few days later, Joey came to my house to pick me up for our date. When he arrived, I greeted him wearing a sundress and sandals—and he greeted me wearing jeans, a very colorful belt, a t-shirt and bright red Sperry shoes. He was the most colorfully dressed individual I'd ever seen. In the Southwestern town where I lived, the guys usually wore jeans or jean shorts, an untucked t-shirt, Redwing leather shoes that came up around the ankle, and visible socks. We jokingly referred to this style trend as farmer chic.

"I don't want to take you to any of the usual spots," he explained. "I want you to remember me." So he took me to a dive bar where we stuck out like sore thumbs thanks to Joey's colorful outfit and my preppy one, not to mention the fact that we both had all our teeth.

The crowd's first reaction to us was suspicion but when Joey noticed them eyeing us, he called out in a friendly voice, "Hey, everyone! This is our first date!" It broke the tension in the room and everyone started clapping. Joey could make friends anywhere.

My initial reaction to being taken to a dive bar on our first date was mild irritation. I thought, *Where are you taking me?* But we had a great evening, laughing together, playing pinball and pool and throwing darts. I loved that Joey was so young at heart.

We ended the evening around ten o'clock because Joey needed to drive straight through to California that night so he could pick up his sons from their mother's house in Orange County. It was a quick date but perfect. As he dropped me off, Joey gave me a great big hug and a kiss on the cheek. I didn't take the kiss on the cheek as any indication of disinterest on his part. There was no denying the wonderful evening we had shared.

Just to make sure there was no doubt in my mind as to his interest level, Joey called me around one-thirty or two in the morning as he arrived at his destination in California, just to tell me how much fun he'd had with me. As time passed following our date, he would call me from time to time throughout the day and say, "Just wanted you to know I was thinking of you."

I really started to fall for him. I had returned home from Rhode Island a little bit embarrassed over my broken engagement with George but, with Joey in my life, I quickly forgot all about George and any embarrassment I was feeling. Joey made it clear that he adored me and this was the first time in my life that I had ever felt truly adored and precious to someone.

When Joey returned from California, he invited me over to his house for a second date. His roommates were gone and we had the house to ourselves. He cooked dinner for me and, afterwards, he sat down on the floor with his back against the sofa and had me lean back against him. He wrapped his arms around me and read me a beautifully illustrated children's book. The book was called *Hope for the Flowers* and it was about a little boy who plants a seed and later plucks a flower to give to his true love.

"I'm so taken with you!" he said. "You're the first person I think of in the morning and the last one at night. And when I'm not with you, I can't wait to see you! And, as crazy as this may sound, I know I'm going to fall in love with you!"

Then he presented the book to me. "I'm giving you this book," he explained, "because there are no flowers in the yard to pick for you."

I loved every word he said to me and everything about him. He made me light up in a way no one ever had before him.

After we had been dating for a couple of months, we went to his parents' house in the California desert. Joey and I were sitting outside on the lawn of their mountaintop home. We had a blanket spread out beneath us and we were looking up at the stars in the night sky. Suddenly he started improvising a song and dance routine for my benefit. It was hilarious and sweet and it made me giggle. As the song ended, he dropped onto one knee and proposed marriage to me.

I was taken by surprise but, at the same time, I knew that we loved each other and would be together.

"I would love to be your wife!" I said. "Of course I will marry you."

He placed a big, clunky man's ring on my ring finger, saying, "I'll fix that soon, but I couldn't wait another minute to propose to you!"

I looked down at the big, gaudy diamond-and-gold-nugget ring which apparently Joey's mother had found in an old jewelry box when he told her he planned to propose to me. The ring was Las Vegas all the way and, in order to even keep it on my hand, I had to wear it on my thumb. He promised that, the next day, he would take me to a jewelry store to look at real engagement rings.

We went inside the house where Joey's parents, brother and sister-in-law were waiting to hear my answer, and Joey announced, "She said yes!"

We all hugged and kissed and laughed with joy and everyone said, "Welcome to the family!"

The next day, Joey took me to a jewelry store to look at rings and brought his mom along with us. We selected a ring and, while it was being made, I wore the chunky gold nugget ring on a necklace. Later that day, we drove to Huntington Beach, California for Joey to pick up his boys, Mark and Jordan, who were seven and ten, respectively.

Meeting the boys for the first time was both exciting and daunting. I really wanted the meeting to go well. Mark and Jordan turned out to be the sweetest boys, every bit as warm and loving as I'd hoped, and all my fears were put to rest.

At the conclusion of this weekend trip, Joey and I dropped off the boys at their mom's and started driving home. While we were driving in the car, I mentioned a certain man I'd met while traveling in Norway and referred to him as "the funniest person I'd ever met."

"What do you mean?" Joey said. "I thought I was the funniest person you'd ever met! Now I'm the second funniest?" He wasn't teasing me—he was seriously offended.

I asked him, "Why are you making a big deal out of this? I didn't mean to hurt your feelings."

I didn't understand why he was taking a comment that had nothing to do with him, making it all about him, and getting his feelings hurt. I thought to myself, *Wow, he's really sensitive!* My next thought was, *Wait a minute…could he actually think I don't adore him as much as he adores me?*

I tried to reassure him by saying, "I really do think you're funny!"

It was no use. He wouldn't let it go and things escalated until we found ourselves in a big argument. I was exasperated and couldn't understand how something so insignificant had turned into an argument.

Finally Joey switched gears and said, "Sorry. Let's not worry about it." But, despite his best attempts to let it go, he continued to pout and became aloof. I had never seen that side of him before but I decided to just move on and didn't spend any time analyzing his behavior.

I remembered his mother saying to me, "Oh, Joey's the life of the party alright, but he can also blow up like a bomb."

I hadn't personally been the recipient of his explosive temper and had only seen little glimpses of it when he was around his mother and brother. I did know that a family crisis early in Joey's life had made a lasting impact on him.

First, let me tell you a little bit about Joey's background. He was one of four children. Greg and Todd were the oldest, born two years apart. Five years passed before Joey was born and, a year later, Caryn came along. Joey always felt that his parents focused all their attention on the two older kids and he and Caryn got the short end of the stick.

Even though he and Caryn got less attention than their older siblings, Joey felt that his parents had especially high expectations of him. For example, Joey's parents pushed him to graduate high school in three years rather than four in order to save an extra year of tuition fees at the expensive Seventh Day Adventist school he attended. He grew up resenting the double standard.

Then, when he was seventeen years old, Joey got his girlfriend, Jeri, pregnant. Joey and Jeri had met through Greg, who was heartbroken when he found out about the pregnancy. He'd always carried a torch for Jeri and had hoped the two of *them* might get together. Joey's relationship with Jeri caused a rift among family members, and this was exacerbated by the fact that Greg was sick and dying with colon cancer during Joey and Jeri's courtship. Jeri happened to get pregnant right around the same time Greg's health took a turn for the worse.

Joey was hit hard and deeply wounded by the knowledge that he had disappointed the family by getting Jeri pregnant. The dynamic between him and his mother had always run hot and cold, anyway, and this didn't help. In many ways, she was the typical Italian mother who alternated between joyousness and explosive anger.

At least they *had* a relationship. This was an improvement over Joey's relationship with his father, who was sweet but distant and never seemed to have any time for Joey.

Joey's parents were against the idea of him marrying Jeri. Nevertheless, Joey married his baby's mother and three years later, they had a second son.

22

$\mathcal{G}$iven that I had just recently moved back home following a failed engagement, my family was a little bit wary of my engagement to Joey. We were all eating dinner together at a Chinese restaurant when Joey and I told my family the big news. When Joey excused himself from the table for a moment, my family expressed to me their reservations over our quick engagement.

"I know, I know," I cried, "but I love him!"

When Joey returned to the table, he explained, "Listen, I love your daughter and I will take good care of her. We want to be together but we don't want to live together without being married first. So, that's why we want to get married as soon as possible."

We agreed to have our actual wedding in December but neither Joey nor I wanted to wait to be intimate until our December wedding. And we didn't want to feel like we were living in a sinful arrangement in the meantime. So we planned to meet at four in the afternoon on October 20th, 1993 at the local courthouse to legalize our commitment.

Right before it was time for Joey to leave his dental office to come meet me at the courthouse, he had a patient who ran late. So Joey had no time to change out of his magenta colored scrubs. The cut-off time for filling out the marriage paperwork was four-thirty, and he arrived at the courthouse at four-twenty in that colorful outfit.

When I saw him, I thought to myself, *Oh, wow, I'm going to marry you in that wonderful outfit?* Sure enough.

We were married by the judge in his chambers and it was a quick, hectic experience. It was very transactional and completely devoid of romance. Everything was cut and dried: "Do you take Melissa to be your wife? Do you take Joey to be your husband? Okay, you're now officially married. And now we're closing so you need to leave!"

That was it—no pictures, nothing. We were actively planning a lovely wedding and this courthouse ceremony was just a formality but it still left me feeling strange. Afterwards, we went out to dinner and then to my place. Now that we were officially man and wife, we could spend the night together.

Joey still had his own apartment and I was still rooming with Cheryl in the condo. Since the condo was nicer than Joey's apartment, that's where we spent our first night as a married couple. We relaxed for a while and then headed to bed. We were both tired and Joey had to see patients early the following morning. Any girlhood fantasies I might have had about the magic of my wedding night went out the window. It was just another night.

Wow, I thought, *I really expected to feel something other than slightly peculiar on the day I was married! Oh, well. Maybe it just hasn't hit me yet and I'll get that feeling later...*

On the upside, my new husband and I could now go to bed together every single night without feeling like we were doing something wrong. We were both too exhausted to consummate our union and, as we fell asleep in each other's arms, we joked, "Well, I guess we'll have to make up for this on our actual wedding night!"

It wasn't more than a few days before my engagement ring was finished and ready to pick up from the jeweler, along with our wedding bands. Now it was time to shop for my wedding dress. Grandma and Jennifer came shopping with me and, thankfully, Mom was also feeling well enough to join us. She had envisioned me getting married in a very specific style of dress.

"Really, Mom? A portrait collar dress? Are you sure?" I asked.

"Yes, honey! It will look great on you. You'll see. Here, try this one on..."

When I walked out of the dressing room in the dress, my mom started to cry. Grandma and Jennifer also loved the dress on me and, standing there in front of all of them, I felt like a princess.

Once we had found my wedding dress, the rest of the wedding preparations unfolded effortlessly. We put about two hundred friends and loved ones on our guest list and chose the Morey Mansion in Redlands, California—a beautiful and picturesque wedding venue. Our wedding date was all set for December 4th, 1993.

Now all I had to do was find long bridesmaid dresses with sleeves so my bridesmaids wouldn't freeze at my winter wedding. I chose a dark emerald green velvet dress with a high portrait collar in satin—the perfect complement to my wedding dress. As you know by now, my sister Carrie (who was only twelve years old) was very sensitive to many things, including the feel of certain fabrics against her skin, and she threw a fit and refused to wear the dress.

I didn't want to deal with having her in the wedding due to all the drama and difficulties that tended to surround her. I would have been fine to excuse her from participating but my mother wouldn't hear of it. She agreed to Carrie's demands to have her bridesmaid dress made in a different style. This infuriated me and, to make matters worse, this whole quick-change with Carrie's dress was happening within just a few days of the wedding.

On the night before the wedding, we had our rehearsal dinner and then I stayed overnight at the Morey Mansion by myself. I liked the tradition of the bride and groom sleeping apart on the night before the wedding. I spent a quiet and contemplative evening by myself and awoke in the morning to a beautiful breakfast and a touching poem written for me by my husband and delivered to me by the innkeeper.

Mom, Grandma and my sisters had slept at the mansion as well, and then Aunt Debbie and my cousins arrived, and slowly but surely my wedding day got underway. I had my regular hair stylist lined up to do my hair and makeup but I found out that she'd gone out drinking the night before and couldn't make it because she was suffering from a terrible hangover.

I became very anxious, knowing that my veil wouldn't fit unless my hair was styled in a certain way. Eventually my hair stylist showed up and I breathed a sigh of relief until I realized she was still completely hungover. She spent no more than ten minutes on my hair and didn't even try to do my makeup.

When Aunt Debbie walked into the room and saw me, she said, "What on earth happened to your hair?"

I started crying.

"Don't worry, Missy," she said. "I'll fix it!" She took the pins out of my hair and re-styled it and I did my own makeup.

When it came time for photos, Carrie balked at putting on her dress for the photos.

I told my mom, "Forget it! I don't need her in any of the pictures! This is my day and I don't need her ruining it!"

Mom insisted on having Carrie included in the photos and I was very frustrated. My wedding day was being hijacked by my mom and little sister. Jennifer played mediator and somehow Mom managed to get Carrie into her dress and into the photos. In every one of the wedding photos, Carrie can be seen with either a frown or a contrived smile. Meanwhile, Grandma's health had started failing and when she finally got comfortable in a gaudy couch-chair, she stayed put. All the photos had to be staged around Grandma sitting in that chair instead of outside on the beautiful grounds or in the stately library.

All of a sudden, everything was going wrong and, for a moment, I lost my mind and became the typical Bridezilla. "I don't care what anyone else wants!" I screamed. "You are all here because I invited you and you need to do what I need you to do! Then you can do whatever you want. And right now, what I need you to do is get these pictures done!"

Adding to the chaos was the fact that our florist, Caryn (Joey's sister) unilaterally decided to replace the winter themed Poinsettias, blood red roses and Christmas greens in my bridal bouquet. In their place were hot pink Stargazer lilies—a flower I would have loved at another time of year and on some other occasion where a tropical theme was appropriate.

When Joey saw the flowers, he leaned in and whispered to me, "When did you tell Caryn you wanted it to look like we were in Hawaii?"

Meanwhile, without budging from the chair where she was still sitting, Grandma said, "Hot damn! I didn't know you were taking us to Jamaica! So much for the winter wonderland."

It was the exact wrong thing to say in that moment—but funny enough to break the tension. "Sorry to disappoint you, Grandma, but we're not going to Jamaica. We're having our tropical wedding right here in California."

With the way things were going, my only thought was, *All I ask is that I make it down that staircase without breaking my neck!*

At last, it was time for the wedding to start. As I was standing on the landing and looking at all the guests seated below, Joey's mom caught sight of a friend of mine who was dressed like she was about to go to a nightclub rather than attend a wedding.

"Who's that putana talking to Caryn?" Mary asked. "Someone needs to tell her to cover up those boobs so we can have a wedding!" Thankfully, someone found her a shawl which she wrapped around herself.

Then the wedding music started and I made my way down the stairs and around to where the guests would watch me walk down the aisle. I was met by my dad whose cheek was swollen to four times its usual size.

"Dad! What in the world happened to your cheek?"

"Paintball." He whispered.

This was the last straw for me and I started laughing hysterically.

"Sorry, Miss," he said, his cheek so swollen he could hardly smile. "I hope I'll still do."   "Come on, Daddy, of course," I said.

I could see that my dad was misty eyed. He wasn't actually crying but this was a level of emotion I had never seen him express toward me before. It really choked me up. In that moment, I felt that he loved me, even though he hadn't spoken the words. For as long as I could remember, I had been waiting for a sign of his love and it couldn't have come at a better time.

23

I made it down the aisle without incident and Joey and I exchanged our vows. The ceremony was a blend of his Seventh Day Adventist background and my Mormon one and included scripture and a prayer. Joey's sons lit candles and then the four of us lit a candle together, signifying our blending together to form a family.

A string trio played as the pastor said, "You may now kiss the bride!"

My husband and I shared a big kiss and, in that exact moment, the three-year-old ring bearer—Joey's nephew, Greg—slipped on the satin train of my dress, fell and hit his head. As he was screaming his head off, everyone else burst out laughing.

My goodness, can anything else go wrong? I wondered.

The wedding party moved outside for the reception and Joey and I began dancing to Nat King Cole's *Unforgettable*. Finally I was starting to relax and feel grateful that the ceremony was over and we had somehow all survived it—and that's when Joey noticed how cold it was outside. We looked around and saw our guests shivering and trying to cover up to stay warm.

"Wait a minute..." Joey said. "What happened to all the heaters we ordered?"

As it turned out, Joey's mother had gotten it into her head to send back ten of the twelve heaters we had ordered. She didn't think it was likely to be chilly on the evening of our December wedding and unilaterally decided that our wedding guests could dine and dance in the open-air outdoor tents with the benefit of only two heaters rather than twelve. Neither Joey nor I could fathom what she was thinking. We were paying the majority of the wedding costs ourselves, so it wasn't a cost issue.

Joey and I had taken dance lessons to be prepared for the occasion but Joey was so frustrated by the heater situation, he forgot his dance steps. As we rotated away from each other, him to dance with his mother, and me to dance with my dad, I could hear him arguing with his mother over why she would have sent back ten of the twelve heaters.

The issue of the tropical flowers now came back into play, with Caryn explaining that she had worried that the poinsettias would wilt in the heat of the house. So, here we had Joey's sister who was afraid it would be too warm inside the mansion for the flowers I'd chosen and his mother who thought it would be too warm outside for us to need the heaters we'd ordered. Everything was growing tense.

"Come on, Joey," I said. "This is our wedding! Let's have a good time!"

He tried to rally so we could make the most of the occasion. He got some guys to help him move the chairs inside so that people could dance and party indoors. At some point, Joey and I made it to our hotel to sleep, once again too exhausted to have a proper wedding night. In the morning, we made our way back to the mansion and discovered that many of our guests had fallen asleep in the overstuffed mansion chairs.

We enjoyed a wonderful brunch with our family and, funny enough, Caryn's flowers held up beautifully. With all the pressure behind us, the mood was lighthearted and festive, with everyone giggling over the numerous mishaps. After saying goodbye to our family and loved ones, Joey and I got into his little, white convertible Volkswagen Rabbit and headed to Arizona for our honeymoon.

Our honeymoon began at the Grand Canyon and then we planned to go to a gorgeous resort in Sedona. We were going to take a hot air balloon ride in the morning and enjoy a beautiful brunch wherever the balloon might land.

As we were heading on muleback down the Grand Canyon to the Phantom Ranch at the bottom, I experienced extreme saddle soreness—not exactly conducive to honeymoon intimacy. Not only was I very uncomfortable, I was terrified that, with one false step from the mule which I was riding, I could have fallen to my death.

Once we got safely to the bottom, we had the best time. We had a lovely little cabin with a fireplace where we could build fires at night. It was very romantic. We went on nature hikes in the most beautiful surroundings and Joey was especially happy, being such a nature boy.

In my everyday life, I was more of an indoor girl and didn't spend enough time in nature, so this was a real treat for me. The experience bonded us even more deeply and, at last, I felt truly married.

I realized during my honeymoon that the fairytale we create in our minds can rob us of enjoying the actual events that take place in our lives. I reflected back on the mishaps at the mansion, remembering how upset I had been over them and how everything seemed catastrophic at the time. And yet, only a day later, we were able to have a laugh over everything and it brought us closer.

This was the first time I had a shift in perspective and saw perfection in a different light. Our perfect honeymoon moments had evolved out of everything falling apart, and that helped me realize that there was perfection even in the chaos because it brought us all together and bonded us.

While everything was going haywire at the wedding, it had seemed like the end of the world but I now saw how perfect moments could be born of imperfect beginnings. Life is messy and we certainly can't orchestrate it well enough to bring about true perfection. There is always a surprise around the corner—and it is life's surprises that give it flavor.

24

*R*eturning home from our honeymoon, I was really excited about building my future with Joey and I felt very much like a wife. I felt loved and adored by him and welcome in his family just as he was welcome in mine. I was at one with my husband and life was perfect.

Joey returned to work at his dental practice and I began taking general classes at the local college. Kevin, the dentist for whom Joey had been working, wanted to relocate to California so when he heard that Joey was planning to marry me, he offered to sell him the practice. This was a win-win for them both. Joey had been working there for a few months, so it was a smooth transition. The patients loved him and the feeling was mutual.

I began working at Joey's dental practice, running the front desk. Having never done anything like that before, I was a bit clumsy with booking the appointments and it took a while to understand how much time to allot for appointments for certain procedures. If I didn't allow enough time, Joey would feel rushed and, if I allowed too much time, there would be gaps in the schedule.

Not surprisingly, discord and frustration arose between us over this. The disharmony had nothing to do with our personal relationship but was a natural byproduct of learning to work together. The problem was, I took the criticism he gave me at work and brought it home with me.

One night in particular stands out in my memory. I returned home from night classes at the college. Joey had made dinner for us and was waiting for me to get home. He was also waiting for me to apologize for overbooking his schedule and keeping him running all day. Meanwhile, I came home pouting and ignoring him as a way of letting him know he'd hurt my feelings at the office.

After about half an hour of him sitting in the den, watching TV, and me sitting in the bedroom, reading, he came into the bedroom and said, "I don't even get a hello, let alone an 'I'm sorry?'"

"What are you talking about?" I snapped. "I've been waiting for you to apologize for being such a jerk to me today!"

"I was not a jerk! You have no idea what a stressful day I had because you can't remember how to book the patients!"

"Well, okay, I'm sorry," I said, not feeling particularly sorry at all, "but your schedule is right there! If there's a problem with it, why don't you tell me in advance?"

"Because I'm only looking at what I have that hour—not the entire day!"

This devolved into an argument over who had the bigger beef, who had the right to be angry, and who was being more impatient and insensitive with the other. We were both insanely stubborn and we each saw the situation quite differently. That really troubled me. We were both so invested in our own hurt feelings and our own pride, neither one of us wanted to be the first to apologize.

"I should just fire you!" he said.

"Well, fire me there, fire me here!" I shot back. "Pick your poison!"

I was only twenty-two years old, still immature, still deeply wounded by my father, and not about to let my husband wound me in the same away. Joey threatening to replace me at the dental practice called to mind so many things I'd lost when I was a kid. When my mom was in California being treated for cancer, my dance lessons were taken away—not because I deserved it but because my dad couldn't commit to getting me there on time. My summertime art program at the parks and recreation center was taken away for the same reason and so were my evening swimming lessons at the community pool.

Joey wasn't trying to exclude me from the dental practice. He really wanted us to work together. He felt that, if we could get in step with each other and work well together, it would enable us to manage the practice in a way that ensured its success. But, despite our best intentions, things couldn't have gone worse.

In addition to our conflicts related to working together at the office, there was the issue of how I was supposed to get my work done and simultaneously look after Joey's two sons when they came to visit during school breaks. This seemed like an unfair expectation to me but Joey felt that I just needed to figure it out.

We fell into a pattern where he would be intolerant of my imperfections and missteps and I would react with rage. He had a real problem with my extreme reactions and I always regretted the harsh words as they were leaving my lips. I never regretted them enough to apologize, however, as apologies were a real struggle for me. I wasn't about to say I was sorry if I felt that a situation arose because my husband had failed to work things out with me.

I lashed out at him and he responded in kind. Our arguments turned verbally abusive and, unfortunately, there were times when they became physical.

"I hit you because it's the only thing that hurts you!" said Joey. "Nothing I can say seems to hurt you!"

My husband used to get the tar knocked out of him by his brothers who were five and seven years older than he, respectively. And his mom was the type to spank first and ask questions later. Joey seemed to be on the receiving end of most of those spankings and developed a tolerance for loud and sometimes physically abusive behavior. He also learned that the way to get attention was to provoke, so he was often the antagonist—within his family of origin and with me.

Meanwhile, I freely shared with Joey the dubious gift I'd been given by my dad—the gift of being able to lacerate someone with my words. It came in very handy.

When we first met, we were so caught up in the euphoria of falling in love that we didn't spend much time getting to know each other. We fell in love hard and fast and ran to the altar so soon after meeting, we never stopped to realize that we were not the best match in terms of the childhood wounds we brought into the marriage.

One day, Joey hit me and I laughed in his face. "You may leave a mark," I said, "but you'll never hurt me! You're not strong enough."

I started to get a good look at myself and I didn't like what I was seeing. I had a lifetime of anger stored up and I was unleashing it on my husband, just as he unleashed his anger on me.

At times like these, I was troubled by the thought, *Joey sure seems to bring out the worst in me!*

25

A moment of truth occurred at the dental office when I made another scheduling error that put Joey in a time crunch. He lost his temper and let me have it, belittling and embarrassing me in front of two dental assistants.

I said, "How *dare* you put me down in front of other people? I'm your wife!" I was incensed.

As far as Joey was concerned, he was the dentist and this was the office where he practiced. He was not going to let me disrespect him by talking back to him.

I wasn't about to let him disrespect me either and, to prove my point, I marched out the back door of the office and headed down the stairs.

To prove *his* point, he locked me out.

When I heard him lock the door behind me, I saw red. I flew back up the stairs and tried to pull open the door and, when I couldn't, I started kicking it. I didn't give a moment's thought to who might be witnessing this—including Joey's dental patients! I just wanted back inside. As I was yelling and screaming and kicking the door, I noticed a woman in her backyard next door, watching me with a horrified expression.

"Open this door!" I yelled. "How dare you try to lock me out of the office? It's my office too!"

Joey had borrowed a sizeable sum of money from my dad to buy Kevin out of the dental practice. This made me feel like, "Wait a minute...I have more of an ownership in this dental practice than you!"

I didn't say those words out loud. Joey had been a little uneasy about accepting the money in the first place and wanted to repay my dad as quickly as possible. And I knew that reminding Joey of the loan would have been childish—not to mention emasculating.

Joey finally relented and opened the door, fearing I might actually break it if he didn't.

"Get out of my office!" I screamed. "You're fired!!!"

"Fine! I won't see patients then. You figure it out!" And he left. It was around lunchtime. His unspoken message to me was, "You think this is your practice? Seriously? Then go ahead and try to treat the patients!"

By calling my bluff and accepting my "firing" of him, Joey sank my battleship. I wasn't a dentist and couldn't very well treat the patients who were scheduled that day. "I'm sorry," I had to explain, "but the doctor will not be able to see you today. We'll have to reschedule."

Once I had calmed down, I felt completely humiliated, especially since our two dental assistants had witnessed my outburst and knew that I had fired the dentist in a moment of rage.

Joey didn't return to the office that afternoon. I knew I had crossed a line and I was not looking forward to the conversation we were likely to have when I saw him again. I really was terrified that Joey would leave me and I masked that fear with justified anger.

Any time I felt like I had a legitimate, valid viewpoint that was being dismissed out of hand, I could become filled with rage. Expressing myself in such an unrestrained, in-your-face manner made me feel powerful and put me on an adrenaline high. As satisfying as it could be in the moment, I knew this was the worst possible way to handle the situation and I was horrified by my own behavior. I feared that my explosive behavior would erode my relationship with Joey—not that he was behaving like a prince himself.

I realized, *I am very much my father's daughter and I need some help!* My father was the last person I wanted to emulate.

Joey never did return to the office. I spent the day paging him and he spent the day ignoring my pages. Around nine o'clock at night, he returned home. It turned out that he had left his pager in the car and gone to the movies to calm down and cool off. When he got home, he headed straight for the sofa to spend the night and I went to our bedroom to sleep alone.

I lay there forever, trying to sleep and, when I could no longer stand Joey not speaking to me, I went to the couch, woke him up and said, "I know I crossed a line with you professionally and maybe even morally, and disrespected you and your staff. I'm really sorry. I was so caught up in my anger, I wasn't thinking straight. Why don't we get some counseling? I don't want to continue on this way."

"I think that's a good idea," he said.

His words stung. By agreeing that we needed counseling, Joey validated my deepest fear—that there was something wrong with me. It was one thing for me to admit my faults but I didn't appreciate him pointing them out to me. It reminded me of my father.

I wanted to lash out at him and say, "You're not perfect, either!" but I didn't want to make things worse. I had just apologized and promised that I wasn't going to let it happen again, and I was afraid I would lose all credibility if I lashed out. So I went back to bed.

Joey spent a little more time on the couch. Then he made his way back into bed with me, wrapped his arms around me, and we both fell asleep. Nothing more was really said between us that night.

The following morning, I had to humble myself in front of our staff and apologize to them. I also had to listen to them tell me, "We've never seen anyone have a reaction like that before and, frankly, we were worried about you!"

As I listened to them talk about what I'd done and how they felt about it, I started to cry. I realized that my meltdown had cost me the respect of my staff and that I'd never again be quite as highly regarded by them. That bothered me immensely. My mother was the quintessential lady and she had taught me better than that. By her example, she had taught me to be graceful, dignified, soft spoken and humble and she never would have behaved as I had on the previous day.

26

I knew I needed to see a professional in order to start working through some of my childhood issues. So, I made an appointment with Steve, the pastor who had married us, who also happened to be a counselor. When I explained to him what had happened at the office, he told me that he believed it was indicative of both a relationship issue and a personal issue. He wanted to help me keep my marriage together and warned, "If you don't find a way to resolve conflict, your marriage is in jeopardy!"

I made an appointment for Steve to meet with Joey and me at our house. When he came over to counsel us, Joey didn't hold back at all. This came as a total shock. For some reason, I'd assumed he would take special care not to embarrass me. When I realized how open he was being, I started to break down and deflect accountability.

Steve told me, "You can't justify your actions based on the actions of another! You have to own your mistakes, take responsibility for yourself, and stop bringing Joey into this."

"See! You were wrong, just like I told you!" Joey said. "You should've listened to me!"

Then Steve jumped in and reprimanded Joey for using this opportunity to hurt me. Joey looked stunned—and then he got defensive and started mouthing off to Steve.

Steve stopped him in his tracks. "If you are more concerned about your pride than your marriage, there's nothing I can do here. If your marriage fails because of your pride, you'll look back on this night and call yourself a fool! Now, I love you both and I'll pray for you but I'm not going to sit here and watch two people tear each other apart. I'm leaving now."

When Steve took off, I felt completely defeated and deflated. A feeling of despondency and despair came over me and I started crying. *Maybe we're not going to be able to work through this, after all. Maybe Joey and I won't make it,* I thought.

Joey was angry that Steve had spoken to him that way in our home, and I was angry that Joey had alienated Steve.

"That's your biggest problem!" I shouted. "You never listen to anyone! You think everything you do is perfect and we should all listen to you and conform to your way of thinking. The world is perfect as long as you're getting what you want every minute of the day. The problem is, the world doesn't work that way! I don't think like you do so I'm never going to be successful at being what you want. I'm not you!"

I continued working with Steve on my own, trying to confront my hair-trigger temper and face it head on rather than run from it. Over time, I reached the point where I was in control of my temper and not the other way around. I began to consider my anger and rage as a sword with the power to make people stop and pay attention. I didn't need to hold the sword in my hand like the archetypal female warriors I'd seen in pictures. It was there in my sheath when I needed it.

Whenever we weren't getting along, Joey and I would leave each other alone for a while and then find our way back to each other. We got into a pattern of saying, "I'm sorry…I love you," and making love. This would make us feel better for a little while but, as we kissed and made up, our problems were piling up under the carpet. Considering how much makeup sex was taking place between Joey and me, it wasn't too surprising when I turned up pregnant in the early fall of 1994.

With a new baby on the way, we knew we needed more room. As it was, when Joey's sons came to visit, we barely had room for all of us. So, we began house hunting and found a home we liked.

As I was helping Joey at the office and trying to get our new house organized, decorated, and ready for the baby, I was having horrible morning sickness. I would spend the first part of the day at home, vomiting, and then come into the office later in the day.

It soon became apparent to me that I wasn't going to be able to manage Joey's office in a way that met his expectations, so I hired Kim. She was a dental assistant and could also help with the front desk. Kim was in her early twenties and lived at home with her parents. She didn't have a boyfriend or husband and was able to devote herself to the dental practice. She assimilated easily into the practice and the office was running smoothly.

Meanwhile, I began to have more and more complications with my pregnancy. For two weeks, I went back and forth to my doctor's office, complaining of terrible abdominal pain. Finally, the doctor admitted me to the hospital for exploratory surgery. Initially, the procedure was performed as a laparoscopy but, during the surgery, they discovered that my appendix had ruptured. They had no choice but to operate to remove it. I was twenty weeks pregnant at the time.

As I awoke in the recovery room, groggy and still intubated, a nurse was explaining to me that my appendix had ruptured and I'd just had surgery. "The doctor will be in to talk to you in a few minutes, and someone's gone to tell your husband he can come in now."

Joey came in and kissed me and told me not to worry. I had a feeling that the doctor was going to tell me that I had lost the baby or it was ailing in some way but, when the doctor came in, he said, "The baby made it through surgery but things can get a little tricky in a case like this. Let's see how the baby's doing..."

The doctor put a stethoscope to my belly and began to listen for the baby's heartbeat. When he couldn't find it, I began to panic. Not only was I growing increasingly upset, I was in terrible pain.

"Now, let's not panic..." the doctor said. "Oh, here's the heartbeat!"

I suddenly had extreme empathy for what my mother must have gone through, feeling sick and exhausted all those years. Alongside the empathy I was feeling for my mother was self-recrimination for not being more understanding of her when I was younger. No doubt my weakened state and terror over the doctor not being able to hear the baby's heartbeat contributed to my heightened emotions.

After a four-day hospital stay, I was released. Joey dropped me off at my mom's during the day when he had to go to work and then picked me up at night. Mom was delighted over the fact that I was pregnant and, being in one of the healthier periods of her life, she was able to take care of me and give me a level of attention she couldn't give me when I was a child.

My appendicitis and appendectomy ushered in this unexpected blessing—a long overdue chance to connect with my mother, something which I had been craving for so long. She made me feel special and loved, for which I was incredibly grateful and appreciative.

On the downside, the constant traveling back and forth between home and Mom's was hard on me because the roads were very bumpy. One day, I decided that I was well enough to look after myself and I told Joey not to take me over to my mom's place. It became obvious very quickly that I'd made a grave mistake when I touched the incision area and noticed it was hot to the touch. I also felt something warm running down my body. I had popped the incision, which was oozing pus as a result of a nasty post-op infection.

I called Joey and then I called my mom. She took me to the E.R. where we were met by my surgeon. Because the wound was so infected, anesthesia would not have taken effect. So, the doctors opened me up without anesthesia, cleaned the wound and packed it with gauze.

Six weeks of pure hell followed. For the first four weeks, I stayed at my parents' house, sick as a dog and in excruciating pain, and a home-care nurse came in several times a day and looked after me. Then I was ready to return home where I could sleep in my own bed.

I spent two more weeks at home, during which time my parents came and took care of me. Dad showed his love by letting me wrap my arm around him as he helped me walk from the bedroom to the kitchen or bathroom. When he asked me how I was doing, I saw a caring and nurturing side of him I had waited my whole life to see.

After six weeks of recovery and care, I returned to the doctor. I had lost twelve pounds because the pain medication I'd been taking took away my appetite. The doctor told me I needed to eat and he also let me know that Joey and I were going to be having a boy.

One month later, I returned to the doctor, fourteen pounds heavier, and was told that I now needed to curtail my eating. Meanwhile, every time the baby moved, he kicked the incision area and caused me tremendous pain.

I discovered that being in the water helped so I often visited the local retirement communities in our area so I could float in their pools. I spent so much time in one particular retirement community pool, I became the pet project of the sweet retired ladies and gentlemen who would show up in golf carts to drive me back to my car and present me with homemade jam and other snacks. If I missed a day at the pool, they called to make sure I was okay and some of them even became Joey's dental patients.

27

As I got further along in my pregnancy, I was devoting even less time to the dental office than when I first hired Kim. Now Kim was moving away and we needed to hire a new girl, so we hired Tammy. Everything was running smoothly but, from time to time, Joey would still expect me to do something which I felt was beyond the constraints of reality and completely unrealistic. Nevertheless he wanted things done the way he wanted them done, and that was that.

By the second week of August, the baby had dropped and seemed to be sitting right on my incision. I was in a tremendous amount of pain and so swollen that the doctors were concerned that the baby might rip open my incision. So, on August 14th, when I was thirty-nine weeks along and close to full term, the doctors decided to induce labor.

The following day, our son entered the world quickly and effortlessly, weighing in at seven pounds, eight ounces, twenty-two inches long. We named him Drew and gave him two middle names—William and Lawrence, the names of our fathers.

When the nurse handed my baby to me, he looked completely different than I'd imagined. My son had a very pointy head, huge hands and feet and two slanted eyes which were barely open. He also seemed to have been born with a suntan, and this was perplexing to me.

I thought, *Wait a minute…this isn't my baby! This baby looks like an alien!*

Joey was in the room with me and he was overjoyed, as was his mother. I wondered, *What's wrong with me? I just had this beautiful baby and now I'm concerned he's not perfect enough?*

I didn't express these thoughts out loud. I privately had my moment of looking at Drew and waiting for the euphoria to hit me. Since I didn't feel I could share with anyone what I was feeling, I had no one to answer my question: "What's wrong with me? I thought you were supposed to instantly fall in love with your baby the minute the nurse handed him to you! Why aren't I feeling overjoyed?"

The nurse took Drew out of my arms, cleaned him up and put a little beanie on him. I thought to myself, *Well, he does look more normal in the hat. As long as we keep his hat on him, he'll be okay.*

Right from the start, Drew was a handful. He was very colicky, prone to screaming fits and didn't sleep soundly. When I took him in for his six-week checkup, the doctor asked me how I was doing. During the time when I was sick with appendicitis, the doctor had become a personal friend and had even gone golfing with my husband. So I felt comfortable around him.

"I know I love my son," I said, starting to cry. "So please don't think I don't. But I don't seem to know what I'm doing. The baby never stops crying! I cry all the time too because I'm so tired and sad. I keep waiting for that moment everyone tells me about where I'm supposed to love the experience of being a mom."

"Sounds like postpartum depression to me," he said. "Your body's going through all these changes and your hormones are playing a trick on you. I'm sure when you imagined giving birth, you saw it going a certain way in your mind. But, in reality, it took a lot of trauma to get here. I want to give you an anti-depressant but you won't be able to breastfeed…"

At first, I was a little resistant to the idea of taking an anti-depressant, especially if it was going to mean that I had to stop breastfeeding.

"It really is in the best interests of both you and the baby," the doctor explained. "You've been through a lot and you need to take care of yourself." He then referred me to Tom, a psychiatrist who confirmed the diagnosis of postpartum depression.

During our session, Tom asked me challenging questions about my marriage and my life, forced me to look at my choices and talked to me about the difference between living and merely existing. He explained that living is something you actively do by making choices whereas existing is something you accept. He felt that there was no greater tragedy in life than simply existing.

"Tell me why you stay with your husband, Melissa. What do you love about him?" he asked.

"He's my soulmate," I explained. "And he's the only person in the world that I have those feelings for!"

"Imagine that I plopped you down in the middle of New Zealand. Within a certain amount of time, you'd find someone that you felt the exact same way about. You feel the way you feel about your husband but you have no idea what the experience might be like if you ventured out and looked at what was out there. You have this magical thinking that makes you believe he is the only man that fits your criteria. And you are using that magical thinking to create the circumstances you want to see. You have to deal with reality."

I found Tom's words to be unnerving and, as I left his office, I was shaken up. I had gone to him to find some peace and instead I was thrown off balance.

Before I left his office, Tom had said, "Stick with me, Melissa. I'm not going to make this easy for you but I am going to help you. You need to be told the truth and you need to see how your own choices contribute to your reality. You're so afraid of being knocked out of the boat but you are a very capable woman without a man."

I had mixed reactions to what he was saying. On the one hand, his candor made him seem like a bit of a jerk. On the other hand, I really liked hearing that I was a capable woman, even if I was terrified to embrace it. I couldn't imagine letting go of Joey—and I flat out didn't want to. I wanted to work on our marriage.

Tom had told me, "Joey is going to have to participate if you want to work on your marriage." Since he only treated patients on an individual basis, he recommended a marriage counselor named Scottie.

We made an appointment and went to see her. In Scottie's office, I explained the situation as I saw it: I was a new mother, tired and overwhelmed, and I had a husband who was a typical doctor in the sense that he could be very demanding. He wasn't always like that, but there were times when he didn't seem to have a good grasp on real-life limitations. He got so focused on wanting things the way that he wanted them to be, he couldn't see beyond that. Although this was occasional, when it did happen, it was awful and led to terrible arguments between us.

I felt that I'd presented myself as a perfectly reasonable person who had a husband who could be quite demanding at times. The marriage counselor didn't see it that way and ended up siding with Joey. When the issue of me throwing that fit and stomping out of the dental office came up during our session, the counselor said to me, "He's a professional! You can't act that way!"

"You're right," I countered. "He *is* a professional and he shouldn't act that way!"

Marriage counseling presented Joey and me with a whole new set of conflict resolution rules we were expected to abide by at home. Yelling and hitting were now strictly out of bounds and, if one of us said we needed a break, the other one couldn't veto it. It seemed like all these rules were designed to modify my behavior, not Joey's.

I felt like the marriage counselor's sympathies were skewed in favor of my husband and I didn't feel particularly heard or understood by her. After we had been going to marriage counseling for about six months, I asked to meet with Scottie alone. I told her that I didn't feel like marriage counseling was working.

"Joey gets to come in and get everything off his chest," I said. "And then once he's done all the talking, he pulls the ripcord and says he doesn't want to talk anymore. That's not fair!"

"The thing is, Melissa, it actually *is* okay for Joey to stop the conversation when he feels he's emotionally at a boiling point. He can end the conversation whenever he needs to. You're going to have to learn how to accept this boundary of his."

Joey and I temporarily stopped going to marriage counseling but, from time to time, we would still meet with Scottie individually.

28

*A*round this time, I started experiencing extreme nausea and was having a hard time dragging myself through the day.

"I am pregnant again and I'm really struggling. I'm tired all the time and I have no energy," I told Tom, the psychiatrist. "I feel like I have the flu."

"Well," he said, "you're going to have to deal with this! Unless you want to terminate the pregnancy…"

"No, I don't want to do that!" Terminating the pregnancy was not even an option for me.

"So you want this baby then?"

"Well, no…I mean, yes, of course I do! But the timing is totally off."

I never even considered not having my second child. Despite my best efforts, I nearly lost Drew due to my appendicitis. After spending most of that pregnancy terrified that I would lose the baby, there was no way in the world I was going to voluntarily give up a baby. I was simply overwhelmed when I envisioned the challenges of managing two small children while also having to contend with a marriage which was proving to be much more challenging than I could have anticipated.

"The timing may be off but have faith in yourself. You can handle this!" Tom said.

As I left his office, I started to identify the ways in which I was contributing to my own frustration. I could see how simply changing my perspective on things could help me calm down and relax. All the way around, Tom was helping me to grow up.

It had never occurred to me before that I had failed to grow up. I often thought to myself, *Well, I did a pretty good job of raising myself!*

As this shift occurred in my outlook, my behavior followed. I was still suffering from mild postpartum depression but I became more patient at home. As a result, Joey and I got along better and had less frequent arguments. Little by little, I began to pull out of my depression and, for the first time in ages, I felt like I had found my groove.

I started to embrace the idea of becoming a mother to a second child and I spent as much time as I could with baby Drew. My sister Jennifer happened to have given birth to a daughter six weeks before Drew was born and had recently moved back to the Southwest. Having my sister nearby was a real godsend. It was great to have her emotional support and it was great for the little cousins to be able to get together for play time. Drew kept me on my toes and it was easier on me when he had a playmate.

Once again, Jennifer became the person I turned to for solace and comfort. She continually encouraged me, saying that, if I could stay positive, everything would work out. At the same time, her natural brutal honesty kept me out of magical thinking and firmly planted in reality.

When Joey and I hit a rough patch, for example, Jennifer said, "You need to pull yourselves together and get help if that's what it takes! You have a family and you have the responsibility to work on your family so you can provide a happy life for your kids."

I couldn't argue with my sister's reasoning and I took her words to heart. When Joey and I were in conflict, we returned to marriage counseling with Scottie.

My pregnancy was a total breeze compared to my first pregnancy, with the only complication being several trips to the hospital with Braxton Hicks contractions toward the end. The contractions were caused by the baby sitting right on my appendectomy scar. I was also very swollen, retaining a lot of water, and getting very little sleep.

Right around Halloween, I took fourteen-month-old Drew out on the front lawn to take a picture of him in his pumpkin costume. I bent down, trying to get a picture of his face when suddenly I felt a tightening in my stomach. I recognized the sensation as a contraction and immediately took Drew back inside the house, got a glass of water and lay down on my side. This was what the doctor recommended I do whenever I got a Braxton Hicks contraction but, this time, it failed to make the contractions disappear.

When Joey got home from work, I told him about the contractions. He called the doctor and told him what was going on.

The doctor said, "If the contractions get to the point where they're two minutes apart, get her to the hospital!"

Because I'd already had several false-alarm trips to the hospital with Braxton Hicks contractions by this point, the doctor put me on bedrest. As the mother of a young child as active as Drew, I found the term "bedrest" laughable. As the holidays rolled around, it became harder and harder to manage Drew while being pregnant. He was always a very active boy and it seemed like I was constantly picking him up and putting him down.

Finally, in the afternoon on December 2nd, I went to the hospital and labor was induced. A little bit after midnight on December 3rd, Devin joined the family. I had always liked the name and Joey liked it too. I had a childhood friend named Devin, so I had good associations with the name in that regard. I also liked the idea of giving my boys names that started with the same letter. For Devin's middle name, we gave him the name Marshall after Joey's physician grandfather.

Given all the challenges of my pregnancy with Drew, I had been anxious that I might lose Devin before he was ever born. Having him born early made me feel like I had somehow put him at risk or failed him. Then there was his low birth weight. He was expected to weigh around eight pounds at birth but he was quite a bit smaller when he was born at six pounds, six ounces. The doctor allayed my fears and assured me that Devin was perfectly healthy.

I longed to hold my baby and, when the nurse put him in my arms, my heart grew to ten times its size. This was the experience that had eluded me when Drew was born. Devin was a perfect little bald-headed baby boy with a peaches and cream complexion. I was now the mother of two little boys.

Devin grew so quickly that, when I took the two boys out in public, people often thought they were twins. He was a big, calm, sweet, loving boy—and his big brother was a live wire. Devin listened to me and Drew did not. Devin was an easier child to manage in that sense and I constantly felt more drawn to him for that reason.

Drew was a very challenging child in terms of his behavior. I was constantly admonishing him not to do dangerous things but there were times I couldn't catch him in time and he'd end up hurting himself. Keeping him safe sometimes felt like a full-time job. He was such a handful and I was often frustrated with him. In my desire to keep him safe, I was sometimes hard on him. I would find myself saying things like, "No, you can't jump off the counter with knives like Peter Pan! You'll hurt yourself!"

And Drew used to play nasty little pranks on Devin. Devin would come to me and say, "Mommy, the dinosaur bit me!" When I looked at his arm, I could clearly see Drew's teeth marks in his arm.

Devin was very sweet and would always quickly make up with his brother, giving him a hug and saying, "Okay, I forgive you."

Drew loved his baby brother very much and talked to him when he was still in my belly. Now that Devin was out of my tummy, Drew sometimes felt jealous of him. He would say to me, "Mommy, don't hold Devin! Hold me!"

Whenever I recalled how it had taken a little while for me to bond with Drew, I was filled with guilt. I worried that Drew sensed that I was more inclined toward Devin and I worried he might feel like I didn't love him as much as his brother.

One night during my pregnancy with Devin, I had been holding Drew in my arms while he slept. Suddenly the thought came to me, *He's not going to be here very long so I'd better hold on to him while I have him!*

That moment heightened my awareness of how special Drew was to me. From then on, I made sure I spent one on one time with him so he felt loved, and I paid closer attention to him and listened very closely to everything he said to me.

When Drew turned four years old and started attending pre-school, he liked it right away. He was very friendly and social and loved to bring his teachers little trinkets and treats. If we made cookies at home, Drew made sure to put some in a little package and bring them to his teacher. And he would encourage me to bring pizza for the entire class, which we did a few times.

Drew was a cute little boy and the little girls really liked him. He would talk to me about wanting to kiss the girls or hold their hands. The feeling was clearly mutual. Little girls in Drew's class would run up to him and try to hug him or give him a picture they had drawn for him.

"Mommy, Jasmine kept trying to hug me today," Drew would say.

"Yes, I saw that, Drewby. The girls really seem to like you and you have lots of friends."

"Yes, Mommy, I'm very friendly!"

Drew said the cutest things and always made me chuckle.

29

*A*round this time, I hired a woman named Gabby as our office manager. She was my age, married to a policeman and had no children. She had previously worked for a periodontist in town and came to us highly recommended. She was not leaving her former employer under any sort of questionable or unfortunate circumstances.

We were told that she was seeking the challenge of setting up a dental practice with computers rather than simply being stuck at the front desk. When Gabby interviewed with us, it was obvious that she was very tech savvy. This was a skill set we knew we were going to need in order to bring our office into the twenty-first century and begin to computerize our system.

Gabby considered herself an innovator and I thought she was articulate and obviously intelligent. Demeanor wise, she laughed easily and loudly. Within months of Gabby's hiring, there was evidence of the good work she was doing. She was working with various insurance companies and involved with Joey in the process of negotiating contracts. The practice was growing very quickly.

Unfortunately Gabby soon began to infiltrate my life in ways that were neither normal nor reasonable. She was violating boundaries left and right and was very dismissive with me any time I voiced a concern.

As the practice grew, Joey asked Gabby to help him with another matter. Joey had purchased a satellite dental practice in a nearby town with an attorney partner, and he enlisted Gabby's help in getting that practice on the right track. Joey and Gabby often left town for the satellite office on a Tuesday night and worked Wednesday through half-day Friday out of town, taking separate rooms in a hotel.

I had no concerns about another woman spending this amount of time alone with my husband but, when he also started spending a great deal of time on the phone with her when he was at home ostensibly to spend time with me and the boys, it led to discord between us.

I had two little boys who were a handful and a husband who was out of town most of the week. So I didn't appreciate it when Joey also spent time on the phone with Gabby during what was supposed to be family time. Joey told me that all their conversations were business related but, as far as I was concerned, the weekends were family time and business could wait.

Invariably, we ended up arguing—sometimes in front of the boys. I tried to avoid this whenever possible and always felt badly when the boys saw their father and me having words. Sometimes it would escalate to the point where Joey walked out of the house. There were times it seemed as if he was picking a fight with me just so he'd have an excuse to leave. At times like these, I would get so exasperated, I would start crying.

Inevitably, Drew would come to me and say, "Please don't cry, Mommy. Daddy's mean but I love you."

"No, Drewby," I would say, "Daddy's not mean." But my little boy was right—his dad *was* being mean to me.

As if it wasn't bad enough that my husband was gone much of the week, he started leaving on weekends to go to California to play polo. Joey's brother, who was quite affluent, was taking polo lessons in Indio and Joey began joining him. It was a sport which had always interested my husband and, now that he had more disposable income, he was able to participate. He boarded some horses in California and kept some at home, as well. These included a trail riding horse, which the boys would ride when their dad took them out riding. (I also enjoyed riding but, as a young mom, it was hard to find the time.)

Any time I voiced an objection or question about the amount of time Joey was spending away from home, he responded with anger and defiance. I wasn't getting any answers from him that made any sense to me, and I couldn't seem to get him to understand my feelings and the position he was putting me in with his constant absences. I was living my life as a single mother and, for all intents and purposes, handling the child-rearing responsibilities entirely on my own. It was hard to function as a single mother while trying to deal with a very angry husband who said he loved me eighty percent of the time and treated me badly the other twenty percent.

We had somehow arrived at a point in our marriage where we no longer spoke the same language and had ceased to communicate effectively. We were really struggling as a couple and experiencing the most significant friction between us since our blowup at the office. Our calm moments outnumbered our upset moments but when we did have friction between us, it was loud and unhealthy.

Whenever Joey was dealing with me, he made me feel like I couldn't do anything right. Yet he seemed to enjoy spending countless hours on the phone with Gabby, talking and giggling, day and night.

Around this time, I found myself wondering, *What is really going on with Joey and Gabby?*

So one day, I decided to pay a visit to Gabby at home. When I knocked on her door, Hugo, her husband the policeman, answered the door. I asked him, "Is Gabby here?"

He said, "She doesn't want to talk to you!" This let me know that she was indeed at home.

"Well," I explained, "I think she may be having an affair with my husband and I believe I have the right to ask her about it!"

Sounding like the cop he was, he said, "No, you don't have the right to come to my house and disrupt my evening. My wife and your husband are *not* having an affair and now you need to get off my property before I arrest you!"

As I was walking away from their house, my cell phone rang. It was my husband calling. He had just gotten off the phone with Gabby and was furious with me for embarrassing him in this way. He was very mean and nasty with me and threatened to leave me.

I cried all the way home. I couldn't believe my husband had threatened to leave me. It wasn't that I'd never considered leaving him before but, considering that we had two small children, I considered divorce to be of the question.

When I got home, Drew crawled up into my lap and wanted me to hold him. He was always the one to want to console me.

I was tired and upset and just wanted to be left alone. "Drewby, Mommy's tired. Please go to bed."

"Please don't cry, Mommy," he said "Don't be sad. Even if Daddy doesn't love you, I love you!"

30

*B*etween Joey and me arguing about Gabby and his constant absences from home, I started to break down. I was not responding well to the conflict between us. I was prone to losing my temper and had to walk on eggshells to avoid provoking Joey's temper. I was living a life of constant stress and uncertainty, just as I had during my childhood. Since my married life mirrored my early life, it didn't feel abnormal to me. It was merely a continuation of life as I knew it.

I had become a nervous wreck and I was extremely sleep deprived. Devin had asthma so I often had to get up in the middle of the night to give him breathing treatments—which would then awaken Drew. Because Joey was constantly traveling and I was alone much of the time, I was the only parent available when the kids were awake in the middle of the night.

In addition to all the other stress in my life, Joey was constantly accusing me of out-of-control spending and he claimed to have the credit card statements to prove it. He was very angry with me over this spending but I wasn't spending the money. Unfortunately, due to our breakdown in communication, there was no way to convince him of this. He would pull his credit report and mine and look at our credit card statements and draw his own conclusions.

Something definitely was not adding up but I was so exhausted that I didn't trust my own recollection of events. I thought, *Well, maybe I did go to Target and fill out an application for a credit card. I don't even know!*

At some point around this time, I talked to Scottie, our marriage counselor, and said, "I don't feel like I can manage all of this anymore. I feel like I need help."

Scottie encouraged me to spend a few days at a mental health facility. The idea of being an inpatient made me very anxious and afraid. In my mind, agreeing to check in to the hospital would mean I was in tacit agreement with the notion that I was unbalanced. I didn't think I was unbalanced—I thought I was reacting in an understandable way to extraordinary stress. Remembering stories I'd heard about my grandmother's suicide only made me more uncomfortable with my decision to go to a mental hospital.

Scottie was strongly recommending that I go and Joey was completely on board and pushing me to go. I felt powerless to refuse and ultimately decided that refusing to go would cause more problems than agreeing to go. So, I said, "I can't take this anymore! If you two think this is what will help me, then fine."

As my friend Christina drove me to the hospital, she let me know how she felt. "If you can find some answers in the hospital, great. But I don't think you need to be in a facility to find answers and I think you're being railroaded! I don't appreciate Joey pressuring you to go." For some time after my hospital stay, she would keep her distance from Joey.

As I checked into the psychiatric hospital, I felt completely broken down from all the turmoil. I had no fight left in me. I could no longer find my voice and was not exactly my own best advocate. Once I had been processed and assigned to my room, the reality hit me and filled me with anxiety and fear. I cried myself to sleep that night and passed a very restless night.

Not only was I extremely upset but I was freaked out over the fact that there were no locks on any of the doors—not even the bathroom door! Anyone could have walked in on me at any time. The staff went through my luggage and wouldn't let me keep a razor to shave. They even removed the laces from my tennis shoes.

I told one of the nurses as she checked my belongings for forbidden items, "Look, I really don't belong here!"

Then again, I seemed to have given up. And, while I didn't have any inclination to kill myself, I also didn't have a whole lot to live for anymore except my children. My spirit was broken.

Christina slept at a nearby hotel and returned to see me the next day. She was permitted to bring me a book and a journal.

"Mel," she said, "please don't think for a minute this is the proper place for you—it's not! But you can still spend this time relaxing."

She could see that I was exhausted mentally and spiritually. As she was leaving, she said, "I love you! And remember, you're strong and you'll fight your way through this."

Christina and I had known each other since childhood, and she had witnessed what I went through with my mom and dad and knew I was resilient. When she said goodbye, the reality of my situation hit me and I started to sob. I spent the next three days working with a psychiatrist.

This doctor asked me many questions, starting with, "So, why do you think you're here, Melissa?"

"I lost my temper and threw a rock at my husband's car," I said. Then I paused and said, "I guess that's not normal. But I was frustrated that he was leaving town one more time. I've been exhausted and taking care of two small children and I really needed his help!"

"Maybe it's not normal where you come from," he said, "but where I come from, it's pretty darned normal!" He started laughing which put me at ease and then I started laughing.

"Do you feel like you have control over your anger?" he asked.

"No, I don't always feel like I have a great degree of control over my anger," I admitted. "I can go from calm waters to a tsunami pretty quickly."

When he told me that he wanted to start me on some antidepressants, I objected, saying, "I don't like the way antidepressants make me feel!"

"Remember," he said, "this is in your best interests."

I was reasonably comfortable with him and could see the wisdom in his approach. Nevertheless, I didn't feel like I needed to be there and I remained skeptical about the entire experience. Participating in group therapy sessions with people who scared the hell out of me contributed to my sense that I didn't belong there. Two men in particular paid entirely too much of the wrong kind of attention to me.

Despite my many reservations, I went along to get along. My fear of exhibiting any behavior that might lead those in charge to determine that I needed to be held there against my will terrified me. I was very measured about what I shared with the doctors and the other patients.

For example, there was no question in my mind that Gabby was telling my husband lies about me and making up a completely false narrative about my spending. But I kept those thoughts to myself. I didn't want the doctors to construe what I was saying as paranoia—and then use that so-called paranoia as a reason to detain me. But I was as certain as I could be that Gabby was up to no good.

When I was assigned a roommate, I objected strenuously and insisted upon having my own room. My objections had no effect and I was paired up with a roommate named Lisa. She was being treated for anorexia and had been at the psychiatric hospital for a month by the time she moved into my room.

Lisa would turn out to be a real blessing. She talked to me about her life and asked me questions about mine. This was the first time I really began to understand anxiety. In my own life, I easily recognized sadness but I had never given much thought to the issue of anxiety.

My roommate let me know that I was a blessing to her, as well. When I opened up and talked to her about my childhood and my relationship with my parents, she said, "You know, you're really helping me. I don't think I ever thought about anyone else having circumstances as difficult as mine!"

As Lisa began to lean on me for emotional support, her doctors paid me a visit. "What have you been talking to Lisa about? We are seeing a radical change in her for the better!"

The truth was, we just clicked. She even ate normally when she was with me—mashed potatoes, of all things! In the three days I was there, she put on two pounds. She had to gain a total of twelve pounds before her parents would allow her to return home.

When it was time for me to return home, she became very concerned. "But what if, after I leave here and you're not around, I don't want to eat anymore?"

"Just call me right before mealtimes. And, if you need to, call me afterwards," I said.

So, that's what she did. And, for quite some time, we wrote letters back and forth. Suddenly her letters stopped coming—and my letters to her started being returned unopened. In her very last letter to me, Lisa had written, "The darkness is starting to invade the light in my world..."

In the few days Lisa and I had known each other, I encouraged her to talk to me or someone else when she was feeling down. "You are so valuable and important to people so remember to take care of yourself! And if you need to be reminded of how valuable you are a million times a day, I will do that for you! Just call me. Or call someone! Don't try to handle this alone."

To this day, I have no idea what became of Lisa. I've often wondered how she is doing. I pray that she is still alive and doing well. It breaks my heart when I consider that she might have decided to end it all. She was only nineteen years old.

Helping Lisa helped me and made being in the mental facility so much easier. By the time I went home, I was feeling much better. My one complaint was that the medication made me very groggy—but that was easily fixed. The doctors lowered my dosage and then switched me to a different medication.

In addition to the satisfaction I felt by helping Lisa, my stay at the hospital resulted in a lifelong painting avocation. During art therapy, I had started to paint and the paintbrush became my lifelong friend.

As I checked out of the hospital with my journal in hand, I had a new resolve. While journaling during my hospital stay, I discovered that I was being manipulated. And I realized that I would need to develop some real inner strength if I was to have any hope of surviving the situation with Joey and Gabby. Whether I liked it or not, Gabby had managed to insinuate herself into my marriage and, unless I wanted to risk losing my mind, I was going to need to develop nerves of steel.

When I returned home, it was a new beginning for Joey and me. While I had been away, my husband was acutely aware of my absence and he was reminded of how much it meant to him to have me in his life.

And, of course, the boys had missed me terribly. "We made you some cookies, Mommy! We missed you and we love you!"

Drew thought I had been at a hotel on vacation. The boys' dad had told them, "Mommy is really tired and she needs a break so she can get some rest." There was definitely some truth in those words.

31

*D*espite the fact that Joey was still spending a great deal of time out of town, I was really happy and feeling pretty good. I resumed my counseling appointments with Scottie and worked with her on becoming more patient and understanding with Drew. She taught me how to direct Drew's energies into positive directions so I wasn't constantly scolding him. I started having an easier time managing my boys and was sleeping better at night.

On May 18th, 2000, Drew and I took a bunch of unpainted wooden birdhouses into his preschool classroom, along with a bunch of paint and brushes. The kids had a great time painting their birdhouses and Drew and I had our picture taken together. In the photo, Drew is sitting on my lap holding his birdhouse, surrounded by all the other kids holding theirs. It was a wonderful and memorable day for me and Drew.

As we left preschool, my son was proudly carrying his brightly painted birdhouse. He loved primary colors and especially "Power Ranger" red. So he had painted his birdhouse red and added some blue, which is my favorite color, and some green. After preschool, we stopped by Burger King and had a wonderful time there.

It was a bright sunny day so, when we got home, I took the boys outside where they could eat watermelon and splash around in the kiddie pool. Meanwhile, our dogs ran around the cornfields surrounding our yard, panting from the heat.

When I heard the phone ring, I went inside to take the call, while keeping one eye on the boys outside. It was Joey who was out of town with Gabby. I told him about our wonderful birdhouse project and he told me about Gabby's latest accusation of me. Our phone conversation devolved into an argument and ended with him hanging up on me.

I was sick to death of talking to Joey about Gabby and fed up with her constantly meddling in our lives. I despised her for it and resented Joey for allowing it, but that didn't dampen my resolve to be a good mom and a better wife.

When I went back outside, Drew sensed that I was upset. "Mommy, let's get Popsicles and make us happy!"

My son had the right idea. I needed to turn my frown upside down with a Popsicle. So, that's what we did. The boys and I ate Popsicles and then they watched *Thomas the Tank Engine* while I cooked dinner. When it was the boys' bedtime, I went to find Drew so that he could brush his teeth.

I discovered him already asleep in the top bunk where he always slept. He was still wearing that day's outfit but I didn't want to wake him by undressing him. I pulled the blanket over him and let him sleep, kissing him on the cheek. Then I lay down next to Devin on the bottom bunk. Once Devin had fallen asleep, I made my way to my own room and fell asleep, alone. I wasn't expecting Joey back home until the following evening.

At some point during the night, I was awakened by the sound of Devin coughing. I went into the boys' bedroom, picked up Devin and brought him into my room with me so I could give him a breathing treatment. It took a while to get him to the point where he was able to breathe freely.

Around two or three o'clock in the morning, I called Joey. I was calling to ask him to cancel his patients for the following day in the satellite office and come home to help me. He let my call go straight into voicemail. I figured he must have turned off his phone right after hanging up on me earlier.

I left him a message, explaining, "I'm exhausted and I really need your help with the boys!"

I knew that, if I couldn't get Devin's breathing trouble under control, I was going to need to take him to the hospital. If that happened, I would really need my husband's help with Drew. I made a couple more attempts to reach Joey but, each time, my call went straight into voicemail. I left a couple more messages for him, saying, "I need you to call me as soon as possible!"

Around four o'clock in the morning, the breathing treatments finally worked and Devin's wheezing eased up. He fell asleep in my bed and I fell asleep beside him.

The next thing I knew, Drew was in my room. In his scratchy little voice, he was saying, "Mama, Mama, the sun's coming up! The sun's coming up!" That was the rule—he wasn't allowed to get out of bed until the sun came up.

"Sweetheart," I said, "Mama is sooo tired! Want to lay down with me?"

"No," he said, "I'm hungry."

He had a habit of waking up hungry, going into the kitchen and helping himself to whatever was easy. His first choice was always ice cream. It wasn't unusual for him to grab a Popsicle or make himself an ice cream sundae for breakfast and eat it before any of the rest of us woke up.

I got up and took Drew into the kitchen. That's when I saw the Rocky Road ice cream out on the counter, starting to melt, and noticed the chocolate all over his little face and hands. "Oh, no, sweetheart," I said, "you can't eat that! It's too early. What else would you like?"

"Bif Raviolays, Mama."

I was too tired to make him a real breakfast so I popped open a can of Beef Raviolios, put them in a bowl, and heated them up for him. Drew wanted to watch *Thomas the Tank Engine* while he ate, so I started the video for him.

Yawning, I said, "Drewby, Mama's going to check on Devin."

I wandered back to the boys' bedroom to see how my youngest son was doing, knowing that Drew was happy watching *Thomas the Tank Engine* and eating his "Bif Raviolays."

I lay down beside Devin, who was already beginning to stir.

Thankfully I was able to soothe him back to sleep.

I startled awake from a deep sleep, gasping and in a panic. I realized that I had dozed off. I would not normally have fallen asleep but I'd only gotten an hour and a half of sleep between the time Devin fell back asleep at four o'clock that morning and the time Drew woke me up at five-thirty. It was now seven-thirty or eight, which meant that I'd been asleep for a couple of hours.

The house was eerily quiet. I thought, *Wait...why don't I hear the video playing? Where's Drew?*

I immediately got up and went into the playroom where I had left Drew. He wasn't there and the video had stopped. We have a one-story house and there weren't a lot of places indoors that he could have been hiding. The dogs weren't inside the house either. Instinctively I sensed that something was very, very wrong. I ran into my room and threw on a sundress and flip-flops. Then I ran outside, calling for Drew.

On my way out the door, I noticed that the sliding glass door was open a little bit. Drew must have opened it to let himself out, which would explain why I hadn't heard the shutting of the back door when he went out. Otherwise, the sound surely would have awakened me.

Our backyard opened onto the cornfields and in the distance were a levee and an open irrigation canal with plenty of water in it. Any time I walked with the boys in the direction of the canal, I would say, "We can't play in that water, Drewby...Mr. Crocodile is in there!"

Drew knew Mr. Crocodile from *Peter Pan*. And he loved Peter Pan more than any other character in the world. If we got anywhere close to the canal, he would say to me, "Oh, no, Mommy! We can't go over there. The crocodile lives in there! It's too scary..."

We always walked in a different direction so as to avoid Mr. Crocodile. So I knew that Drew had to be playing out in the cornfields because he wouldn't go anywhere near the canal. If the cornfields were wet from having been watered, it was even more fun for him. He loved to walk through deep mud. He would become simultaneously exasperated and proud of himself whenever one shoe got stuck somewhere in the mud and he had to pull his foot out of his shoe and return home with one shoe.

32

I ran in the direction opposite the levee, racing alongside the six-foot stalks of corn, looking down each row to see if I could catch a glimpse of my son.

"Drew! Drew!" I yelled into the nothingness.

It never even occurred to me that Drew could have gone in the direction of the canal until I saw his little footprints in the dirt. Seeing them, my heart sank and I felt dizzy and disoriented. I knew that something unusual had happened to take him in the direction of Mr. Crocodile.

Breathless, I reached the levee and looked down at the canal below me. That's when I saw our dogs and noticed that two of the larger ones were wet. As I ran down toward the water, I could see Drew's footprints in the dirt. I could also see where a large clump of dirt had given way and crumbled right at the top of the canal.

I put two and two together and realized that Drew must have come down to the canal and stepped on a soft patch of dirt which probably gave way beneath his feet. I figured that the dogs must have gotten wet trying to help my son.

I collapsed on the canal bank. I heard screaming coming from my mouth but it was as if it were coming from a great distance. "No, no, no, no! Please, God, NO!"

A border patrol agent slowly rolled past and asked, "Ma'am, do you need help?"

"Yes, sir, my son's footprints led me to this canal! It looks like the dirt gave way and I'm afraid he's fallen in…"

I had been feeling completely panicked. Suddenly I felt this palpable calm come over me. I felt as if Drew were letting me know that he was okay.

There he is! I can see him—his spirit! I thought to myself. *His eyes are incredibly sparkly.*

"Mommy," he seemed to be saying to me, "I love you so much! I never want to be without you. Now I get to be in your heart forever."

I felt deeply saddened but strangely calm. *Please come back…please come back…please come back!* I was willing him home.

The border patrol officer kept asking me, "Are you okay, ma'am?"

"I don't know if my son is here any longer," I explained. "I think he fell in the canal. But I can't find him…"

"When was the last time you saw him?" he asked me.

I recounted the timeline to him. Then, as if they'd been crouched down out of sight, hiding and waiting for just the right moment to appear, policemen, deputy sheriffs and members of the FBI Search and Rescue team materialized on the scene. A Border Patrol helicopter began circling overhead, searching the cornfields and up and down the canal.

The sheriff was not yet on the scene but his deputy sheriffs were and they asked me for a description of Drew and the clothes he was wearing at the time he disappeared. The last time I had seen my son, he was still in his clothes from the day before because that's how he had fallen asleep. So, that was the outfit I described to the deputies.

Gabby's husband, Hugo, being a police officer, happened to hear the report over the police scanner and called his wife—who was actually answering his calls. As I said, Joey had been ignoring all of my calls the night before. Hugo told Gabby what was going on and she told Joey, and someone told me that Gabby and Joey were on their way home. They were driving, so it was going to take a while.

Given that we lived in a small rural town, word spread like wildfire and people began arriving at my house. Everyone was there to support me but no one really knew what to do with themselves. They asked me, "Do you want us to go help with the search?"

"No," I said reflexively, without really thinking about how it would sound, "I know he's already gone." This statement would end up causing law enforcement officers to turn in my direction and start questioning me.

It seemed like people were just popping up out of thin air. I blinked and there was my housekeeper. Then my sister, Jennifer, arrived and immediately joined the Search and Rescue team, riding her horse up and down the canals, looking for Drew.

My parents also showed up. *How do all these people know what's happening?* I wondered. *I don't remember making any phone calls.*

I was living in a bad dream. I needed Drew's pillow. I went into the boys' room and lay down on his bunk, snuggling up to his pillow and his shirt. I knew they would smell like him and, when they did, I started to cry.

That's when I noticed that Drew's clothes from the day before were lying crumpled up on his bedroom floor. By that time, the sheriff had appeared at our house and I had to tell him that I was mistaken about the clothes Drew was wearing when he disappeared. I hadn't even seen Drew in the outfit he had chosen for himself that morning before he went wandering off by himself.

33

My pastor walked into the room and I said, "Rick, I just know he's gone. He came to me...in spirit."

The sheriff was standing outside the bedroom door with my dad and heard me say I knew Drew was gone. So he started questioning me.

I tried to explain that Drew had come to me in spirit and told me that he was okay. "He said he was going to live in my heart forever and never leave me."

It was hard to read the sheriff's expression. He listened intently and showed compassion—but he was also there to do a job and solve the mystery of my son's disappearance and death.

Around one o'clock in the afternoon, Joey showed up. (Thankfully Gabby was not with him.) I had already made my way into our bedroom by then.

"When was the last time you saw him?" he asked me.

I told him and then I said, "I kept trying to call you to get you to come home and help me with the boys!"

He didn't explain himself. He just said, "I'm sorry. I'm going to go look for Drew."

"Okay," I said. "I'll stay here with Devin." I went into the living room and sat down with Devin. I couldn't believe how many people were in my house.

After some time had passed, I could feel the energy in the room shift. My dad came and sat down next to me. "Miss, they found him," he said. "He's gone..."

I started to sob and shake.

"He was about ten miles from the house in the canal," my dad continued. "Some children saw him floating by."

Joey came in, sobbing quietly, and it was clear that he was heartbroken. He had been with the Search and Rescue team when they pulled Drew out of the canal, and he got to hold him before he was taken to the hospital. I didn't get to hold him or even see him—not in his physical form, anyway. But there was no question in my mind that he had come to me, his eyes shimmering, to let me know that he would live forever in my heart.

"Is he okay?" I asked. It must have sounded like a strange question but Joey understood my intent. I wanted him to tell me about the condition of our son's body.

"Well," Joey said, "he has scratches on his face and his forehead is bruised. I don't know if he hit his head and then fell in, or hit it as he was falling in, or got the bruises from going through the canal. But at least he is peaceful—sleeping."

"I didn't mean to fall asleep!" I said. "I didn't mean for this to happen! Are you going to leave me? I'm sorry...I'm so sorry..." I felt off kilter and completely disconnected from my body.

Joey hugged me and held me, saying, "Don't worry. We're going to get through this."

My doctor prescribed a sedative so I would be able to sleep that night. In the meantime, I really needed to feel Devin close to me. The poor little guy was still so young and had already lost his big brother.

I sat with Devin, holding him, and he asked me where his brother had gone.

I explained, "I'm very sorry, sweetie, but Drewby's not coming home. He's gone to Heaven."

"He's gone to Heaven to be with Jesus?" It seemed to be both a question and a statement.

"That's right, sweetie. That's right. Drewby is in Heaven with Jesus."

Devin didn't seem sad. He seemed to instinctively understand that it was okay for his brother to be in Heaven.

Before Drew's passing, our family had been attending a nondenominational Christian church. (It was at this church that we had met Pastor Rick, who counseled Joey and me on how to handle stress in our marriage.) Both boys loved going to Sunday school where they would color pictures and get a fun snack of some sort. Drew often spoke of God and Jesus.

The news crews showed up that afternoon, wanting to film our house and the canal where Drew died. They wanted to speak to me but somebody told them I couldn't talk. I was later told that there was a piece about Drew's death on the evening news. I couldn't bear to watch the news, myself, but our loved ones kept telling me that they were sorry the media was being so hard on me.

I would come to find out that they were referring to media reports stating that Drew's death was a result of the fact that I'd fallen asleep and I was lucky that neither child endangerment nor manslaughter charges were filed against me. After one particular newspaper article mentioning the fact that I'd fallen asleep on the morning of Drew's death, a friend asked me whether or not I was under investigation.

Some days later while shopping in town, I would run into the sheriff and he would ask me how I was doing.

I broke down and started to sob. "Are you going to arrest me, Sheriff?"

"Arrest you? For what? For falling asleep? Oh, no. I know you didn't hurt your child."

I recalled the day the previous year when I was holding Drew as he slept and this thought came to me: *He won't be with us long and I need to enjoy and treasure every moment!* That's when I realized that I had been told in advance what was coming—and told that I needed to become a better mom.

I did. I tried harder, endeavored to be more patient, and spent more time with Drew than before. I was grateful for the advance notice. I was even grateful for the few days I'd spent in the institution and the counseling that followed, because they had led to me becoming a better mom.

As that endless day turned into an endless night, my mind wandered back to my pregnancy with Drew. He was such an active baby in the womb and ten times more active once he entered the world.

When Drew learned to talk, the voice that came out of him was almost impossible to associate with a child. It was a low, raspy George Burns voice—a whiskey-and-cigars type of voice that was completely unexpected and totally hilarious when coming out of the mouth of such a little guy.

He had his father's larger than life personality and didn't spend a lot of time sitting still. He threw himself into playtime with gusto and loved to make loud noises. Even though he was all boy, he was also sensitive. Like me, he loved to paint and do arts and crafts projects—like the birdhouse he painted with his class on the day before he passed. And one of his favorite things to do with me was to lie down in bed, cuddle up together and have me read to him. He had a few favorite books that we must have read together a few hundred times.

Drew loved to be naked, wearing just his cowboy boots and hat. He also loved to clomp around naked in his daddy's cowboy boots. He would stand in front of the TV in just his cowboy boots and hat and dance to the rhythm of the Louis Prima song featured in *The Jungle Book*. (His two favorite Disney movies were *Peter Pan* and *The Jungle Book*, which was my favorite.) It made me so happy to watch him dance. When he laughed, he would throw his head back and his hat would fall backwards on the floor.

He was delightful and charming and had a devilish smile but he seriously tested my patience. He never listened to one single rule I set for him so he was often in "time out." Being in time out never bothered him. He would be upset for a moment and then quickly acclimate to it.

"I'm sowwy, Mama," he would say in his baritone voice.

I used to think to myself, *This kid is such a character, with his raspy George Burns voice!*

Drew was such a loving child. Even when he was as little as one year old, he would comfort me. He'd put his hand up to my face, pat my cheek, and say, "Wuv you, Mama." Or, "It's okay, Mama...it's okay."

34

I went into Drew's room, gathered up his boots and pillow, and grabbed the birdhouse he had painted the day before. Looking at the birdhouse, I remembered the conversation between Drew and Devin in the car on the way home from preschool.

Drew was holding his birdhouse and said to his brother, "I added some green for your favorite color!"

"No, Drewby, green is *not* my favorite color!"

"Yes, it is!" It was so funny to hear Drew trying to convince Devin that his favorite color was green.

As we pulled away from the preschool, Drew set his sights on the Burger King next door. "Mama? Jesus wants us to get burgers and fries. He likes families to eat burgers and fries!"

"Oh, really?" I'd said. "Jesus wants us to eat burgers and fries? Then we'd better go get them!"

After we ate, the boys played in the outdoor play area and had a great time. They got along great and, as we left there, I thought, *This was such a wonderful day! What a gift. And what a shame Joey wasn't here for any of it. He's missing out on so much by being out of town and it's really sad.*

Looking at the birdhouse now, it occurred to me that Drew had left it to remind me that I really was a good, loving mom to him despite my self-doubts. I held and kissed the birdhouse and realized what a gift the days leading up to the accident had been.

I took the sleep medication the doctor had prescribed and, as I started to get sleepy, I thought to myself, *How remarkable for a little boy to talk about Jesus on the day before he dies. It certainly wasn't his usual Power Rangers speech. He must have sensed that he was close to Heaven and been trying to give me what I needed with that burgers and fries memory...*

Drew often said "God loves us" or "God's inside me." Now I could hear him saying, "God's inside me, Mommy, and I want to be in your heart too and be with you forever."

As I drifted off to sleep, my last thought was that my son knew that I loved him. After I fell asleep, Joey lay down with Devin. I went to bed around seven in the evening and later that night, Joey's family began to arrive from California.

Thanks to the sleep medication, I slept for thirteen or fourteen hours straight. I awoke the following day between eight and nine in the morning, still in a fog of disbelief. I asked myself, *Did that really happen or was it a horrible dream?*

I got dressed and walked out of the bedroom. Our house was still filled with friends and family. Having a house full of people was a stark reminder that I wasn't dreaming. They were all there because Drew had died. I broke down and started crying.

Joey came over and sat next to me, holding my hand and comforting me. "I love you," he said, "and we'll figure this out together. I know this is going to be hard but we have to go to the funeral home and make arrangements for his burial."

I looked at Joey and asked, "Can I hold him when we get there?"

I really wanted to see my son. I hadn't seen him since I'd fed him his "Bif Raviolays" and put him in front of the TV on the morning he died.

"Umm...I'm not sure. Pastor Rick will meet us there and he'll know."

"I want to see him and hold him," I repeated.

On the way to the funeral home, Joey played me some songs he thought we might want to use in the funeral services. I used to sing to Drew *Beautiful Boy*—the song John Lennon wrote for his son, Julian. As Joey played it and I listened to the lyrics, I thought about how

Drew had been so impish and mischievous, living his life to the fullest like Peter Pan. Joey also played the Eric Clapton song, *Tears of Heaven*, which he wrote for his young son who died tragically. Then, Joey played *The House on Pooh Corner* by Kenny Loggins.

"So, I'm thinking maybe those three songs," Joey said.

Suddenly I remembered Drew's funny way of counting: "One, two, too many, too much, five..." Three was always "too many" rather than an actual number. Remembering this, I started laughing and then I was bawling again. I realized, *He's really gone. This is real and we are on our way to say goodbye.*

Then I realized I needed to bring Drew his Power Ranger and write him a letter so he could take those with him on his journey.

When we got to the funeral home, my mom, dad and sister Jennifer were waiting there for us. I was anxious to see Drew right away so they brought Joey and me into the room with him. I explained that I wanted a minute alone with Drew. Rick went outside the room and told my family that I'd like them to wait there. Then he came back into the room and said to me, "But Melissa, whatever you do, don't move the sheet!"

Joey and I both looked at Rick, not quite understanding what he was getting at.

"Remember," he said, "there was an autopsy...I don't want you to be upset."

"Oh, I understand," said Joey.

Drew's neck was exposed but his shoulders were covered. He had bruises on his face and scratches on his forehead but otherwise he looked like my little boy. He was just sleeping. I bent down and kissed him and pressed my cheek against his. I put my hands on his shoulders and got as close to him as I could. He was freezing.

"Joey," I said, "they need to give him a blanket. He's so cold!"

"No, sweetheart. They have to keep him cold."

I don't want my son to be cold! I was thinking. So I asked the staff to bring in another sheet and at least drape that over him so he'd be warm and comforted. Then I noticed that the sheet that was already covering him was not entirely opaque. Beneath it, I could see a wide incision, stapled shut. Joey followed my line of vision and saw what I saw.

"Why? Why did they have to do that to him?" I asked my husband. On the surface, it looked like my son was only sleeping. But beneath that sheet was a whole different story. *I never knew death looked like this,* I thought to myself.

Being a dentist, Joey was better able to handle that moment than I. "Just think of it like he had a little procedure done—some kind of surgery. They did the procedure because they needed to make sure the cause of death was really drowning and not something else covered up by the drowning."

"Oh..." I said. "They thought I killed him." At this thought, my body went sort of limp and I wanted to cry. "Oh, Joey, I didn't hurt him...no, no, no, no, no..."

I felt Drew come to me in spirit in that moment and I was able to grasp the fact that my son was still my son. Only, he had somehow been freed and was no longer limited by his body.

It's just his body lying there, I told myself. *It's not who he is. He is with me and he is now free to do the things he always wanted to do. No harm can come to him anymore. He is finally free to be the little boy he always wanted to be.*

I understood that Drew was no longer bound by the laws of physics. At last, he was free of all constraints. I imagined him jumping off something and skinning his knees and crying and then getting right back up and running headlong into his next adventure.

I remembered Drew dressed up as Peter Pan and Devin dressed up as Captain Hook, and how much fun we all had that Halloween. Drew loved Peter Pan so much and he loved battling his brother as Captain Hook. *Now he really is Peter Pan,* I thought, *on a never-ending adventure in Neverland! And, as Peter Pan, he will always return to my window.*

When I left Mormonism, I became like a leaf blowing in the wind. I wanted to know about all religions and couldn't quite find anything to fit me. As I explored various religions, I discovered that I am extremely spiritual and function on a spiritual level. Organized religion struck me as more of a business, a song-and-dance show, than an opportunity for real spiritual communion. My soul was seeking something serene and peaceful and I never found a religion or an external place that felt like my spiritual home. My spiritual home is internal.

A day and a half after Drew died, a woman from the Mormon Church came to the house with food. "If you live your life righteously," she said, "you will be in the presence of God and your son again." She made it clear that I needed to prove myself worthy.

No, I thought, *I just want to get to Heaven to spiritually be with my son.* And my next thought was, *I hope God forgives me for feeling this way. I'm sure he does. The God I know and love in my heart would never keep me from my son.*

Realizing that our spiritual home is both internal and eternal made saying goodbye to Drew's body easier. I knew I wasn't saying goodbye to the true him.

Well-meaning loved ones kept saying to me, "Well, now he's in Heaven with Jesus and he's your guardian angel!"

I would think to myself, *No, that doesn't feel right. That's not Drew. He will be having an adventure, not sitting at Jesus' feet, worshipping. He could never sit still that long.*

I didn't say it out loud but that's what I was thinking. I also understood that everyone in our entire family and circle of loved ones was suffering and in pain and they needed to cling to whatever they needed to cling to in order to get through their own grief.

Pastor Rick told us, "Drew is saved...he is with Jesus now...the Lord has him."

Then Jesus has his hands full, I thought, *because Drew is not about to be one of those angels who sits there, happy just to be in the Lord's presence. Jesus would have to constantly be going to get Drew down off a tree.*

I had a clear vision of a really large hill, the highest peak in Heaven, and atop this hill was a tree. I knew that Drew would be swinging from that tree, jumping from the swing and running to get right back on it. That was the Heaven where my Drew was living. *I'll meet you there, Drewby,* I thought.

We had a tire swing at our house and it was suspended from a tree atop a hill. "Higher, Mommy, higher!" Drew would yell as I gently pushed him on the swing and he pumped his legs to go higher and higher. When he got as high as he could go, he would jump off the swing, roll on the ground laughing, and run back for more.

"We have to be careful, Drewby," I would say. "If you go too high, you're going to get hurt!" It didn't matter what I said—he always wanted to go higher.

Even though I was certain that my son was very much alive in spirit, I knew that I definitely did not want to place his body in the hard ground. I couldn't bear the thought of him being cold, and that's what I envisioned when I imagined burying him in the ground.

It also seemed terribly claustrophobic. *That would be the worst thing in the world, to be underground and confined to this small space. He'd feel trapped in there,* I thought.

The funeral home offered us the option to have Drew interred in the mausoleum. That was the only option that I could handle. At least that way, I'd feel like Drew had simply been put to bed. Joey had no objections so our decision was made.

After all the funeral arrangements had been made, we returned home. I was exhausted. Our house was full of people and noise and our kitchen was full of food which well-meaning loved ones had brought over. It was all too much for me. I felt completely overstimulated.

While we were at the funeral home, I had been told to bring Drew's burial clothes when I returned. When I went into my son's bedroom to get his clothes, I also began collecting his toys. There was his red Power Ranger, a stuffed lion and a stuffed bunny I had bought for him when I was pregnant with him.

Then I remembered that I wanted to write him a letter. I found some crayons and paper, wrote Drew's name at the top in bold, bright letters, and wrote him a letter. On the day of the funeral, Joey put a St. Christopher medal around Drew's neck and I took the small children's Bible we used to read to him and tucked it in next to him with the letter inside. Devin drew him a picture of fun, brightly colored scribbles. Devin wanted to make sure his brother knew the picture was from him so I helped him sign his name.

I was planning to leave the toys I'd collected, as well, but at the last minute, I realized, *No, Drew would want Devin and me to keep some of these things.* So I left Drew's stuffed lion but kept the stuffed bunny. I couldn't bear to part with it. I also held onto the red Power Ranger for Devin. Over time, I would be so glad I'd held onto it, as it was one of the only direct memories Devin had of his brother.

Most of the memories Devin would carry of Drew would be through stories told to him by others. But Devin specifically remembered watching *Power Rangers* on TV with Drew and playing Power Rangers in the yard with him. Any time they played Power Rangers, they both wanted to be the red one.

35

$\mathcal{D}$rew's funeral services were held at the chapel at the cemetery and officiated by Pastor Rick. The entire community seemed to have turned out to mourn with us. The place was so packed, there was standing room only.

I sat in the side alcove of the chapel, completely numb. Any time I looked at the casket—which had been open during the viewing but was now closed—I thought, *I'm never going to physically see him again!*

I didn't want to fall apart in front of everyone so I averted my gaze from the casket and focused all my energy on Devin instead. I wrapped him up in my arms and held him.

I need to be strong, I thought, *and make sure this moment is about Drew's life and about how wonderful he was as a person. If I fall apart, I will be taking something away from the moment I want for my son.*

As the services started, I had the sense that Drew was guiding me. I had an out of body experience in which I was walking toward Drew, toward that heavenly tree with the swing. I knew in my heart exactly where I was going to meet him.

I watched my father go up to the podium, as well as my brother-in-law and father-in-law. When my father spoke, I saw the vulnerability that lay beneath the steely exterior he put out into the world. As he read a poem he had written for Drew, tears were rolling down his face.

Seeing Dad mourn his grandchild who was taken from the earth too soon shook me up and made me cry. I had never before seen my father cry—not even at my wedding.

Devin looked up at me and wiped a tear from my face. The congregation, witnessing this, stirred and I could feel their outpouring of love.

Immediately after my father finished speaking, it was time for the brother of a friend of mine to sing *Beautiful Boy* while accompanying himself on guitar. It was clear to see how much this moved everyone present and I felt overcome with gratitude.

They're never going to forget you, Drew. This is something that will stay with everyone forever, I thought.

Joey's father, a very quiet man by nature, went up to the podium, spoke, and read some Bible scriptures. Then Joey's brother, Todd, spoke, sharing with the congregation his memories of Drew. "He was always dirty from playing. And his hands were always sticky from candy or melted ice cream he would scoop out of the carton with his hands…" He chuckled as he shared his memories and everyone laughed along with him.

He really didn't need a spoon! I thought. *He was that way about life in general—he just reached in and grabbed whatever he wanted. For a little boy, he sure lived boldly. From the moment he was conceived, his life became an adventure.*

I learned so much in the nearly five years Drew was with me. He was one of the greatest teachers I've ever had. He taught me to be patient. He taught me to quiet myself so I could see clearly and respond out of love instead of reacting emotionally. I was not always successful in responding to Drew from a place of love and I was often hard on him. There were times I was simply unable to provide for him the love I craved as a child.

As the funeral services came to an end and everyone began to make their way out to where Drew would be interred, I stood in front of the casket. I wanted to thank everyone there for sharing in my son's life. So many people loved him. As I've said, he was a beautiful child, a little bit larger than life. We would be out in public and people would stop us to talk to Drew and comment, "What a striking young man!" Or, "What a handsome little guy!" Those comments were sugar for my son's soul and he ate it up.

I greeted and hugged each person as they exited and thanked them for coming. This was unplanned and I'm sure it took Joey by surprise but he followed my lead. Out of the corner of my eye, I noticed Devin behind me and saw him put his hand on the casket and say a few words to his brother. Devin caught my eye, looked up at me, smiled and turned back to the casket. I noticed that he didn't look sad and it made me wonder whether perhaps Drew's spirit was there and Devin was able to perceive his presence.

If Drew's presence was familiar and palpable, the concept of death and the fact that it was a funeral wouldn't have registered for Devin. It was amazing to me that my son looked not only fine but happy. *If I know Drew,* I thought, *he is probably amusing Devin by pretending to jump off the casket!*

I was envisioning Drew alive when he came to me in consciousness, saying, "Mommy, I'm fine! I'm still playing."

I started to cry. It was bittersweet, knowing that, even though I could no longer hold or hug Drew, he was every bit as much alive as he had ever been on earth.

When Devin is awake, I'll be with him here on earth but when he is asleep, I'll be with Drew in Neverland, I thought to myself. That is how it's been ever since Drew's passing. Drew has never been gone from me—he's just not here physically. From the time Drew passed on, I began to think of him as being on this grand adventure where there was no way to communicate with him except through love and memories of love. I discovered that the love transports you back to the person.

Until you experience the transition of someone incredibly dear to you, and until you are forced to rely upon the love that existed in the physical world, it's impossible to really grasp that love is a gateway to a spiritual connection that never dies. Any time I talk to Drew or about him, he draws closer and I feel him with me.

I cannot send him a letter or call him on the phone but I am never really separate from him. Drew's words in the moments after his death still ring true for me today: "Mommy, I'm going to be with you forever."

As I stood in front of my son's casket and prepared to walk to the mausoleum where he would be interred, I realized I was feeling better emotionally. I thought to myself, *I hope and pray I can hold onto this knowing that Drew isn't really gone—he's alive in spirit. If not, this is going to be the worst pain I have ever experienced in my life.*

Some of our loved ones went to the mausoleum for the interment and some left. Following the services, we had a lunch at our house for everyone. A group of my female friends took care of everything from top to bottom—planting flowers in the flower bed, cleaning my house, making sure there was enough food for everyone. They took such good care of me. These friends stayed overnight and, the following morning, they served me angel food cake with berries and whipped cream for breakfast.

It really tickled me. "This is the perfect breakfast! Drew would have loved this. The only thing he would have thought was missing was vanilla ice cream!"

My friends loved me through it all and, in so doing, they pulled me through. Every morning, someone would either show up at my door or call me on the phone and say, "Hey, let's go get you dressed!" And then they would say, "Let's get Devin to school" and "Tell us what groceries you need from the store." If I was having an especially bad day, they would take me on a gentle walk and hold me and let me sob.

One of my girlfriends came up with the idea to create Drew's Garden in our backyard. Friends would randomly show up at the house, make their way around to the back, and leave beautiful wind chimes, birdhouses, garden gnomes and tiles and stones with engraved sayings. And of course, many people brought angel sculptures.

Drew's Garden turned out to be a magical place and attracted hummingbirds and many beautiful butterflies. *They look like fairies— like little Tinkerbells in Drew's Neverland,* I thought.

I would go out there and sit with nature all around me. Sometimes I fell apart and sat out there, sobbing. Other times I sat there, peaceful and joyful. Devin absolutely loved to water the plants in Drew's garden so we did that together. It was a tremendous gift to have this beautiful sanctuary.

36

*I*t was about six to eight weeks after Drew's funeral and everything had gone back to normal—or what now passed for normal. Everyone who had gathered around and held us so close when Drew first passed had now returned to their usual routines. I understood that our loved ones couldn't remain on high alert forever but understanding this did not make the transition any less difficult. I was in terrible shape and I knew I had to pull myself together.

Devin had gone from being Drew's baby brother to being an only child. He needed someone to play with but I just didn't have any energy so I enrolled him in preschool—a brand new preschool. Drew's preschool had held a memorial service for him, planted a tree in his honor, and tied ribbons to the branches. I knew that, if I took Devin to Drew's preschool, it would break my heart to have to see that tree every day.

There were certain things that unraveled me and I owed it to myself and my family to avoid such things. It was my only hope if I wanted to remain functional for those who needed me. I also thought it would be better for Devin to be in a brand new preschool so he wasn't constantly having to field well-meaning questions like, "Where's your brother?" Knowing how candid kids can be, I also knew it was entirely possible that someone might come right out and say to Devin, "Your brother is dead!" Or, "Your brother died!"

Devin was only three and a half and was still such a little guy. He would ask me, "Drewby died, Mommy?"

"Yes, Devin…Drewby died."

"But, Mommy, Drewby's okay?"

"Yes, honey. Drewby's fine," I would say.

"Mommy, I know you're sad," he said. "Drewby doesn't want you to be sad." I realized that Devin was probably able to talk to Drew.

Right away, I could see that switching Devin to a new preschool had been a good decision. When I dropped him off in the mornings, everyone was genuinely happy to see him rather than solicitous and concerned. As much as I appreciated the love and support, there were days that I just couldn't take one more person asking me, "So, how are you doing? And how is Devin doing?"

One day, I dropped Devin off at preschool and then I drove to the cemetery, parked and walked over to the spot where Drew was interred. I sat down on a bench right in front of his spot and looked down to see a bunch of flowers—and underneath the flowers was a very small, square box. I opened it up and a song started playing. A music box! It was not a fancy music box but I could see how it might catch a child's eye.

On the box was the word "Mom" and the "o" in Mom was created by a red heart gemstone. There was no one buried on either side of Drew at that time so I knew that this music box was from him. I figured he had "borrowed" it from someone else and left it there for me.

As I listened to the song play, the music box wobbled and warbled like it had really taken a beating. I started to sob. I put my hands against the marble and then lay my head against it.

"Drewby!" I said, half laughing and half crying, "you borrowed this from somewhere for Mama, didn't you? That's stealing, honey!" Talking to my son, I felt a spiritual surge that I understood was an unspoken exchange between us, a conversation.

Any time Drew would "borrow" something from a store for me and I'd reprimand him, he would say, "No, Mommy…*not stealing*! I borrowed it for you."

He often "borrowed" lip gloss or funky earrings from the store and gave them to me. One time, we were at the Dollar Store and I saw him put some hoop earrings in very bright reds and yellows in his pocket for me. So, the music box didn't surprise me too much.

From that day forward, the sound of a music box playing instantly brought with it the close presence of my son and made me smile, remembering that day at the cemetery. And any time I found myself swaying to music, I would remember Drew insisting, "Dance with me, Mommy! Dance with me!"

"Mommy's making dinner, Drewby," I would protest. But he didn't care. I loved to listen to music with him and he loved to dance with me around the kitchen.

As July came to a close, I began to panic. Drew's birthday was August 15th and I didn't know how we were going to face his birthday without him for the first time. I envisioned what grieving together as a family would look like but grieving was not something Joey and I could do together. My husband managed his grief by immersing himself in his work and staying as busy as possible and I dealt with my grief and remembered Drew by talking about him and looking at photos. Unfortunately, our differing approaches did not mesh well. Joey's need to work through his pain and my need to express myself caused us to have some very potent and toxic arguments.

The truth was that Joey was very angry with me and blamed me for falling asleep on the morning of Drew's death. I first started to notice his anger toward me about three weeks after the funeral when he seemed short-tempered with me. We had started seeing a grief counselor right after Drew died, but Joey's anger wasn't expressed during those sessions, only at home.

"What's wrong?" I asked. "You seem like you're mad at me."

"How could I not be?" he said.

His words were a kick to my gut and they took the breath from me. *Oh, my God! He blames me!* This was the first time I'd had that thought. I was already struggling with the desire to have that fateful morning back in my control so I could do it differently, and now I was finding out that my husband blamed me for our son's death.

Joey's anger built to the point where any little thing I did could trigger a venomous response from him. He swung from one extreme to the other, vacillating between being completely absent and totally filled with rage. He was unable to calmly express his feelings. Even if he got annoyed or irritated with me over an issue that had nothing to do with Drew, his feelings would quickly turn to anger over my falling asleep on the morning of Drew's death. Joey's outbursts reminded me so much of the temper tantrums that children often throw.

Whenever Devin would hear us fighting, he would say, "No fighting! No fighting! Daddy, you're in time out."

"You're right, Devin. Daddy does need a time out!"

Then Joey would leave and I would fall apart.

And just like Drew had done, Devin would say, "Mommy, please don't cry!"

It got to the point where Joey and I were not doing anything well together and it was clear that we needed marriage counseling. (We were already in grief counseling but the focus was different.) During our marriage counseling sessions, it came to light that Joey wanted to separate.

I said, "I just buried my son and now you want to *leave me?*"

I thought that losing my son was the greatest pain I would ever have to bear but the pain of being completely abandoned at such a time was even more painful. I would wail in pain and be utterly unable to breathe. The heaviness of the despair made me feel like an elephant was sitting on my chest. The depth of the pain was primal and beyond anything I'd ever experienced.

One day, Joey and I were fighting and I said, "You seem to hate me so much, you hate *everything* about me!"

"How could I not?" he said. "You killed my son!"

I was stunned speechless. When I regained my voice, I shouted, "Get out right now! I did *not* kill him!"

He told me that he was already going and then he started carrying the TV set out to his car.

I wasn't telling him to move out, just to get out for the time being. *Oh, my God!* I thought. *He's not just taking his clothes, he's taking his TV! He's not coming back! Wherever he's going, he's planning to stay there.*

I felt a piece of my heart die and I realized I had lost everything that was dear to me except Devin and a few friends. I wanted to die. Thankfully, my friends circled the wagons and never left my side. They were frankly appalled that Joey would leave me at such a time.

I tried to explain to them, "He's in so much pain, just like me."

A friend of mine pointed out, "That's the problem, Melissa. He doesn't see your pain!"

I couldn't envision us reconciling and I began trying to mentally and emotionally prepare myself for divorce.

37

*J*oey and I did end up getting back together—but Gabby had greater control over the dental business than ever and she remained a huge source of contention between us. Joey had allowed Gabby to assume complete control over the business finances and checkbook.

The seed for Joey's decision to turn financial control over to Gabby was planted way back when I first started working at our dental office as a newlywed. As you may recall, I had to learn on the job and made mistakes that reflected poorly on Joey. So, from then on, he decided it was better to have somebody else taking care of that side of the business so that we wouldn't argue.

Then there was the fact that, while Joey and Gabby were working together, the dental practice grew exponentially. The practice became very, very successful and Joey regarded Gabby as someone instrumental in that success. He consulted her for her ideas and opinions as to how to grow the business and valued her input immeasurably. The business grew so significantly and became so successful, it turned into a big conglomerate and Joey had to hire more dentists. All of this led to Joey giving Gabby more and more control, and Gabby edging me out of Joey's decision making process to the point where my input was no longer welcome.

By 2002, Gabby's entire family was working at the dental office: her sister, Juanita, her mother, Cathy, and her sister-in-law, Diana.

Joey and I argued almost daily about Gabby's family's involvement in our marriage and our lives. I found it deeply disturbing.

One day, I tried to talk to Gabby about it but she was dismissive and confrontational with me, to the point of rudeness.

"Look, Melissa," Gabby said, "I work for your husband, not you! If you don't like it, talk to him!"

The underlying message was, "I don't have to deal with your crap, so stop bothering me!"

Whenever I went to the office and Gabby treated me dismissively, I became incensed. I wanted Joey to say to her, "Hey, that's my wife! Don't talk to her like that."

Instead, my husband would say to me, "I told Gabby to do that! And I don't care if you don't like it. I feel like *you* are the problem here and you're the one who needs to leave."

Joey may as well have said to me, "Look, I am trying to run my business and Gabby is a huge help to me! I need her to do whatever I need her to do, and I expect you to just take the money I am working so hard to earn and keep your mouth shut!"

Joey expected us to live together and function as husband and wife but, when it came to our finances, I was supposed to just take the money and shut the f*** up. His attitude toward me caused constant arguments between us and fueled Gabby's defiant attitude toward me.

Shortly after getting back together, Joey and I decided that we wanted to have another baby so that Devin would have a sibling living under the same roof with him. (As I mentioned earlier, Devin's half-brothers lived all the way in California). Joey had already undergone a vasectomy so we found ourselves involved in the long, drawn-out, painful process of in vitro fertilization.

Between trying to be a good mother to Devin, grieving my other son, trying to hold onto my marriage and undergoing in vitro fertilization, I felt like I was constantly on the brink of losing my grip. After three unsuccessful embryo transfers, I still wasn't pregnant. I was going to need to undergo another egg retrieval process—which meant incurring more expense.

Joey said to me, "Well, I'll have to talk to Gabby to find out where we're at financially with all this."

Gabby had Joey's ear and was constantly saying, "This whole in vitro process is so expensive!"

As far as I was concerned, whether or not I underwent the process of in vitro fertilization was flat out none of Gabby's business, and not up for discussion. It irritated me to no end to have this woman involved in such personal aspects of our married life. More than anything in the world, I wanted to have another baby and I didn't see why she should get a vote on the subject.

"Why are you involving her?" I asked Joey. "Is she the one calling the shots on whether or not I'm going to have this done?"

"Well, I run the business with Gabby," Joey said. "I do the dentistry and she runs the business."

"That's the problem!" I said. "Gabby shouldn't have knowledge about our finances that I don't even have!"

We had started out talking about in vitro fertilization and, the next thing I knew, Joey was accusing me of overspending again. Any time any financial issue came up for discussion, Joey tended to throw in the kitchen sink.

"I know all about your credit cards," he said. "You just spend without thinking about it. You seem to just want, want, want..." That's how the argument would always start.

Then I would say, "What are you talking about?" Sure, I had certain credit cards which I used but he seemed to be referring to expenditures which were a total mystery to me.

"Well, Gabby gets a copy of our credit report from the bank any time we need to apply for or renew our line of credit, and the report shows all the stuff you're doing! She showed it to me."

"Great!" I said. "Then show it to *me*. Show me all this money I'm supposedly spending!"   At first Joey refused to let me see our financials. When he finally relented and instructed Gabby to forward the information to me, the answer was always the same: "Gabby says she'll get it to you."

Of course, she never did. "I don't think she's the person you believe she is," I said. "I think she's stealing!"

"No way!" he said. "Her husband is a police officer. If she were stealing, it would ruin not only her career but his!"

The fact that Gabby was married to a cop was all the proof Joey needed that I was the one who was taking the money—not her. In Joey's mind, Hugo the police officer was some sort of insurance policy against any potential misconduct by Gabby.

Whenever I said anything about Gabby, Joey would tell her what I'd said and she would become incensed.

"She doesn't know what she's talking about!" Gabby would say. "That would ruin Hugo's career!"

This was Gabby's typical reply and it only served to cement the lily white image of her that Joey had in his mind. He firmly believed that Gabby would never do that to Hugo and Hugo would never stand for it. Gabby was counting on Joey's perspective of the situation. She knew it would create absolute trust between them.

By now, I despised Gabby. I couldn't bear the sound of her voice over the phone, hated running into her at the office, and even the sight of her car in the parking lot of the dental office was enough to raise my blood pressure. She was on my nerves to such an extent that I began to nit-pick her outfits and her shoes, making comments to myself about her lack of style. In short, Gabby's meanness toward me was wearing me down to the point where I hated everything about her. She had pushed me right to the edge of my patience.

As if her treatment of me wasn't bad enough, I had to deal with her sister Juanita, whom she had hired to answer phones and schedule patients at the dental office. Now, when I called the office to speak with my husband, Juanita answered the phone. Just like Gabby, Juanita was rude and condescending in the way she spoke to me and generally treated me like a royal pain in the ass. She had palpable disdain toward me and it came through loud and clear.

38

*M*y husband and I were having significant marital problems but I was going along to get along. I was weary of constantly arguing and I also knew that it wasn't good for Devin to witness it. So I kept my mouth shut in the face of the daily insults I suffered at the hands of Gabby and her family.

Having to bite my tongue and keep quiet when so many outrageous things were going on reminded me of being a little girl and having my father tell me, "Shut up and do what you're told!" In many ways, I was receiving the same message from Joey.

Living in a small town, everyone knew everyone and this was especially true in my case because I'd lived in the same town since I was a child. One day, Dana, a friend of mine who worked in the dental community and also owned the preschool attended by Gabby's son, was at a Bunko game where Gabby also happened to be present. Dana had to listen to Gabby brag about how she had taken Joey's "failing dental practice" and turned it into a multi-million dollar business.

"They really owe everything they are to me!" Gabby said, modestly. Then she started talking about me and saying, "She's crazy—totally unstable! She was the cause of her son's death, you know! If it wasn't for her husband intervening, she'd be in prison!"

Needless to say, when I heard what Gabby had said about me, I was livid. I had reached my breaking point and I couldn't take much more. When Joey came home from work that night, I told him what Dana had told me. He initially began defending Gabby, as he usually did.

"Well, maybe Dana got it wrong," he said.

I let him know that I was irritated that he would defend or condone any part of Gabby's miserable behavior.

When Joey realized how upset I was, he softened just a bit, saying, "Okay, okay...I'll talk to her. She shouldn't say those things about you. But she *did* help build up the practice."

The next day when Joey spoke with Gabby, she predictably denied ever having said any of the things reported by Dana. "I don't think Dana likes me very much. She must have made this up!"

Joey believed what she was saying.

"You know, Joey," I said, "she could tell you anything and you'd believe her! If it comes from her, it might as well be coming from the mouth of Jesus, as far as you're concerned!"

I was so angry, I let my temper get the better of me. "I hate her! You keep her the f*** away from me and tell her to shut the f*** up about me, or I'll divorce you!"

"I'd love to see you try!"

Our relationship was drifting into dark and stormy waters even as I was continuing with in vitro treatments and trying to get pregnant. I often asked myself, *What am I doing, trying to get pregnant with this much conflict between us?*

Before I could even answer the question, I turned up pregnant. Suddenly the situation in which I found myself really hit me. *Oh, my God! This is really, really bad! I'm going to end up divorced with two children, one of whom is a newborn!*

By the time I was eighteen or nineteen weeks pregnant, it became routine for friends of ours to see Joey and Gabby out in public together and ask me, "Is Joey having an affair with her?"

I would say, "Well, Gabby has gotten herself so embroiled in our lives that she might as well be sleeping with my husband! But no, she's not."

Having sex with my husband was the one and only area of my life where I believed Gabby was not trespassing. I would think to myself, *Thank God. At least Joey still feels like my husband, not hers.*

Just to be sure, I asked Joey whether he was sleeping with Gabby.

He seemed totally grossed out at the thought. "Absolutely not! You and I have our problems but that doesn't change the fact that I love you!"

As our marital problems mounted, Joey continued accusing me of overspending and financial recklessness. He often talked about the cost of in vitro fertilization and how it was putting a financial burden on the dental practice. It seemed like he was constantly assigning blame to me and I began rejecting it outright. I noticed that I was becoming emotionally healthier and I smiled when I thought about my few days at the institution and how much the therapy had helped me.

"I regret having this baby with you!" I said one day. "It was supposed to bring us together but all I ever hear is how much it's costing you!"

This comment really wounded Joey, who pointed out that we got along fine except for issues related to money and Gabby. He was right.

At twenty-two weeks pregnant, the constant stress I was living under finally proved too much for the baby. I had to be taken to the hospital with a fever and ended up in spontaneous premature labor. I felt like I needed to use the restroom and, when I did, a tiny stillborn baby literally fell out of my body and into the palm of my hand. I started screaming and crying hysterically.

A nurse quickly swept in and took the baby from my hand. I couldn't have even told you whether it was a boy or a girl. I saw the head, the back, and the limbs—and I could see that the baby was not alive.

My spirit was broken and I couldn't stop wailing. The staff at the hospital knew what had happened to Drew and they started crying right along with me. I didn't know where my husband was—as usual. I had driven myself to the hospital. Finally Joey appeared in my hospital room.

When I saw him, I said, "I can't take this anymore! I can't handle the stress. It just killed my baby! I don't know if I can ever get past this. I am so brokenhearted and so tired of the fights."

Joey didn't say much. He seemed completely numb. His inability to connect with me over the terrible loss of this baby was further confirmation of the fact that we had serious problems. I felt totally alone.

I asked the nurse whether the baby had been a boy or a girl and she told me it was a boy. "I had a feeling the entire time I was pregnant that it was a boy," I said. "I was going to name him Peter. After Peter Pan."

My family arrived at the hospital and grieved right along with me. No one could believe that I could be losing another child and everyone was heartbroken. I could not wrap my head around what was happening. *This can't be happening to me! I've already done this! I don't deserve this!*

Then I thought of my son. *Oh, God—poor Devin! He was so excited about having a baby brother or sister!*

Joey spent some time comforting and consoling me and then, as was his way, he was ready to drown his grief in work. He turned his attention back to work and to Devin.

It seemed that, any time we were facing a life altering tragedy, Joey left me alone while he returned to work. I felt totally abandoned. I didn't get angry until I left the hospital. As I was wheeled out in the wheelchair, I was a changed person—heartbroken and determined to change my life. I was crystal clear on one thing: I was not going to live like that anymore!

39

*A*fter Drew died, I needed Joey in a way that didn't register for him. We are different people and we grieved in different ways. What I would learn from this was that, when it came to mourning, I was on a solo flight. I had no co-captain. I also had no auto-pilot switch and had to be alert and on point at all times. There was no one there to save me from my grief—not even my husband. It was one of the loneliest experiences I have ever had to confront. In the process of doing so, I learned and grew more than I ever thought possible.

Meanwhile, the days of me keeping my mouth shut and taking the abuse Gabby dished out—and the apathy my husband demonstrated when he failed to stop her—were over. My miscarriage had put an end to the tolerant version of myself. It had also put a halt to our intimacy.

Joey definitely noticed the change in our relationship. There was no way he could have missed it. About a month after my miscarriage, he came to me and said, "It's like you don't even love me! You don't show any interest in me. So, what are we doing? If you think you can find someone else who will put up with your shit, then go find him!"

"Consider it done!" I said. "You are no f***ing prize yourself!"

Hearing Joey imply that he was the only man willing to "put up with my shit" was so insulting. I became defiant and lost interest in what Joey thought of me. His words meant nothing to me anymore.

I no longer held back with him. I said what was on my mind and, depending upon the particular interaction between us, I became alternately indifferent, indignant and belligerent. I was bold and fearless in a way that was brand new and felt spectacular.

Joey definitely sensed that something had changed in me and came to the conclusion that I was planning to leave him. I had no intention of doing so—but I also had no intention of letting him know that and losing my leverage. And the fact was, I was still pretty upset with him over Gabby's continued mistreatment of me and his continued endorsement of it. In my mind, his failure to put a stop to it was as good as endorsing it.

I asked him to move out again, saying, "I need some time and space to figure out if I want to save our marriage or pursue a new life."

I had no intention of ending my marriage. At the same time, there was a tiny part of me that wanted so badly to be rid of Gabby that I was willing to endure a divorce from Joey if that was the only way to get her out of my life.

It had gotten to the point where my husband was so convinced that Gabby was indispensable to the success of his business that he was willing to risk our marriage over her. He was willing to deal with conflict at home and the possibility of divorce rather than jeopardize the perceived benefit Gabby brought to his dental practice. I found the situation to be pathetic.

Everything reached a boiling point due to an incident with my brother's then girlfriend (they have since married) who worked in Joey's office. She told me that Gabby was spreading gossip around the office about my affair. The amount of detail that my brother's girlfriend overheard Gabby recounting let me know that it had to have come from Joey.

I took this as a complete and total violation of the trust between Joey and me, and I lost it. I was done being manipulated and emotionally tortured by this woman.

"That's it!" I told Joey. "It's her or me!"

"Well, I'm not going to fire her!" he said.

"Fine. Then I want a divorce!" We were already separated but we'd been trying to work our way back together.

I'm sure Joey thought this was just one more salvo in our ongoing war of arguments—but I was deadly serious. I'm also sure he figured I didn't have the money to hire a divorce attorney. I knew that my dad would loan me the up-front costs of getting the ball rolling with an attorney. After I took care of the basic retainer fees, I knew I would have to get the rest of the money for the attorney from Joey, and I was perfectly prepared to do so.

I was sick and tired of the triangulation of my marriage and I wanted a new life. It wasn't that I didn't love my husband—I did—but I needed control over my own life. So, in 2002 or 2003, I hired the most ruthless attorney in town and had him prepare papers for service on Joey.

Joey and I decided that we would try to have a civilized discussion to see if we could work things out before they got too far out of hand. So, he came to the house and we sat down together at the kitchen table. (We were separated at the time and he was not living at home.)

"I want you to know that I did find an attorney," I said, "and I filed for divorce. I am not doing this because I want to—but I can't live like this! I won't raise Devin in a house where we're constantly fighting and I will never be okay with Gabby being a part of my life or having control over my finances."

"Okay," he said. "Well, let me know when the papers are ready."

"But how are we going to pay my divorce attorney?"

"We will get a check for you," he said.

I was incredulous. "After everything I just said to you, you're going to tell *Gabby* to write me a check? Seriously? It's not her money! You should be able to write a check from our checkbook without having to ask that bitch for permission—and so should I! This is exactly why I can't do this anymore!"

"Well, I don't see how I can just fire her! I rely on her to run the office and we need a successful business if I'm going to make enough money to support two households."

When he spoke these words, everything clicked for me. Gabby wasn't going anywhere—period. It didn't matter whether Joey and I remained married or not.

A couple of days later, I called my husband and let him know that he could pick up the divorce papers.

When Joey saw the divorce papers with his own eyes, he broke down and cried. He called me from the car, begging me not to divorce him. He told me how much he loved me and Devin and promised that things would change. He promised that he would never again violate my trust by sharing our personal business with Gabby and that he'd never again allow her to say a disparaging word about me. He would stop traveling with her, spending time with her after hours, and talking with her on the phone after work. But he needed me to understand that he still needed her to run the business.

"...And I want us to have another child!" he said. This was 2003, six months from our ten-year wedding anniversary.

He said everything I wanted to hear him say except "I'm firing her." I let him know that it was hard for me to sign up to continue in a life where she had any involvement at all.

"I'll keep her under control, I promise," he said. "And you'll have access to everything."

He told me in so many words that Gabby would start answering to me and not the other way around. I would no longer be an outsider in my own life. I didn't decide immediately but, after giving it some thought, I agreed that we could try again if he was willing to go to marriage counseling.

Joey moved back home and we returned to marriage counseling with Scottie but, before long, we realized that what we really needed to do was practice the wisdom she had already imparted to us. Joey started making a concerted effort to be a better husband and was changing for the better. He was more attentive to me and less grumpy. I had presented him with two choices: a life with me or a life without me. He had chosen a life with me and went out of his way to reassure me that he needed, wanted and loved me. He made me feel really special.

Seeing these positive changes in Joey renewed my hope in our relationship. It felt like a new beginning for us as a family.

For our ten-year courthouse wedding anniversary, Joey took my original one-carat wedding ring set to a jeweler and had them create a three-stone past-present-future ring for me, featuring a three-and-a-half-carat stone in the middle. It was impressive, definitely a show stopper, but it was the thought that Joey put into it that really made it a meaningful gift.

Meanwhile another egg retrieval process resulted in a pregnancy which filled me with hope and elation—but the pregnancy lasted only twelve weeks before I once again miscarried. This time, I felt numb. All I could think was, *I must have done something to offend God. I must not have been a good enough mother.*

It was excruciating to suffer two miscarriages after first losing Drew. It was as if each loss compounded and magnified the other losses. I told Joey that I couldn't continue with the in vitro fertilization treatments and, if we were going to have another child, we had to find another way.

As I mentioned earlier, he had gotten a vasectomy right after Devin was born. Now, he sought out a doctor to reverse his vasectomy and, within two months of his surgery, I got pregnant the old fashioned way.

Something about this pregnancy felt different to me. I had a calm assurance that I was perfectly healthy and would carry the baby to term. I had sought out the finest scientific minds in the country to help me force an outcome via in vitro fertilization—but things didn't turn around until I got to the point where I put everything in the hands of God.

Suddenly it was clear to me that there was divine timing at play. No matter how many times I had tried to force or hurry the outcome, it was already in the divine plan to happen at a certain time. And despite my manipulations and the good intentions of the best doctors our society has produced, nothing was going to change that divine timing.

One day, Devin lay down to take a nap and, being pregnant and constantly tired, I decided that I would join him. I snuggled up beside him, drifted off to sleep and dreamed that Devin was on the floor, playing with a toddler. I awoke with a smile on my face and a deep certainty that the baby would be just fine.

When we found out we were having a girl, Joey suggested the name Hope.

"That's so fitting," I said, "considering that the first book you ever read to me was *Hope for the Flowers*. And she is our hope for the future!"

Our unborn baby became exactly that—the hope that pulled our family together. Slowly she healed our hearts of the wounds we all suffered when we lost Drew so tragically, and the devastation of the two miscarriages that followed. Our family was growing closer and there was renewed excitement and happiness in our home.

Devin had asked me after the second miscarriage what happened to my tummy and where the baby had gone.

"Sweetie, the baby went to be with Drew," I explained.

"Oh, good," he said, in his sweet, beautiful way. "He needs a brother in Heaven. I have my brothers, Mark and Jordan, here. Drew needs a brother up there."

I couldn't help but smile. "You're so right, Devin! You're so right."

For all the marital issues that Joey and I have endured and all the things we've gotten wrong, there is one thing we've always gotten right—we have raised wonderful children and we have a wonderful family. We have always laughed together, and that silliness is one of the most important ingredients in our successful family.

I know it sounds incongruous to say that we have always had a wonderful family, even during those difficult periods when our marriage wasn't working. I'm not sure how to explain that phenomenon except to say that our kids have always inspired us to dig deeply into the best parts of ourselves and bring that forward. With our kids as our inspiration, we have always been able to rediscover our capacity for kindness.

Both Joey and I dearly love our family. Any time we have been presented with the option to split up, this love prevented us from leaving. The family connection has always remained intact and loomed larger than any justifications for leaving.

40

My pregnancy continued along an easy path and I was perfectly at peace and worry-free. Gabby was even making an effort to be friendlier to me and I thought she might have turned a corner.

Then, six months after the tenth anniversary of my courthouse wedding, Gabby celebrated her wedding anniversary, and suddenly turned up wearing a nearly identical ring to the past-present-future ring Joey had given me. She also bought a GMC Denali, the very vehicle Joey and I had discussed buying in order to have more room for our growing family. I also found out that she was pregnant and expecting a baby within a few months of my late August due date. It reminded me of the movie *Single White Female*.

Meanwhile, a new dentist came to work at the dental practice and wanted to form a partnership with Joey. I was opposed to having a partnership in the main dental practice but I didn't object to Joey and Chris, the other dentist, forming a partnership in a town thirty minutes outside where we lived. I gave the green light with the assumption that they would be the only two partners in the practice.

You can imagine my shock when I found out that they had made Gabby a one-third owner in this new satellite office. (I should note that our first satellite office was a small denture practice which ended up being absorbed into the main dental practice.)

I knew that Joey was growing his dental practice in such a way that he would have passive income, no longer be the only one performing dentistry, and no longer have to work such brutal hours. But Joey didn't tell me that they'd included Gabby as a partner until after it was a done deal and, needless to say, I was not happy about it.

"She demanded it!" Joey explained. "She said, 'If you're going to have me doing this work, I want a piece of it!'"

Chris had no objections and neither did Joey. The truth was that neither of them necessarily wanted to manage the new practice and so they were happy to have her in that role. It was a pretty sweet deal for her.

As I said, I'd initially given the green light on the out-of-town dental practice under the assumption that Joey and Chris would be the only two partners. My other stipulation was that the main dental practice not be used to fund the building of the second dental practice. Both of my stipulations were ignored. Whether I liked it or not, it was a done deal and it was too late for me to pull the plug.

Including Gabby in the second dental practice annoyed me but I was not irate over it. In any case, I needed to turn my attention toward my pregnancy and prepare to give birth. I also focused on the major positive changes taking place in our lives and our marriage and the fact that, for the most part, I was really happy.

A little bit after midnight on August 27th, 2004, Hope was born. The delivery was smooth and incident free. We started calling her Baby Hopey right away. She was six pounds, eleven ounces and perfect in every way. She was dainty and beautiful with sweet slender hands and long, skinny feet. Devin was almost eight by now and, when he met his little sister, he was thrilled. He hugged her and fell in love right away.

From the moment Hope was born, she seemed to be quietly and calmly observing the world around her. She wasn't prone to crying fits but didn't smile much either. She just took everything in.

I hugged and kissed her and said, "It's so nice to finally meet you, little one!" She met and held my gaze with her intense gaze. We locked eyes for the longest time and then she slowly closed her eyes and fell back asleep.

I am so grateful, I thought to myself, *that I know deep down that this beautiful baby girl and I are going to be part of each other's lives and we're not going anywhere. She's going to grow up and be a fine adult, just like Devin.*

With both Devin and Hope, the minute I set eyes on them, I knew that they would grow into adulthood. I never worried that they would be taken from us.

With Drew, I had this deep, instinctive sense that he wouldn't be with us long. There was so much to accomplish in so little time. Everything felt hurried with him and it left me depressed and anxious. It was never that I didn't love him—I loved him completely. But somehow I had the understanding that, *This experience is going to hurt* and that understanding brought with it a bit of guardedness. I could never entirely relax.

Of course, this clarity came only in retrospect. When Drew was first born and I had that alarming response to him, I blamed myself and believed there was something wrong with me. It was only later that I realized that there was nothing wrong with me. It wasn't that I didn't love, adore and cherish my baby. It's that I was tuning into a higher source and getting information that was too intense to process or properly interpret until much later.

If I had known then what I know now, I would have looked at Drew and known, *We have so much to do in very little time. I love you completely and you love me completely but at some point, we will have to say goodbye. So, we'd better get busy.*

It has taken me fifteen years and a lot of heartache to finally understand that the greatest gift my son Drew gave me was the absolute knowledge that love never dies. It evolves and changes as the love we experienced in physical form is carried over into spirit. Drew has never felt gone from me or lost to me. He's just not physically present. But he's on a journey I will one day join.

We are far too hard on ourselves. We must realize that we don't get to control the universe or the outcomes in our lives. We are given opportunities for a finite amount of time. Nothing lasts forever in physical form. Everything comes to an end at some point. We are responsible only for doing our best every day and creating as much love as we can in this life.

Love is the only thing that anyone is going to remember after we're gone. When I am no longer here, the love and interactions I have shared with my children will be with them and that's what will keep me present in their lives. That's how it is with Drew and me—and Devin and Hope, as well.

I have derived a lot of joy from knowing that I'm getting this part of my life right. I know how hard it is for people to understand that the painful education I was given in the form of Drew's tragic, early death is a blessing. It's true and, as painful as it's been, I'm honored.

I have so much love in my heart for all five of my children, my family and my friends. I have been wounded in the past and it's caused me to recoil but now I am reemerging. I am getting back into the habit of embracing love and being loving despite the possible out-comes. I am not responsible for the outcomes, only for being loving and bringing forth love. That's what I choose to do every day—to find a way, to the best of my ability, to love every person in my life.

41

I was, on the one hand, deliriously happy to have my new, beautiful baby girl. On the other hand, the three-way partnership between Joey, Chris and Gabby was going forward and I was definitely having a reaction to it. I was not in support of Gabby being included in the partnership and I felt blindsided by the entire situation, which made me mistrustful of Joey.

Unfortunately this disharmony related to Joey's work began to trickle into our marital relationship and further affect our already fragile intimate life. We were still enjoying a good friendship and partnership and a great family life with the kids, and we functioned well in public, but at home, we were feeling the strain. We had made such strides toward greater closeness but now we were turning away from each other and heading in our own directions.

We still had great moments but inevitably they segued into arguments. These arguments were often triggered by something said by Gabby or one of her family members on staff at our dental practice. These comments were often directed at me. Here was one comment that really infuriated me: Gabby told my friend Dana that she owned the dental practice and Joey actually worked for her.

Adding fuel to the fire was the fact that Joey had struck up a friendship with Gabby's husband, Hugo. When he wasn't on duty as a police officer, Hugo played polo and this became a basis for friendship between him and my husband. Joey had him over to the house quite a bit and this was very hard for me to swallow. I considered both Hugo and his wife to be bloviating idiots and I sure as hell didn't want them around.

Joey was also invited to their home, and he and Hugo rode horses together. Then there were the company parties where they would all be in attendance and I'd also be expected to attend. I didn't appreciate being forced to stand in a room with people I detested, and I hated every minute of it.

One day, I came to an unfortunate conclusion: despite all the positive changes my husband had made, one thing hadn't changed. He was still so addicted to the success he had achieved at work that he was unwilling to jeopardize it, even if it meant he would have a happier family life and marriage. As long as Joey believed that Gabby was a part of the equation that resulted in his successful professional life, he seemed willing to accept any and all damage it caused to his family life and marriage.

Joey didn't seem to care about the disparaging things Gabby said about me in public. He didn't seem to care about the fact that she took all the credit for his business success. His attitude seemed to be, "What difference does it make what she says or does, as long as she makes my life easier?"

I did! I cared! After all, Gabby was saying and doing these things at my expense—and Joey's. Her so-called attempt to be friendlier was short-lived and not terribly sincere, and much of what she was saying about me was very derogatory.

In order to stop thinking about Gabby and these insurmountable issues and problems, I turned my entire focus toward Hope and Devin. I put my head down and just kept going. I loved our son and our new baby daughter and so did Joey. Hope really did help to heal our hearts but, at the same time, my husband and I were essentially living two different lives. We were having a wonderful experience as co-parents but, as a married couple, we were completely divided and incapable of coming together on anything.

We didn't want to separate our family so we maintained the status quo. And, as I said earlier, despite our inability to function as an intimate married couple, Joey and I did have an underlying love for each other that manifested itself in a deep friendship. We accomplished an awful lot together and enjoyed our friendship and our family.

Every few months, we'd have a terrible, destructive blowup. Then we would return to being fine again. The problem was, I couldn't stand just being fine. Hope and I would watch Disney movies at home and I'd long to once again be the princess who was swept off her feet by Prince Charming and saved from the evil stepmother who, of course, reminded me of Gabby. I longed to be loved that deeply and profoundly.

I often thought of the plight of the late Princess Diana. I felt like Joey and Gabby were the workplace version of Prince Charles and Camilla. I recalled interviews with Princess Diana and one in particular where she appeared to be very upset. She let it be known in her very dignified and ladylike fashion that having a third person in the picture made her marriage feel very crowded.

The fact that Joey and Gabby weren't actually sleeping together was cold comfort to me. Joey's refusal to extricate Gabby from the triangle she had made of our marriage made me seriously question the depth of his love for me and left me with a profound feeling of loneliness.

One day, I realized that I was the loneliest married woman I knew. Joey and I had a friendship but there was no passion left. Whenever he tried to reach out for me, I went cold because I felt that his true loyalties lay with Gabby and the success they had created together. I used his snoring as an excuse to sleep in the guest room. I felt and functioned like an outsider, separate and apart, and not like one half of a couple. Sadly, my childhood had given me the ability to easily slide into that mode and begin to see it as normal.

In 2009, I got a Facebook friend request from Aaron, the brother of a childhood friend of mine. We had always had a big crush on each other and there was chemistry between us but we were so young, we never acted on it.

We started texting and messaging back and forth and soon it progressed to the phone. I felt invigorated by his attention and interest— young again, like a high school girl. *This is my chance,* I thought, *to act on my crush!*

Joey and I were leading such separate lives at this point, he barely noticed anything was amiss. It was great to feel alive again. I knew that it was absolutely inappropriate to be flirting and carrying on with Aaron while I was married—and if I forgot for a second, my family reminded me, saying, "Hey, Melissa, what's going on with you and Aaron?"

"Oh, it's nothing," I lied. "That's just how Aaron is—he's flirty."

His flirting with me seemed to awaken my inner voice and now it wouldn't be silenced. *I'm tired of living this lonely existence,* I thought to myself. *I want out of this marriage!* The little bit of attention Aaron was giving me was just the catalyst I needed.

I didn't feel any remorse over flirting with Aaron. If anything, I felt insulted at the thought that Joey would be bugged by it. After all, Joey and Gabby spent every day together at work, traveled together, and had resumed their habit of talking on the phone, day and night. As a result, I once again felt like an outsider in my own marriage.

I didn't want my flirtation with Aaron to result in my children being embarrassed or ashamed of me. I wouldn't have been able to bear that. But I didn't feel guilty for how it might affect my husband. I was only doing what he had done to me. Joey wasn't sleeping with Gabby and I wasn't sleeping with Aaron, but we were both focusing our attention on others when we should have been focused on each other.

I only came clean with Joey when he caught me on the phone with Aaron one night. "Yes, I met someone I care about and I don't want to be married anymore!" I said.

Of course, the truth was more complex than that. I was tired of living with Gabby as a third member of my marriage. I hated having her play such an integral role in my life and I hated Joey's absolute loyalty to her.

Joey and I decided to switch to a new marriage counselor. During a session, I told Joey that I had no intention of cutting ties with Aaron. After all, what was the harm? We were only communicating by phone.

"I'm working so hard to provide you with a great life," said Joey, "and I need to understand how you could develop feelings for someone else!"

I didn't deny having feelings for Aaron, whom I hadn't even seen in person since reconnecting on Facebook. Given all that Joey had put me through, it made perfect sense to me that I'd developed feelings for another man.

"I am sick and tired of Gabby and her family!" I said. "You have been putting this person between us for years! And you're *still* putting her before me even after you promised me that you'd absolutely stop. Now you have her as your partner in a new satellite office and I feel totally and completely betrayed!"

Issues related to our finances also surfaced in counseling, with Joey once again telling me that I needed to take a cold, hard look at my budget. "You really need to cut back on spending!"

I had heard this refrain too many times and I was sick of it. "Why don't you start by looking internally and reducing the staff before you start looking at my budget, which is nothing, comparatively speaking!"

He absolutely refused.

"Okay, FINE! Then I want to see the statements so I can see where the money is going!"

Again, he defiantly refused.

"Okay! Then I'm done."

42

*G*abby had been feeding my husband a steady stream of supposed proof that I was regularly having money transferred into my personal account and overspending. (All the money was funneled out of our business accounts and into our personal accounts.) The truth was that there *were* things going on that I didn't know how to explain at the time.

I would get calls from the bank, letting me know that I was a couple of thousand dollars overdrawn in my personal account. Any time I got one of these calls from the bank, I was mortified—and baffled. When I called the bank to investigate, the banker told me that Gabby's sister, Juanita (who worked in the bookkeeping office for Joey's dental practice) had transferred funds and inadvertently had it come out of my account.

The strange thing was, our bookkeeping office didn't have any financial documentation at all. Gabby was turning over the bank statements and her *interpretations* of the checks and their purpose, rather than turning over the statements along with the canceled checks. Her pattern was that all the information was first received by her and then turned over to Joey.

"If I have to," I told Joey, "I will get a divorce so I can subpoena the financial records. I am calling bullshit and calling your bluff. And I don't care if it's alright with you or not! One way or another, I plan to get those records. I don't need your permission. You can give them to me nicely or I can have my attorney subpoena them—it's entirely up to you. And once I get my hands on the records, I will know where the money is going. And I have a feeling this isn't going to go so well for Gabby!"

Joey told Gabby that I had a list of demands and, in an act of desperation, Gabby and Hugo began meddling in my marriage at a whole new level. They started trying to pressure Joey to divorce me rather than produce the documents I was demanding.

One day, Joey came to a session we had booked with a spiritual advisor named Pastor Steve and handed me a report given to him by Gabby to give to me. "Here you go!" he said.

"A QuickBooks report? Are you kidding me? That's not what I asked for!" I said. "I am not doing this anymore! I am out of here!"

I was ready to walk out of the session and this upset Pastor Steve.

"Look," I told the pastor, "you are not qualified to stand in judgment of me. You have no idea what I have been through with Joey and Gabby! Anyway, I can't trust you, knowing what good friends you are with Gabby."

I thought Joey had chosen our marriage counselor but it was actually Gabby—a fact I was unaware of until I arrived at the first session. I could only imagine what Gabby had told the counselor. She was diabolical in the way she managed to present me to the world as insane while she hid behind a veil of Christianity. She had set it up perfectly so that I had to simultaneously fight two battles: getting my husband to see her for what she was, and getting the rest of the world to see me as sane.

I was so fed up with Joey that I decided that there was no reason not to transition my relationship with Aaron from the phone to in-person visits. So, I began traveling out of town to see him. At the same time, I began to receive invitations from out of town galleries to show my paintings. Art had always been a passion of mine and now I started having showings and enjoying success as an artist.

As I sold my artwork, painting became not only a means of expression but a career. A gorgeous soul melody was pouring from me onto the canvas and my soul was singing. Even as my marriage seemed to be falling apart, I was experiencing this rebirth and finding myself in the process. To enjoy success while doing something I loved was wonderful.

I embraced the areas of my life which were working for me. I immersed myself in my art career, my new friends and my friendship with Aaron, which restored my confidence in myself—a gift that I would carry forward into the rest of my life.

Meanwhile Joey turned to my family, imploring them to put pressure on me to stay in my marriage. My family was not exactly in support of my wonderful new friendship and, to some extent, they turned their back on me. The more Joey turned to my family to bolster his position, the more I ran toward Aaron. At the time, I wasn't really conscious of the fact that, any time I left my husband and spent time out of town, my children were also without their mom.

After a while, I realized that what I was doing wasn't fair to the kids so I asked Joey to move out of the house. (Up until that point, Joey would spend the night in a hotel whenever things between us got tense.) Then I went and saw an attorney and filled out divorce paperwork. (I had used a different divorce attorney previously but he had since retired.)

"Sounds like you're going to have a war on your hands!" The attorney said. "I recommend you get the retainer paid as soon as possible so we can get the ball rolling." So I told Joey that I needed a check to cover the attorney's retainer.

Within a week of the conversation I had with Joey where I demanded our financial records, Gabby stopped showing up for work. And Hugo called my husband and told him, "You're an idiot! Your wife's crazy and she's going to bankrupt you! You'll be out of business in six months. If you are fool enough to let your crazy wife ruin the business, go right ahead, but my wife has no intention of showing up to work under that kind of stress. She refuses to work under such conditions. Either you divorce your wife or Gabby's not coming back to work."

Gabby and Hugo were putting an ungodly amount of pressure on Joey to divorce me. Even though he was living outside our home at the time, my husband had no intention of divorcing me and was working toward reconciliation. He now had the task of weighing and putting into proper perspective this doom-and-gloom scenario that Hugo was trying to sell him. He had to ask himself whether or not he was about to sabotage his business success by choosing his marriage over his work relationship with Gabby.

Slowly the lights started to come on for Joey and he began to put two and two together. He wondered, *Why are Hugo and Gabby pushing me so hard to get a divorce?*

Finally the documents started showing up. Right away, it became clear that Juanita was manipulating the books in such a way that benefitted Gabby at the expense of the dental practice.

Joey came over to the house (we were still separated at this point) and really wanted to talk to me. I could tell that he was on the verge of an emotional breakdown. Everything was coming off the rails for him. The economy had shifted and that was beginning to impact his practice, and dentists from the nearest big city were moving into our town and setting up offices, which meant that Joey was facing stiffer competition. Now everything with Gabby was blowing up in his face and I was making demands and no longer going along to get along.

Every area of Joey's life was spinning out of control and he was no longer sure what the hell to do. I could see him starting to crack and my heart went out to him. I continued to see Aaron but I stopped pushing Joey quite as hard.

Sadly Joey believed that everyone was jumping ship because he was now making less money. From his perspective, Gabby was look-ing for a better and more lucrative opportunity and I was leaving him because I had not been given the lifestyle I wanted.

Joey had misinterpreted what I was saying when I told him, "I am not giving up any money from my budget until I understand the reason why it appears that I am overspending in the first place. I am constantly being blamed for spending money I am not spending and I am sick of it!"

I had instinctively known for some time that Gabby was bad news and that something was terribly, terribly wrong. I was done. I could not—and would not!—live like this for one more minute.

43

On July 27th, 2010, Joey came home from work, walked into the house and collapsed on the floor. "Hugo says Gabby's not coming back to work anymore! I have no idea how to run this practice without her!"

Hugo had made it clear to Joey that, unless he stopped asking questions and divorced me, Gabby would not be returning to work. Gabby must have finally realized that, no matter how she tried to wriggle out of it, she was not going to be able escape scrutiny. And, no matter how she fought it, I was going to get my hands on our financial documents. Joey was going to request the documents from the bank and I'd get my hands on them in that way or else I'd subpoena them. Either way, Gabby would be caught—at last.

I had been waiting years to hear Joey tell me that Gabby was no longer working at the dental practice. I was elated over this news. By demanding to see the company financials, I had essentially doused the wicked witch with a bucket of water and she was finally starting to melt.

The only problem was, Gabby really did handle a lot of the daily operations for the office. So Joey was understandably concerned when he found out that she would no longer be showing up for work. He decided to reach out to Jenna, a former employee. He asked her to step into Gabby's position and help him manage the business, and she agreed to start work the following Monday.

Now that Gabby was no longer working in Joey's office, I had full access. So, within a couple of weeks of her July departure, I began regularly going in to the office and opening the mail. Meanwhile, Joey went to the bank, removed Gabby as signatory from all our bank accounts, let the bank know that Gabby was no longer working on our behalf in any capacity and should not be granted any sort of access to our accounts, and asked the bank to deal only with me.

The bankers asked Joey, in confidential, worried tones, "Are you sure your wife is okay?"

They had been listening to Gabby's story about me being a lunatic and bought it, hook, line and sinker. I am not qualified to make the clinical determination that Gabby is a sociopath but I can say as a lay person that she is a diabolical and masterful manipulator.

Joey convinced the bank that I was indeed of sound mind and asked them to give me the benefit of the doubt.

In addition to going through the office mail, I had Jenna—who was now working with our accountants to manage the office payroll—to give me access to QuickBooks so I could look at the payroll. When Jenna returned to our employ, I laid down the law, telling Joey that no one was ever to be granted a signature stamp again. Only Joey was to sign the checks.

When I opened QuickBooks and started going through everything, I could see that Gabby had unilaterally given herself a fifty thousand dollar annual raise eighteen months prior. And Gabby's mother had been double billing us for her time, claiming duplicate hours in two locations and being paid ridiculous amounts of overtime. (No one in Gabby's family was working for Joey's dental practice by this point in time.)

I now had actual proof that Gabby and her family had been engaged in full blown embezzlement, and I was really angry. I had endured Gabby's meddling in our lives and our marriage for thirteen years, and this was the first time I could see in black and white the damage she had been doing. I had removed the first card and the entire house of cards was beginning to crumble. And I couldn't wait to show Joey proof that Gabby was every bit as unscrupulous as I had suspected.

I waited for my husband to come home from work and made sure the kids were otherwise occupied. As soon as Joey walked into the kitchen where I was waiting, I showed him the contents of the folder.

"Here you go!" I said. "She's been lying to you. She has been taking fifty thousand a year more than she was owed and her mother's been taking another twenty-five thousand in overtime wages she wasn't due. And I have a feeling that this is just the tip of the iceberg!"

My husband was stunned speechless. He couldn't believe what I was saying—or what he was seeing with his own eyes. Joey had clung to this idea of Gabby as a moral person who was beyond reproach.

After the hell Gabby had put me through for so long, I thrilled in the knowledge that I had knocked the halo off her head.

"I just want you to know I was right," I said. "For years, I told you—no, I *begged* you—just to look into it! Just to make sure what she was telling you was true."

I really let him have it. Now that I had actual proof, I unleashed thirteen years of pent-up anger on my husband.

"Well," he said, "we're going to have to prove this."

I took this to mean that he was questioning me and that further incensed me. "Look, I want her arrested and put in jail! And I want my name cleared. You've really screwed things up between us because of her and, all this time, she's been lying about me! She drove us to the brink of divorce—more than once!"

Joey said, "All I'm saying is that we're going to have to get everything in order and make sure we have everything we need before we start making accusations."

I knew that he was right. If we accused Gabby of embezzlement, things could go very badly for her police officer husband, Hugo, and that's what Joey was trying to avoid. He was concerned that Hugo might try to retaliate against us, and rightly so. Hugo wielded his badge, his firearm, his power and his authority like a bully. He was a dangerous man with enough power and authority to take our freedom from us. I knew we would have to tread lightly.

"Okay," I said. "Just so everyone knows I'm not making this up, I will take my findings to our accountants and attorneys and let them decide what this means."

"That's fine with me," Joey said.

Now that I had this little bit of information, I began to piece things together in my mind. Gabby had systematically convinced Joey that I had been running up credit cards and pathologically spending money, and I was now certain that I would discover that she had been behind it all. I went on a crusade to clear my name and repair my credit, which had been damaged by whatever she'd been doing in my name.

As I promised Joey I would, I took the information to our accountants and attorneys and let them make sense of it all. I started by calling our CPA's office.

"Amy," I said, "I want to confirm that Gabby's salary was $100,000. If I've done my math correctly, she was actually being paid $150,000. What can you tell me about this?"

Amy defended Gabby, calling the payroll situation a "crazy oversight." She was very hesitant to accuse Gabby of any wrongdoing whatsoever. She put me through my paces to make sure I wasn't lying. Gabby had been so successful in creating this narrative where I was an unstable liar driving my family into bankruptcy, everyone was skeptical of everything I said and treated me with kid gloves.

Ultimately Amy agreed to look into the matter and get back to me. She pulled all payroll reports for January through July of that calendar year and concluded that, if Gabby had finished out the year, her salary would have totaled between $150,000 and $200,000.

"Great," I said, "thank you. Next question—when did she start paying herself that increase? The previous year?"

Amy told me that the increase began in 2008 and, during 2009, Gabby earned a salary of $156,000.

With this information in hand, I then called our attorney.

"Okay, Jack," I said, "we now know for sure that Gabby's been overpaying herself and her mother. So let me ask you something. She didn't have an employment contract reflecting that raise, did she?"

Our attorney let me know that he was unaware of any employment contract—for the main office, anyway. He never mentioned anything about the satellite office where Gabby had been given one-third ownership interest along with Joey and Chris, the other dentist, and I didn't think to ask.

The satellite office partnership had been formed in 2005 and lasted about a year. Then Chris left the practice due to a crisis that had arisen in his personal life. When Chris left, Joey had said to Gabby, "You're not a dentist and I'm not going to become fifty-fifty partners with you. It's my license at stake—you have no skin in the game. Once we find a replacement for Chris, we can resume the partnership with each of us having a third."

Well, Gabby didn't like that so she called our attorney and told him, "Joey said he wants to become fifty-fifty partners in the satellite office."

Naturally our attorney, Jack, called Joey to confirm this—but Gabby's mother intercepted the call. She told Jack, "Joey is with patients and he wants you to deal with me. Just send over the paperwork and he will sign it."

When Jack sent over the paperwork, Gabby simply took the signature page and made a point to put it in front of Joey while he was doing dental surgery. "This is to renew our lines of credit," she lied and handed him a pen.

Gabby then returned the "signed" document to the attorney. Next, she had to figure out how to file a new operating agreement with the Corporation Commission. That document, once filed with the commission, had to be published. Gabby knew that getting that signed by Joey wasn't going to be easy. The document's contents and its signature line were all on one page, so she couldn't simply put the signature page in front of Joey while he was preoccupied with a patient. Instead, she flat-out forged his signature.

Gabby was no longer coming in to work but she and Joey remained in touch as he transitioned her out of her position. Gabby had a lot of information that Joey needed and he and Jenna had many questions they needed answered by Gabby.

"I need to make you aware," Joey told Gabby, "that Melissa put together the fact that you've been paying yourself $150,000, not your regular salary."

She simply said, "Oh, okay."

"Is there any reason why that would be?" Joey asked her.

"Well, Juanita took care of payroll. I wasn't really paying attention."

Gabby didn't say that she knew and she didn't say that she didn't. It was an absurd game of cat and mouse. She was careful not to implicate herself in anything illegal but, by this point, everyone knew. She had been downright reckless in her actions, figuring that she was safe from discovery because all company mail was opened by her. Joey never saw any of the mail before it went through her hands or those of her sister Juanita.

44

*A*s I continued to go into the office to open and sort through the mail, I noticed something strange. We were getting bank statements from Wells Fargo Bank and yet we did all of our banking at Bank of the Foothills. We had once kept our business accounts at Wells Fargo but we had moved all our accounts to Bank of the Foothills.

When I looked closer, I saw that we had a merchant account open at Wells Fargo Bank. Not only was the Wells Fargo merchant account still open, there were hundreds of thousands of dollars being funneled into this account and then transferred into another account that I didn't recognize.

Joey had no idea that this Wells Fargo account was still open. He agreed to go to the bank and ask them to give me access to all the bank statements for the merchant account. I had the one statement that had come in the mail, but I needed the entire history of the account.

Meanwhile I called Amy at our accountant's office. She told me that she was aware that the old Wells Fargo merchant account was still open.

She explained, "Any time a patient uses a credit card, the money goes into the merchant account. But I was under the impression that all the money in that account was being swept into the Foothills Bank account."

I read her the last four digits of the mystery bank account that was receiving all the transferred money from the Wells Fargo merchant account. "Is that the Foothills bank account?"

"No, I don't recognize that account number."

I believed her. She had been working for our family for a while and I had no reason not to trust her. "Well, the money is going into this other account!" I explained.

Amy suggested that I go to Wells Fargo in person and see what I could find out about the mystery bank account. So that's what I did. When I explained the situation to the Wells Fargo banker, he called me by Gabby's last name and said, "You're the dentist's wife, aren't you?"

I was startled by him calling me by Gabby's last name, and I made it clear that I was the dentist's wife, not Gabby.

"In any case, this other account is a joint checking account," the banker continued. "Your husband and this other individual are listed as joint tenants with rights of survivorship."

I couldn't believe my ears. *My husband and Gabby opened a joint checking account, as if they were a married couple?* I was completely baffled and disturbed by this. *Is Joey lying to me?* I wondered. *Is there something he's trying to hide from me?*

"May I see the signature card?" I asked.

When the banker showed it to me, it was clear that Gabby had forged Joey's signature, just as she'd done on the operating agreement for the satellite office. Being such a small town, banking relationships where we bank tend to be pretty casual, not governed by the formalities one would encounter in a big city. Everyone knows everyone else in town and transactions are done on the basis of face recognition and a handshake. Even taking all that into consideration, it is fair to say that the bank failed to do their due diligence.

It turned out that all the bank statements for their joint checking account bore Gabby's address and were delivered electronically—not via postal mail to the dental office. Since Gabby was a signer on both accounts, she was able to electronically transfer money from the merchant account into the joint account she held with Joey.

Before I left the bank, I told the banker what I needed and he agreed to put together the entire history of the Wells Fargo accounts and call me when these things were ready for me.

Meanwhile I took the document proving that Joey and Gabby had a joint checking account and put it in front of Joey.

"Look at this!" I said. "You need to ask Gabby about this because the bank is telling me that this money went into this joint checking account…"

He looked completely dumbfounded, and said, "I knew nothing about this joint account!"

I looked at Joey and was quiet for a moment. Then I said, "And you're sure there's nothing else you want to tell me?"

"No," he said, putting his head down. "I don't know what to say…I don't know. I'm ashamed. You'd better tell Jack and Amy about the joint account."

I wasn't going to let it drop that easily. "Are you having an affair with her?"

"Hell, no!" he said. "That's gross and disgusting! She was my business colleague. We made money together—that's it. I had no romantic interest in her whatsoever." But something about his tone rang an alarm bell deep inside of me. I couldn't articulate it, not even to myself.

When I picked up the bank records compiled for me, I spread them out on the living room floor and barely slept for the next couple of months as I pored over everything. I was like a bloodhound, determined to follow the scent wherever it might lead me.

As I spent sleepless nights doing my investigation, all I could think was, *Thank God for that bank statement! Otherwise, I never would have figured this out!*

I was repulsed by the fact that my husband shared a joint checking account with this woman who had created so much conflict and stress in my marriage. During these nights on the floor, going through papers, I noticed something strange. On the next business day, I went into the bank and spoke with a banker.

"Every single time Gabby transfers money out of the merchant account into the joint checking account," I explained, "it is transferred the very same day into this *third* account. Where is that money going?"

"I'm sorry but I can't give out that information," said the banker. "All I can tell you is that there is only one named individual on this account and it is not your husband."

"So, what you're telling me is that it's Gabby's account."

With his words, the banker said "I can't confirm that" but there was something in his expression that made me wonder.

I said to myself, *I knew it!*

Gabby had apparently closed this personal account at Wells Fargo on July 30th, 2010, three days after she quit coming in to work. But she couldn't completely destroy the evidence because she didn't have the authority to close the merchant account. That would have required Joey's involvement.

I went straight to Joey, saying, "Remember how Gabby was always saying I was spending all our money? And remember how she said that the business was being negatively impacted by my so-called irresponsible way of living? Well, take a look at this! Gabby was transferring money into this joint account you say you know nothing about—and then it was being funneled into this *other* account where only one of you is the account holder…and it's not you!"

All the bitterness in my heart came through in my words. For thirteen years, I'd been told how I was spending too much money and hurting our company, and I'd been living with the knowledge that my husband hated me for it. I knew I hadn't done the things I was accused of doing and now Joey knew it too.

As a result of Gabby's blatant lies, I had been injured and suffered terribly and so did my family. She put her greed above my family's wellbeing and obviously had no problem ruining my life, my marriage and my children's lives. I hated her and I hated my husband for failing to protect me by taking even the most basic steps to determine whether or not what she had been telling him about me was true.

"…Hundreds of thousands of dollars went into this account," I continued, "so you need to talk to Gabby about this and tell her we need that money back!"

It would be an understatement to say that Joey was shocked to learn of this third checking account, just as he'd been shocked to learn of the joint checking account Gabby had opened by forging his signature. When Joey realized that Gabby had been duping him all along, he looked like someone had taken all the life out of him. It was a completely genuine and honest reaction.

I began scanning and emailing the information I'd uncovered to Jack and to Amy. Each time I sent over a new batch of material, I said, "Here's what I think. I think Gabby has been stealing money but please, by all means, look these things over and decide for yourselves. If you can somehow account for this, Amy, and if it all seems like it's on the up and up to you, Jack, just let me know."

I was very careful never to outright accuse Gabby of anything. I always made sure that all of my suspicions were relayed to our attorney and accountant so I would have the cover of a third party. That was my only hope of keeping my family safe from the wrath of Gabby's police officer husband. I never for one second lost sight of his ability to destroy our lives.

45

"There is an IRS agent here and he needs to speak with you," said one of our employees.

I thought, *Oh, my God! What now?*

It turned out that the IRS agent was paying us a visit over an issue that had come to my attention just a few weeks prior: Gabby had been stealing the money allocated to pay our payroll taxes. To be exact, one hundred and five thousand dollars had gone unpaid.

"We need to collect these taxes today," the IRS agent said. "Otherwise, we will have no choice but to put a lien on your business accounts and levy your assets. Is there some place we can sit down while you write a check for me?"

The agent very calmly explained the legalities of failing to pay our taxes and let me know that doing so was a federal crime. He was an interesting character, in his short-sleeved button-down shirt, khaki pants, tennis shoes, and bolo tie. He was very nice but he was also very straightforward. He made it clear that the IRS wanted their money, plain and simple.

Thankfully I had already been working with our CPA to make sure that the matter was handled, and had made a payment on the government tax-payment website EFTPS just a few days before the IRS agent's visit.

"I appreciate your help with this matter," I told the agent. "Here's what has occurred and here's what I've done to resolve it. I believe this payment confirmation will bring us into compliance."

Having an agent from the Internal Revenue Service show up at our office was one more indication to me of the seriousness of the problems caused by Gabby. Joey was also in the office at the time of the IRS agent's visit. With every new twist and turn in this Gabby situation, he sank deeper into depression. He felt totally betrayed by Gabby and foolish for having allowed himself to be duped.

My husband had grown up with a mother who was a small time gambler and played fast and loose with the family's finances. He was used to bill collectors calling the house, looking for money. Because of the acute embarrassment Joey felt over knowing that the family was usually late on paying their bills, he made sure that, when he became an adult, he always paid his bills on time. He prided himself on this habit.

Then, along came Gabby, and he placed his full faith, trust, family, marriage and business in her hands. He believed her to be a trusted friend and colleague and, having turned everything over to her, he then stuck his head in the sand, convincing himself that it was not in her character to create a disaster of this magnitude.

From the day of the IRS agent's visit forward, we were meticulous about keeping up with our payroll taxes, and we continued to gather our bank records. Meanwhile I continued trying my very best to piece everything together with the help of our accountants and attorneys, while allowing them to draw their own conclusions.

Both Joey and I were clear that we needed to be very cautious and measured in our approach with Gabby. We didn't want to swat at the proverbial hornet's nest and provoke Hugo. We agreed that we would wait and present everything at once rather than presenting a series of allegations.

Once Joey had wised up to the fact that Gabby and Juanita were being dishonest in their bookkeeping, he decided it was time to fire Juanita. Without Juanita in place, Gabby couldn't steal. He had fired Juanita in May, a couple of months before Gabby completely stopped coming in to work.

During June and July, while Gabby was still technically employed and being paid, our accountants worked with her to try to get Juanita to turn over the books. Even with Gabby's help, no one was having any success. Of course, it wasn't entirely believable that Gabby was sincere in her efforts to help us get the books from Juanita.

We faced so much resistance in trying to get the books back from Gabby and Juanita, we realized that our only hope was to go directly to the bank and request every single canceled check written during the history of these accounts. Online banking had been available to us since 2010 but we had no idea how far back these issues went, so we needed to request hard copies of everything.

Even if Gabby and Juanita *had* turned over the books without a fight, I wouldn't have been able to rely on the accuracy of anything I got from them. So we requested statements and canceled checks dating back to 2007 from both the Bank of the Foothills and Wells Fargo Bank. It wasn't long before both financial institutions had boxes of bank statements and checks ready for me. (This was a different load of documents than the ones I pored over on the living room floor; these were archived records.)

These documents were quite a revelation. They showed that our dental practice had been paying for random living expenses for Gabby, Juanita, and their mom, Cathy. When questioned about these expenses, Gabby matter-of-factly said, "Yes, because I occasionally worked from home, I thought it was okay for the business to compensate me." Needless to say, this was not an agreement that Joey had ever made with her.

Meanwhile Joey was having meetings with Gabby at the local Barnes & Noble to request the passwords and log-in info for various payer systems, including the state Medicaid and Medicare programs, along with other information we needed. She had complete control over the dental office and Joey couldn't function without her cooperation.

Being fully aware of Gabby's capacity for defiance, I was surprised when she agreed to turn over the passwords to Joey. Perhaps she started to realize that things could go very badly for her. Or, perhaps she started to feel some remorse over what she'd done. Given that she was exhibiting a spirit of cooperation, I decided to adapt my approach to her change in demeanor. I had a feeling that, if I went for the jugular, she would shut down completely and refuse to help us in any way.

She and I corresponded very occasionally via email when I needed to ask her a question. I never spoke to her during this period of discovery and I have not spoken to her to this day. Every time I made a new discovery related to Gabby's misconduct, I presented it to Joey.

"I know it's my fault we're in this mess," he said to me one day, "and I'm working my ass off to get us out of it! But I can't know every way she screwed me over! You and Jack and Amy need to be the ones to deal with it."

My husband was riddled with guilt, shame and self-loathing. The fact that he had believed Gabby's lies about me for thirteen years and taken her word over mine was eating him alive. He couldn't bear to know every single thing she had done. Not only were we in a huge financial hole because of her, but Joey was heartbroken over the betrayal.

The next discovery was related to our dental supply vendors. I discovered that Gabby had quit paying their bills and we now owed them $140,000. They had cut us off and were unwilling to work with us any longer. I had to call them up and fall on my sword.

"We're in the middle of a storm here," I explained. "After being a customer of yours for the past fifteen years, I need you to bet on us the way we've bet on you in the past." To their credit, they agreed to work with us—but it wasn't easy to repair these damaged business relationships.

I knew that Gabby had painted an image of me as a lunatic and I was not about to validate that with my actions or my words. Even though I had private moments where I lost it, I endeavored to be professional when dealing with others, asking for their patience and understanding as we tried to recover from these devastating circumstances. There were only a few people who refused to work with us.

Having grown up in such a stressful environment, I instinctively learned how to read situations and modify my approach accordingly. Those hard-learned lessons served me well now. I knew that, while I was perfectly capable of flying off the handle and going for the jugular, it wasn't the most effective approach. I was smarter than that, and capable of handling situations in a manner that worked for everyone.

I forced myself to listen to people and hear what they were saying before I responded. I remembered my counselor, Tom, telling me years before—during what now seemed like an entirely different lifetime!—that I was going to need to learn to act on my intellect rather than my emotional responses, and I did so now. Still there were times when the stress got so intense that it affected my health and I began to implode. I would spontaneously pass out because I'd forgotten to breathe.

I could still hear Tom saying to me, "You are more than capable of this, Melissa! I promise you. You are everything you need to be in order to be self-sufficient, self-actualized and successful. You can bring anything you need into your world—you just need to learn to master your emotions and lead with your intellect."

Gabby had maxed out our line of credit at the bank, left huge balances with our vendors, and opened and maxed out numerous credit cards in our name. Slowly, little by little, we dug ourselves out of the hole.

Meanwhile, Joey continued meeting with Gabby to discuss her misconduct and get the information we needed from her to run the dental office. During one of those visits, Joey told Gabby that he didn't understand why she had never apologized to me for everything she had said about me and done to me.

The very next day, I received an email from Gabby in which she described embarking on a journey of spiritual evolution and fasting for twenty-one days. She said that, during that fast, her conscience really began to get the better of her and she realized that she could no longer continue living the life she'd been living. She talked about the experience of doing something you know is wrong but being unable to stop yourself from doing it.

She went on to offer me "a sincere apology" and acknowledged that I could have made this period of time during which I discovered all her wrongdoing very difficult for her and her family. She said she was eternally grateful that I had not done so.

She should have quit while she was ahead but, instead, she went on to describe an agreement she believed she'd made with my husband wherein they would split, fifty-fifty, all revenues over a million dollars earned by the dental office. She went on to blame our book-keeper, Louise Pine (who had been employing Juanita) for telling her that I was "spending the money faster than Joey could make it" so Gabby had better start taking her share.

I figured she was lying about the fifty-fifty split on all revenues over a million dollars. I took the email to Joey to see what he had to say.

"Yeah, we had a discussion like that," he said, "when we had a three-way partnership in the satellite office but it never applied to our main office." The truth was, Gabby was stealing before there even *was* a satellite office.

"...Anyway," continued Joey, "we didn't come to any kind of for-mal agreement—not at all. It was more like one of those 'If I ever win the lottery, I'll split the millions with you.' kind of conversations. It was pie in the sky. It wasn't real."

Gabby followed up her first email with another email detailing specific revenues earned by the business. She went on to explain that, according to the "we split everything over a million, fifty-fifty" so-called agreement she had with Joey, she was owed $900,000!

I took this email from Gabby as a sign. It confirmed what I had suspected. Before receiving this email from her, I had come to the conclusion—based only on instinct and what I'd uncovered so far—that the amount of money Gabby had stolen from us was in the high six figure range. Now that I saw this statement that, in her mind, she was owed $900,000, I knew the actual amount of the theft was going to be huge. I knew that we were talking about millions of dollars—millions, plural!

I also knew that she knew that she was caught to some degree. And she was smart enough to throw out a number that was in the ballpark of what I would have found without exhausting every resource.

This email was an obvious attempt by Gabby to keep from look-ing quite so bad but it was far from a true confession. At least I now had something in writing from Gabby related to her embezzlement. The first thing I did was forward copies of the email to my attorney and CPA. Both Amy and Jack were dumbfounded when they saw it.

46

Once our attorney, Jack, had the email in hand, he called Gabby.

"Sure I took nine hundred thousand dollars," she admitted. "I felt that Joey had promised it to me!"

"You don't just take money because you feel entitled," Jack pointed out, "and leave someone else with the tax burden. That's embezzlement and theft! How do you propose we work this out?"

"Well, I'll have to talk to my husband. I don't really know." She went on to say that they were having marital troubles and she wasn't even sure whether or not they would be staying together.

Our attorney, Jack, and our CPA, Amy needed Gabby to cooperate and show us what she had done and how she had done it so that we could begin to correct our books and make sure our tax burden for the current year was accurate. At the conclusion of that phone conversation, Jack asked Amy's boss, Gary, to send out an email memorializing the thefts Gabby had admitted to during her phone conversation with Jack.

"Attached is a spreadsheet of all the different ways you've been taking money you're not personally entitled to. Please reply with confirmation." Gary copied Joey, me, Jack and Amy on the email.

To everyone's amazement, Gabby replied with the word "Correct."

At that point, we started asking very specific questions, including questions about credit card statements on unauthorized credit cards she had unilaterally opened without our consent. We asked her about $75,000 worth of furniture and found out she had purchased it to outfit her home and that of her brother who was going through a divorce and needed new furniture. There were trips to Hawaii for Gabby and Hugo as well as another couple they invited along as their guests. There were also hunting trips and trips to Disneyland for Gabby and her family.

At this point, Hugo inserted himself into the situation and began to use intimidation tactics in order to muddy the waters.

"Well, hold on a minute," he said, "my wife is not admitting any guilt! She had a verbal contract with Joey which entitled her to that money! Therefore, taking those funds was not a crime. You may dispute that in a civil suit but there's nothing criminal here."

"I am telling you," Joey said, in one of the many phone conversations between him and Hugo that ensued, "that we had no such agreement! I will not have you insist that happened when it didn't."

"Well, no matter what," said Hugo, "you're going to have to buy Gabby out of the satellite office. We own fifty percent."

Joey was incredulous. "What are you talking about? I didn't sign anything that made her fifty percent owner!"

"Yes, you did! I'm looking right at a page with your signature on it, showing that Gabby is a fifty-fifty partner! And by my calculations, the business earned $1.5 million while she was working there. So you need to write us a check for half the value—which is $700,000."

This was the moment our suspicions were confirmed about Gabby forging Joey's signature. It was ludicrous and laughable to think that we'd write them a check for that amount of money after Gabby had stolen so much money from us. Hugo knew that perfectly well but he was trying to make a point.

Interestingly enough, Hugo initially thought the amount Gabby had stolen was around $300,000, and he demanded an accounting and agreed to make monthly payments in order to pay us back. Once my investigations revealed that the figure was well over a million dollars, he completely changed his tactic and started claiming that we actually owed Gabby money and needed to buy her out of the satellite office. Everything turned on a dime.

Hugo then began to communicate with our attorney in writing, setting forth his interpretation of what had transpired. In so many words, he described a situation in which Gabby had been manipulated by Joey into engaging in criminal conduct and committing insurance and tax fraud, all in an effort to keep money hidden from me. He described me as a crazy woman and stated that Joey and I had marital problems and Joey was trying to keep from losing huge sums of money to me in a divorce settlement.

Hugo went on to characterize Joey as a criminal, his reasoning being that Joey had committed insurance and tax fraud and used unaccredited dentists to treat his patients. He set forth a laundry list of accusations, putting us in a position where we had to answer for each one.

A police officer was making these accusations after evaluating the situation. In conclusion, he stated to our attorney that, "I would be happy to open an investigation into my wife's conduct but it will not go well for your clients."

In response, our attorney sent Hugo a letter to this effect: "No, we will not be addressing all your nonsense. Let's get back to the fact that you owe Melissa and Joey $1.3 million. Your wife has already confessed to stealing that amount..."

The $1.3 million was representative of everything we could substantiate by documentation, following six months of investigation, and we knew that it was a figure that would stand up in court. We knew that the figure had to be airtight in the event that the matter proceeded to trial. The $1.3 million figure represented only Gabby's theft and didn't even take into account that of her family.

In conclusion, our attorney stated, "We will not entertain any of these other threats or intimidations. You need to focus on getting a plan together. You will need to turn over all your personal financial statements and make a settlement offer if you hope to avoid a criminal investigation."

Hugo responded with another letter of his own, stating that he didn't believe for a second that our accounting was unbiased. He went on to state that he felt our accountants were cooking the books, so to speak, to produce an outcome favorable to us. He claimed to have the "true books" and assured us that he and Gabby would be vindicated while Joey and I would be exposed as liars.

What Hugo somehow failed to realize was that, with each email he wrote, he was corroborating and acknowledging the truth, and he was doing so in writing. It was beautiful. In his estimation, Hugo was smarter than all of us idiots and yet he couldn't seem to get out of his own way.

He also couldn't seem to resist the temptation to try to intimidate us. Around this time, he began parking his squad car on the road leading to our house. I would leave the house and there would be Hugo's car. I'd return home and he'd still be there. Any time I saw his car parked there, the hair on the back of my neck stood on end. He was letting us know that he was watching us, and I found it very disturbing.

It wasn't just Hugo's car parked on the road outside our house, either. Other frightening and strange things began happening around that same time. Someone took a shotgun and shot out the windows in our business office. Someone punctured a tire on my car. These things seemed like more than coincidences and they were scaring the hell out of me.

I was calling my attorney every other day in tears, saying, "I can't take this! This is just not okay!"

In February of 2011, Joey was on his way home when he got a call on his cell phone from Hugo. When Joey answered, Hugo said the following: "I will spend twenty years in prison before I pay you a dime!"

"Are you threatening me?" Joey asks.

"I am threatening all of you!" Hugo said. It was a clear death threat—although, being a law enforcement officer, he was careful to walk right up to the line without crossing it in the way he phrased the threat.

Joey was dumbfounded. "Dude, I don't even know what to say to you!"

After that phone call with Hugo, Joey walked inside the house and began to unravel in a way I hadn't witnessed even when Drew died. Joey was truly petrified that Hugo was going to harm the kids and me.

"I can't do this anymore," he said. "The money's not worth it! I can't live like this. How am I supposed to work hard enough to dig us out of the hole if I'm constantly worrying that he's going to kill you or Devin or Hope? I need to be done with these people. We need to just let them go…let them walk away. I can't take it anymore!"

After Joey's meltdown, I spoke with our attorney, Jack, and told him about Hugo's threat. By that point in time, Jack had already had many conversations with Hugo in which Hugo tried to justify Gabby's actions using legal logic that was beyond ridiculous.

"I really have to question his judgment at this point," Jack said. "And I am concerned for your family's safety. He seems very volatile."

Hugo had made it clear that, if we pushed him too far, we needed to be prepared to be randomly pulled over by the police, who might mysteriously discover drugs in our vehicles—drugs that had been planted. And we needed to be prepared to find ourselves arrested for trumped up charges like resisting arrest.

"I could put cuffs on you and shoot you and no one would question me," Hugo warned.

"Listen," I told Jack, "I do not want to provoke this guy. He is certifiable—crazy! I need you to file the complaints on our family's behalf. I have children and I need to stay as far away from him as I can get!"

Jack began to theorize that Hugo was complicit in Gabby's theft. Otherwise, as an officer of the law, he would have gone to any lengths to make sure his own reputation and name remained untarnished. But Hugo refused to cooperate with us even when his wife was cooperating. Ironically, at that point in time, Hugo's job involved investigating financial crimes.

During the conversations Joey and I were having with Jack, we made it clear to him that no amount of money was worth putting our family's lives in jeopardy. We considered Hugo to be unhinged and dangerous and Joey and I never forgot for a moment that Hugo had the authority to take away our freedom. Jack agreed with our characterization of Hugo and encouraged us to hang in there and let him intercede on our behalf. He also said, "...and avoid Hugo and Gabby entirely!"

Had Joey and I been able to leave town at that time, we would have done so, but we couldn't for several reasons. For one thing, we had purchased the building in which Joey had his dental practice. As owners of the building, we would have had to sell the building in order to leave. There was also the fact that Joey was not exactly a one-man operation—we employed thirty or forty people at the office, all of whom would have been out of a job if we had decided to relocate. Then there was the fact that, thanks to Gabby's embezzlement, we had debt racked up. We needed to either dig ourselves out or declare bankruptcy—those were our choices.

We chose to dig ourselves out of the hole Gabby had dug for us rather than file bankruptcy. We paid back every dime she ever stole— all the money we owed our vendors, all the money she had racked up on our lines of credit, and all the taxes on the money. It took a huge toll on us. It would have been so much easier to file bankruptcy, but that wasn't in keeping with the values Joey and I share.

As Jack was working with Hugo to reach some sort of settlement agreement, I resumed individual therapy. The therapist I worked with was a spiritual counselor and, through the soul searching I did in our sessions, I would go from wanting vengeance to learning that I can go deep within and come to love even my enemies. I would also discover a beautiful secret: it is completely disarming when you can say to someone (even if you only say it in your own heart), "I'm sorry for whatever pain you were in that caused you to act so horribly toward me. I'm sorry for whatever was done to you to cause such pain."

I was mad as hell at Gabby and Hugo and had spent so much of my energy hating them for what they did to me and my family. My life had become a series of frustrations, disappointments and setbacks. My life was turned upside down more than once and I became completely hopeless. Yet, now, I am eternally grateful for every angry moment, every disappointment and every time I felt like I had been kicked in the stomach.

In the midst of it all, I found the capacity to internally say to Gabby and Hugo, "I am sorry for your pain." And I found a capacity for love that exceeded anything I'd known before. I learned to love myself enough to say, "I'm in pain but this pain is teaching me something and I'm grateful for it."

When I was a child, living with so much emotional and psychic pain, all I knew how to do was run from it. I wasn't running anymore. I started embracing the pain and realizing that every time I felt hopeless and in pain, I deserved more love, not less.

Any time I was able to give Gabby and Hugo to God and the universe, feel their pain and feel empathy towards them, and wish them only love, I was able to walk around feeling more peaceful and joyful and loving—and more loved than I ever have in my life.

47

*J*ack told Hugo in the course of a phone conversation, "Joseph and Melissa want nothing more to do with you so, from now on, please direct all communications to me on their behalf." Jack also addressed the fact that Hugo had been parking outside our house and gingerly tried to confront Hugo about threatening our lives. Jack was careful with his words because he didn't want to exacerbate the situation.

Hugo neither confirmed nor denied anything. In fact, he didn't really address anything at all. While Gabby had actually admitted things, Hugo would say things like, "Well, if that's really what they are claiming, they should prove it. Let them step forward with evidence supporting that claim."

Joey and I were walking on eggshells, never able to anticipate what Hugo might do next. Even when we were able to freely drive around town without seeing a police car, we knew that when we got home, we might find either Hugo's truck or a cop car parked across the street from our house. Hugo didn't respect any boundaries, so I had to assume that, at any moment, he might show up at our home or knock on our door or call us on the phone.

We were already living under extremely stressful conditions thanks to the situation with Gabby and Hugo and we started to feel like we were trapped in a fishbowl. The strain on our marriage was proving to be too much for Joey and me. Both of us were struggling under the weight of it all, barely making it through each day, but I was managing the stress a bit better than Joey. He was not thriving at all. He was anxious, tense and exhausted all the time because he could barely sleep at night.

Something had to give. We needed a change in our circumstances if we had any hope of making it through this difficult time. Joey had made it clear that he couldn't take the stress and strain of fighting it out with Gabby and Hugo and I felt the same way. We knew it was going to wrap up at some point but we both needed to know that day was coming sooner rather than later.

The truth of the matter was that, despite Jack's efforts to reach a settlement agreement with Hugo on our behalf, it was clear that Hugo was never going to come forward with a resolution or a workable proposal. He and Gabby were never going to do the right thing. Both Joey and I knew that Gabby and Hugo would never honor a monthly plan for repayment of the stolen monies. In fact, unless we wrapped things up, the odds were good that things would continue to get worse, not better.

The moment that Hugo threatened our lives, Joey became a changed man. It unsettled him in a way I had never seen before. The fact was that Joey—who knew Hugo better than I did—was terrified. That was all I needed to know and I conducted myself accordingly.

Joey and I agreed that I couldn't carry a handgun for protection while Hope was still so little, so he bought me a taser. We knew that a taser wasn't going to save my life in a gunfight but, if Hugo tried to approach me, at least I would have something with which to defend myself.

Meanwhile, we were heavily relying on Jack to act as our agent and he did so, reaching out to people he knew at various law enforcement agencies in the Phoenix area. Jack was also the only one interacting with Hugo at this point, and he found him to be unreasonable and irrational.

"If we call the police and initiate a criminal investigation of Hugo," Jack said to me one day, "that will only set Hugo off and put your family further at risk. In order for you to even consider doing such a thing, your entire family would need to move—and you'd need to move the dental practice, too."

As I said earlier, Joey wasn't able to move his business. That meant that our only other avenue of recourse was to continue our efforts to reach some sort of settlement agreement with Gabby and Hugo. I found this to be a hard pill to swallow.

For me, signing the settlement agreement was tantamount to signing away every opportunity we would ever have to see that Gabby and Hugo were held accountable for what they'd done. It was so infuriating and disappointing to think that, after everything we'd been put through, this was our only remedy. Then again, I knew that we couldn't live under the constant stress caused by dragging out the situation.

When all was said and done, everyone signed on the dotted line. There was a nondisclosure clause demanded by Gabby and Hugo and included in the settlement agreement, so I can't speak about the details. Suffice it to say, they made such nominal financial restitution, it didn't even cover our attorneys' fees. (Both Gabby and Hugo signed the settlement agreement because, as a married couple, they had joint assets.)

On the upside, signing the settlement agreement got Gabby and Hugo out of our lives, got Gabby off the operating agreements for both dental practices and stated clearly that she had no ownership interest in the businesses.

I found that the signing of the settlement agreement brought up a wave of anger toward my husband. *If only he had listened to me all those years ago and looked into what Gabby was doing,* I thought to myself, *we would not be in this position now.*

We were living under an enormous financial strain as a result of Gabby's embezzlement and I resented the hell out of it. I tried not to but I did. There were times when I was less than my best self and I unleashed torrents of anger in Joey's direction. We had very heated arguments but, to my husband's credit, he withstood it without walking out on us. Somehow we got through it. And, as I continued in therapy, Joey also continued along his journey to becoming a better man.

"I know I've gotten things horribly wrong," he said. "I never should have listened to Gabby and trusted her and I feel terrible about what was done to you as a result. But, I believed her. Everything she put in front of me was so convincing. But I will spend the rest of my life trying to make this right. I will make this up to you. I'm going to prove to you I'm capable of being a good husband—someone you can trust and love."

I was skeptical and I didn't make things easy on him. But he was longsuffering and, every day, he would do something special to show me how much he loved me. For example, I might wake up to find roses in my car with a note. My husband was of service to me in every possible way and asked for my forgiveness for putting me and the kids under such stress.

Our children really loved their dad—and he was a great father. I knew he wanted to be a great husband but I was conflicted. I felt like, for thirteen years, he had been loyal to another woman over me. So, I struggled with my feelings but we did our best to keep our family intact and living under the same roof. We still needed to work toward deeper intimacy in our marriage. It was a process of learning how to communicate again, learning to laugh again, finding ways to reconnect and laying the foundation for a successful parental partnership and business partnership.

I still had a profound need for Joey in my life but the romantic side of things remained a struggle for me. The trust had been severely eroded and damaged by the situation with Gabby. As a result, I had my guard up to such an extent that I couldn't seem to lower it. Ironically, as a family, we still laughed together, had fun, played and talked.

Life carried on and our relationship grew stronger despite the gaps in our intimacy. There were times when Joey expressed to me his profound frustration over the lack of intimacy between us. He may have been frustrated but he also understood that what had transpired with Gabby was tremendously traumatic and he was going to need to be incredibly patient with me.

Joey also realized that his decision to love me could not be predicated upon my ability to reciprocate. And he did love me. He was repentant and dedicated himself to me and to our family in a way that I couldn't ignore.

We traveled with the kids and spent time as a family and that always went very smoothly and, within certain parameters, we functioned very well as a couple. But it was going to take time and an abundance of patience if we were ever going to get back to each other on a more intimate level.

As Joey and I somehow managed to flourish within our ambiguous marriage, I continued to spend time with Aaron. I had no illusions about having a future with Aaron, or replacing Joey with him. In order to bring Aaron fully into my life, I would have had to bring him into the lives of my children and I wasn't prepared to do so. Any time I tried to envision what my children's lives would look like if I were to divorce Joey, it stopped me in my tracks. I could never bring myself to dismantle our family.

I would ask myself, *What are the most meaningful things in my life? What can't I live without?*

I would be struck by the extent to which Joey had dedicated himself to me and the kids, and committed himself to our family. In his dedication to our family and his own personal growth, he forced me to see him through new lenses.

Joey was a wonderful dad and he loved the kids and they loved him and we all loved each other. The four of us—me, Joey, Devin and Hope—worked. We brought out the best in each other. We definitely had been through hell but that was okay. I've always been willing to walk through fire for my family.

Not a day went by that Joey didn't tell me, "You're the most beautiful woman in the world."

I so appreciated his love for me—and yet I felt guilty. *Why can't I fall back in love with him?* I would wonder. *Why can't God just flip that switch back on?*

I knew that Joey and I loved each other, and we both loved our family and had their love—but there was something troubling me, and I couldn't quite put my finger on it. Something was off.

"I'm all in," I explained to Joey, "but there is something not letting me have access to those deeper feelings for you."

"I understand," he said. "And I'm not going to ask you to do anything that doesn't feel right. It's like forcing a person who doesn't like broccoli to eat broccoli. Let's hold hands. I'll take just holding your hand and laughing." He always had a way of phrasing things that would make me feel less guilty.

Strangely enough, during this period where we were abstaining from intimacy, we were closer than we'd ever been. For four and a half years, we lived this way.

48

One day in November of 2012 when I was in the dental office and tried to run a collection report, I ran into an "access denied" error code. I couldn't figure it out.

I called our dental software rep, Jordan, for help. "I'm probably just not familiar with this software," I explained. "I must be doing something wrong. It makes no sense that access would be denied to me, since I'm the administrator and should have access to everything!"

At Jordan's recommendation, I directly contacted the company that provided the dental software program used to manage both the financial and clinical side of patient accounts at our office. Their tech support people worked remotely to see if they could uncover the problem. This is when they discovered that someone had changed all the security settings. The way the settings had been altered, all the reports were filtered to show me only credit card and insurance payments. All cash payments were edited out of my view. I had the software company re-set everything so I was able to run the reports with all the data intact.

As I hung up the phone with them, my heart was heavy. My intuition told me that someone—or maybe more than one person—had obviously been stealing from us. I needed to find out who was in on it. I already knew that Jenna had to be involved, based on the date range of this activity. It would take some digging to get to the bottom of it and I was going to have to be discreet. I had no intention of letting the girls in the office know until I was good and ready.

I slowed my breathing and calmly walked up to the front desk, trying not to appear agitated. I didn't want to arouse suspicions. "Hey, guys," I said, "I need the keys to the cash drawer."

Their faces went blank, which was very telling. I took the key, opened the drawer and took the cash. "I need the deposit book, too," I said. "I'm going through the cash drawer and I'll be back."

When I counted out the cash, it amounted to seventeen hundred dollars. This told me that our staff was blatantly ignoring our office policy that no more than a hundred dollars would be kept in the cash drawer at any one time. Kim was now the office manager and, as I was looking at the deposit book, beginning with the day Jenna left, it was obvious that Kim was doing the very same thing Jenna had been doing.

I took the cash and approached Kim, saying, "Do you care to explain to me why we have so much cash in the cash drawer?"

"Well," she said, "the girls at the front desk didn't tell me that much had accumulated. Normally, I deposit it in the bank."

"It's interesting you say that," I said, "because I spoke with the girls at the front and they told me that you come and look at the cash drawer every day. In any case, this isn't right. This kind of money needs to be deposited in the bank. You need to perform a cash reconciliation of your drawer every night and morning so you're starting each day with the same balance. That's how we discussed doing this. This is not good management policy and I'm not happy with it!"

She claimed that she didn't have the reconciliation sheet so I told her not to worry, that we'd start a new sheet. I wanted her to think that all was well.

"I'm going to just deposit this cash," I said, "and starting today, let's leave a hundred and five dollars in the drawer—that's a hundred in paper and five dollars in coins. There needs to be a hundred and five dollars at the end of every day."

"Okay, I understand," she said. "Sorry."

I created a new cash reconciliation sheet, initialed and dated it, and put it back in the cash drawer. Then I took everyone aside and said, "Okay, from now on, here's what we're going to do…"

They all played dumb and I did too. I wasn't ready to completely tip my hand. I decided to let a few days go by so they would think the storm had passed and let their guards down. I waited three days and then casually announced that I had to go out of town for a few days. I did stay away from the office for a day or two but, before I was expected to return, I popped back in, opened the cash drawer and took the cash back to my office so I could count it. Once again, several hundred dollars was sitting in the cash drawer!

So I ran the audit trail reports for the days I was out of town. Thanks to the user log-in information, it was easy to track who was taking the cash and which patients were submitting it. I needed to know the extent of the theft so I ran the audit trail reports beginning with August of 2010, the time when Jenna took over. I discovered that almost two hundred thousand dollars in cash had been stolen. This was money I desperately needed as we tried to recover from Gabby's embezzlement and pay our debts, our vendors and our loans.

I had hoped that, by paying very nice salaries to our employees, I might buy myself some loyalty for a change but apparently I was wrong.

I set up a meeting and told the entire staff to attend. That was the way Joey wanted me to handle the situation—to talk to everyone simultaneously. I waited until the lunch hour so that, in the event some sort of melee ensued, there wouldn't be any patients in the office. Our staff was all smiles—joking and talking, having no idea about the purpose of the meeting.

"I'm so glad you're all here," I said. "I have a problem. Someone in this office is stealing from us. I know that all of you have taken cash payments. If you'd like to go through all five hundred pages of this report, you are welcome to do so…"

I had the five-hundred-page report sitting in the middle of the conference table.

"…But, trust me, I know who's been handling the cash. And I know that one of you has been stealing—or all of you. So, one of you needs to start explaining things. If it was simply a mistake or a lapse in judgment, let me know and we can discuss it. Absent that, I am going to call the police and let them sort it out."

Every single one of the girls went white as a sheet. No one said a word. The entire group seemed to be dumbstruck.

"Well, unless the tooth fairy took it," I continued, "someone knows where that money went! If that kind of money is coming in, it's going somewhere. It's certainly not here!"

One by one, they all tried to lie their way out of the situation. When I called them on their lies, they started to turn on each other and, before long, they were bickering. Each one claimed complete ignorance of the theft, saying, "I don't know what happened!"

"Well, I do know that someone knows what happened!" I said. "And we may not figure it out today in this meeting but I can assure you that, when the police arrive, they will find answers. So, it's best to try to work it out with me now. I need to know where this money is and get it back. I also need this information for my tax returns because I am not about to pay taxes on stolen money!"

Two of the girls broke down and started crying.

At this point, I said, "Okay, guys, I have a good sense of what happened here. And unless someone wants to come forward by the time I'm done counting to three, I am calling the police. One, two, three..."

No one said a word.

"Okay, everyone. Well, thank you for your time. I'm sorry this is stressful but here's what is going to happen. I'm going to call the police now and you're all going to get back to work and attend to the patients."

Everyone left the conference room. Then Kim came back in, bawling her eyes out. "Melissa, I don't know how to tell you this but I had a thousand dollars in cash in my desk drawer and now it's gone! Someone must have stolen it. I was afraid to tell you because I was afraid you'd think I took it."

"You put a thousand dollars in an unlocked desk drawer when there's a locked cash drawer?" I asked. "That makes no sense to me."

She also admitted to using the office debit card to reload her Starbucks card—a relatively insignificant theft compared to all the money that was actually missing. I don't know what she was hoping to accomplish by admitting to that small theft.

I told Kim that she was no longer the acting office manager and, for the time being, I was reassigning her. "I will wait to decide whether I am terminating anyone's employment until the police conclude their investigation. And now I need you to leave my office so I can call the police."

She left crying, "I'm so sorry...I'm so sorry."

Sorry for what? She hadn't admitted to what she had done!

The police department sent out a couple of officers to investigate and, through the officers, I found out that Hugo had retired from the police department.

Here's how I found out: One of the officers asked, "Didn't Gabby used to work here?"

"Yes, she did. Are she and her husband still living here in town?"

"Hugo retired," the officer explained, "and I think they wanted to move but I believe they're still here in town."

One of the officers took the reconciliation reports from our office along with my original deposit books and promised that a detective would be assigned to the case and would return to question the staff. "Someone will be in touch with you," he promised and left.

I told the police that, when they did question the staff, I wanted them to put the fear of God into everyone who worked for us. After all, only those who had done something wrong would have anything to worry about.

We had never reported Gabby to the police and it was now perfectly clear to Joey and me that, in allowing such an egregious act to go unreported, we had become a magnet for thieves. We realized that, until we made our office a less attractive place for thieves to work, they would keep coming back. It was like having a cockroach problem in a household. Until the family puts down roach poison, the roaches will continue to return and multiply.

Through the glass window of my office, I could see Kim pacing back and forth. I waved her in and let her know that an officer would be back and would have questions for everyone.

"I need you to cooperate with him," I said. "And give him all the information he's requesting."

"Oh, absolutely, absolutely," she said. "Sounds good. I want to do everything I can to help. I know this looks bad for me but I assure you I've done nothing wrong and I look forward to clearing my name."

"That's wonderful, Kim," I said. "I really appreciate that. Someone will be in touch."

All the girls finished out their workday despite the fact that they were each complaining of ailments—two stomach aches and one migraine headache.

As I left the office to pick up Hope from school, I could feel the tension that had arisen between the girls. It was obvious that there was a whole new dynamic in play and that they had been arguing.

49

I realized that Jenna had begun stealing cash from us on the very first day she returned to employment with our office. She limited her theft to the cash collected from patients covered by Medicaid, the state insurance program.

Let me explain. Whenever we performed dental services for Medicaid patients, we were prohibited by state law from billing the patients directly. So if we submitted a claim to the insurance company that administers the plan for the state, and the claim was denied, we had to write it off.

However, if we knew in advance that the state would not pay for a particular procedure but the patient wanted the procedure anyway, they had the option to pay for it out of their own pocket—and those were almost always cash transactions. I had been told by our staff that such cash transactions occurred no more often than once or twice a year. In actuality, these cash transactions happened frequently and, when they did, the girls in the office were fixing the books in such a way that it appeared that the money had never changed hands. Then they pocketed the money.

When Jenna was brought back into the office after Gabby left, she put together this group of girls who helped each other steal from us and watched each other's backs.

Detectives Ruiz and Richardson were assigned to work the case and began interviewing the suspects. During the course of their investigation, they began asking me very specific questions, including: "There were widespread rumors within the department that Hugo's wife, Gabby, stole over $2.0 million from your practice. Is this true?"

"Well, detectives, due to the fact that Gabby and Hugo demanded that we include a non-disclosure clause in the settlement agreement we signed with them, I am afraid I am not at liberty to say."

When I told the detectives I was "afraid," it wasn't just a figure of speech. I did not want to invite a lawsuit—or worse!—from Gabby and Hugo by violating the nondisclosure clause in the settlement agreement. I knew that Hugo was capable of making our lives a living hell.

"Don't worry, ma'am. Should our interviews with your employees reveal that Gabby had anything to do with the theft by your current employees, then she will become a part of *this* case, and we can investigate her without violating the nondisclosure clause."

The detectives asked me point blank how I would feel if, during the course of the investigation, they were able to look into the embezzlement by Gabby. I told them I would check with my attorney but that it was my understanding that any questions posed to me formally by an official government agency would fall outside the scope of the nondisclosure clause. When I spoke to my attorney, Jack, he confirmed my understanding.

Detectives Ruiz and Richardson began interviewing our employees and Maggie confessed. They arrested her, she was charged, and the crime is now part of her permanent record. She is unable to work in any capacity where she handles money. She was put on probation but never served time, and was ordered to pay restitution. Since she isn't currently employed, it's unlikely that Joey and I will ever see that money.

The police questioned all the girls on staff, took them to the station for further questioning, and confiscated their phones to retrieve the text messages. Everyone was questioned and released. The detectives actually arrested Jenna and Kim, who spent one night in jail and were released pending further investigation. Both Jenna and Kim were bailed out and told that the court was not prepared to move forward at that time, so the arrest was being dropped—but charges were pending, and the outcome of the investigation was yet to be determined. The prosecution wanted to investigate the matter further and, along those lines, they issued financial subpoenas. Upon receiving those financial documents, they would later decide to move forward with prosecution.

Apparently, the police can arrest someone but if they formally charge them, the person must be tried within one hundred eighty days or the case is permanently dropped. Because of that, the police always endeavor to wait until they have a strong enough case before they formally charge someone. (The investigation into possible wrongdoing was ongoing as of the date of this writing.)

I expressed my frustration to Detective Richardson over all the girls being released after their questioning—and, in Jenna and Kim's case, after their arrest.

"Keep in mind," he said, "that this is like having a noose around your neck and never knowing when it's going to tighten!"

While waiting for compliance with the financial subpoenas, I received a phone call one day from Detective Richardson, saying, "I've been contacted by Special Agent Smith with the FBI and given this case involving Hugo and Gabby and another theft that occurred. Since the agent was aware of some crossover between this case and your case, Special Agent Smith wants me to work with him on the FBI case."

So, now, Detective Richardson from the local police department was working as a special consultant to the FBI!

"…and Special Agent Smith has requested your phone number."

A subpoena from the FBI followed, requiring me to submit copies of Gabby's confessions, along with all the correspondence between us and Gabby and Hugo. I had binders filled with information ready to go and was able to provide them with over two thousand pieces of paper, including email correspondence between Gabby and me; Hugo and me; Gabby, our accountant and me; and Gabby, Hugo and our attorney. I also submitted in spreadsheet format our bank records detailing the money that Gabby had stolen. It had been prepared by my CPA so it was very neat and tidy.

At this point, I was doing somersaults and the happy dance. In fact, I might have done some actual cartwheels in our yard. I thought, *Finally, finally, finally Gabby is going to have to answer for what she's done!*

I was told by Detective Richardson, "If Gabby and Hugo still have assets and this goes the way we think it will, their assets will be seized as restitution, sold, and given to the victims—you and your husband!"

I couldn't wait to tell Joey.

"Wow!" he said. "After four years? Maybe Gabby and Hugo will finally be held accountable!"

When I told him, "The FBI is going to need to sit down with us," I could sense some apprehension.

"Apparently," I said, "an anonymous informant contacted the FBI and claimed to have special and intimate knowledge of Gabby's crimes. And the informant also claimed that you and Gabby had been having an affair. So, we're going to have to go in there and discuss our personal lives when all we should be discussing is Gabby's crimes! It's embarrassing, infuriating, and very frustrating to me that, after all these years, I am still dealing with rumors of you and Gabby having an affair. It doesn't make me feel too good when I think about having to talk to the FBI about our marital troubles caused by you not listening to me about Gabby!"

From the moment that Joey learned that he was going to be interviewed by the FBI, he became depressed and exhausted. I wasn't in a much better mood, myself. Every time I thought about having to discuss with the FBI my husband's failure to question Gabby about her financial dealings all those years and his failure to protect me, I felt humiliated.

At last, the day of the FBI interview dawned. When my attorney and I arrived, Special Agent Smith said to me, "I'm confused as to why your husband is not present."

I explained that I was under the impression that we were going to be interviewed separately and he said, "That's fine. We'll interview him at a later date."

I was dreading having the FBI raise questions about my marriage but I was prepared for it. I was taken off guard, however, when they started questioning me about possible insurance fraud. Apparently the subject of insurance fraud was raised by the nameless confidential informant.

"I have no knowledge of any insurance fraud," I said, "and I see no evidence of any."

Strangely enough, we had recently undergone an exhaustive state audit, no doubt triggered by the FBI informant. I now saw the timing of the audit as a remarkable twist of fate. While we were being audited, it was such a headache—but it turned out to be a strange blessing, as we were able to provide the FBI with a totally unbiased state audit that cleared us of any suspicion of insurance fraud.

At the conclusion of the audit, the state found billing errors but no insurance fraud. (The billing errors resulted in us owing $26,000 on four million dollars' worth of dental claims.) Thanks to the audit report, the FBI ceased their line of inquiry related to possible insurance fraud. We were totally in the clear.

I now saw the recent theft by our office staff as miraculous. When we first discovered the theft, we felt horribly let down and betrayed—not to mention burdened by a major financial loss at a time when we could scarcely afford it. Yet, that very embezzlement became a remarkable and strange blessing. It led to Detective Richardson and Special Agent Smith joining forces, and the light being shone on Gabby's crimes.

50

*M*y FBI interview was out of the way and now it was Joey's turn. Detective Richardson contacted me to let me know that he was going to need to sit down and ask Joey some questions in advance of his interview with the FBI.

Detective Richardson also reminded me, "This informant is claiming that your husband had an affair with Gabby."

"I am absolutely sure that never happened," I said.

"You just need to understand that this is something that is going to come up. I don't want you to be blindsided if your husband has a different answer to that question when he talks to the FBI. If he lies, he will be prosecuted."

"That's fine," I said. "Joey will tell the truth. And I'm sure he won't have anything new to say to you. I believe he would tell me if it was true, and I've asked him about the rumors many times, including during marriage counseling. He never has anything to say other than 'Oh, my God, that's gross! I would never sleep with her!'"

When I hung up with Detective Richardson, I immediately called my attorney and let him know that these rumors about the affair had to be shut down. (At the point at which we had received the FBI subpoena, my attorney Jack recommended that we retain an attorney named Duke so we were now dealing with him.)

"This is turning into some kind of character assassination of Joey!" I told our attorney, Duke. "I don't know how we've moved away from the fact that we absolutely and definitively know that Gabby stole this money. She admitted it!"

I was getting very stressed out and frustrated over the fact that the FBI seemed to be spending a lot of time focusing on peripheral issues like my marriage rather than on Gabby's crimes.

Meanwhile I had a sick little girl on my hands, and I had taken her to the doctor. While Hope was in seeing the doctor, I called Joey. "I need to talk to you about what I discussed with Duke and he's also going to need you to call him tomorrow. See you at home."

Hope fell asleep in the car and, when I got home, I carried her inside and put her to bed. Devin was out with friends so Joey and I had the house to ourselves.

"You need to understand," I told Joey, "that this informant, whoever they are, continues to insist that you had an affair with Gabby. Duke is going to do everything he can to limit the FBI's questions to the actual events related to Gabby's theft and not let it turn into a three-ring circus, but the FBI is going to ask you about the affair! I am so tired of dealing with these rumors!"

I was standing at the kitchen counter talking to Joey, who was sitting in our great room. He had his back to me and was mindlessly flipping through the channels with the remote. With his eyes still focused on the TV, he said, "Except there's a problem—the problem is that it's true about the affair."

Suddenly, I thought I might faint. "What?" I said. "You're telling me it is *true*?"

"Yeah...off and on for ten and a half, eleven years."

"Oh, my God! You were sleeping with her when Drew died?" I said. "That's why you didn't answer your phone—and she didn't answer hers?"

"Yes, I was."

"You motherfucker!" I screamed. "You have put me through hell and made an absolute fool of me! I cannot believe you! So, did she steal this money or did you give it to her?"

"No, I never gave her any money!"

"Are you sure?" I said. "Because all this time, you've claimed you weren't sleeping with her, either! The FBI is involved now so you have to come clean. You're going to have to go in there and tell the truth so I'd appreciate knowing everything now."

"That's why I'm telling you."

"You do realize," I said, "this changes everything between us."

"I know and I'm very sorry. But it's been five years since I've been with her. I'm ashamed of who I used to be and I've spent the last five years trying to be a better man and show you I'm worthy of being your husband."

"Do you love her? Did you ever?" I asked.

"No, no, I never loved her. I got along well with her and we were able to make a lot of money together in business. She was a friend—at one point, my best friend."

"Your *best friend?* That's one of the most hurtful things you've ever said to me!" I said. "She ripped me apart and you stood on the sidelines and let her do it, and you're calling her your best friend? I can't believe you!"

A slide show of my life began playing in my head. Memory after memory came at me, lightning fast, and I questioned every recollection. *At what point did I lose my husband to this woman?* I wondered.

Joey and I had married in 1993. He and Gabby had started sleeping together around 1997 and didn't stop until 2009 or 2010.

I could not even comprehend it. "Your math is wrong," I said. "That is more like twelve or thirteen years! That is most of our marriage! I really am Princess Di and you're the asshole Charles, sleeping with Camilla this whole time..."

The thought that was torturing me the most was that my husband had been in bed with Gabby when our son died. I had spent the previous fifteen years having to listen to Joey, Gabby and Hugo say that I should have been in prison for Drew's death. I could still hear Joey saying to me after Drew died, "You killed our son! You may not have murdered him but you're the reason he's dead!"

I knew that pain could cause people to say horrific things but those words still deeply wounded me. I tortured myself over Drew's death, unable to forgive myself for falling asleep on that fateful morning. But now it had come to light that Joey was in bed with Gabby on that terrible night. I had left him those voicemail messages, begging him to return home and give me backup so I could get some sleep, and he had ignored my messages.

I had never in my entire life felt capable of hurting another person but, in that moment, I felt like I could have killed my husband with my bare hands. I was filled with an anger more consuming than anything I'd ever felt before.

"I never in my life envisioned a moment where I would be this woman in this position," I said. "You have robbed me of who I rightfully am! And now I am going to go rediscover the woman I am meant to be. I am going to give myself that much. I don't know what that means for you or this family but I'm not worried about this marriage anymore. I can't be. I'm going to heal myself—and that's the only thing I'll promise you, is that I'm going to be happy. I will not let what you and Gabby did defeat me. And you will never again have the satisfaction of breaking my heart."

Joey couldn't bring himself to turn around and face me, and it was just as well. I didn't want to see his face.

"You need to leave now, and you need to stay gone until I can find a way to talk to you!" I said.

"I understand," Joey said. "But I'm hoping you'll understand that I've worked so hard to keep this from you because I'm ashamed. I never loved her—it was just sex. I was a different man back then. I know I'm not worthy of you…I've never been worthy of you. I can't tell you how sorry I am. I was self-centered and I fell in love with the power of being successful—and I saw Gabby as a part of that success. She helped me gain a lot of success and that was the attraction."

"Well, she really did screw you, literally and figuratively! So congratulations," I said. "The only problem is, Joey, there were an awful lot of casualties along the way—me being the most obvious one. And our children suffered and our home suffered. Our family wasn't the happy family it should have been, due to the continual stress and strain of what you were trying to keep hidden and sneak off and enjoy. The consequence is that we have this troubled marriage as a result!"

I told him that I would have appreciated being told the truth so I could have made my own choices. At the point at which Gabby's crimes began coming to light and the house of cards started to collapse, I would have divorced Joey had he leveled with me about his affair.

"The one thing I never questioned until now," I said, "was that you were faithful to me. Was there anyone else? You'd better tell me now if there was anyone else."

"There was no one else!"

Any time I become highly emotional, I see colors with words, and this is intensified when anyone touches me. I was seeing red, literally—a flaming, intense orangey-red.

"Joey, at this point, it doesn't matter what you've done," I said. "You need to start dealing with the reality of having to be completely honest with the FBI. I'm furious but I'm just your wife. You're about to talk to an FBI agent and tell him about these things. You can't perjure yourself or you'll go to jail and that will really hurt our family and our children!"

I let him know that he had better take a long hard look at himself, do a gut check and evaluate what was important. And he needed to be ready to answer the FBI's questions. I also reminded him that I had just finished telling the FBI during my own interview that my husband had never slept with Gabby.

"Do you realize I could get in trouble for that?" I said. "I have no choice now but to let them know that you just told me this. When Detective Richardson brought up Gabby and the possibility of an affair between you two, I got upset with him and told him that there was no way this could be true!"

I grabbed my phone, dialed Detective Richardson, and told him that my husband had something to tell him. Then I handed the phone to Joey.

"I just told my wife about an affair with Gabby that lasted for twelve years…" He went into detail with the detective, and said, "Melissa didn't know about it until today. She didn't lie to you. I was lying to *her* and I would have gone to my grave denying it. But, I knew it would come out during my FBI interview and I didn't want my wife to hear it from you. So I told her."

Joey handed the phone back to me and Detective Richardson asked me if I needed anything.

I told him I would be alright. I was absolutely sure of one thing: the last thing I wanted at that moment was the comfort of a man.

51

*J*oey honored my request and left the house, and I went into my bedroom and lay down next to Hope. I immediately started to cry but my tears were for Drew, not for my marriage. I had spent so many years hating myself and feeling guilty for falling asleep on the morning of his death. Now I knew that, while I was home alone—overwhelmed, exhausted and needing help with the children, my husband was out of town and in bed with Gabby. This knowledge wounded me deeply.

How unfair of you to go off and be so selfish! I thought. *And how selfish of you to let me go on being plagued by guilt when you knew it was eating me alive!*

Oh, my God, I thought, *everything could have been so different!* This was the thought that kept returning to my mind as I lay there crying. Joey's confession had taken me right back to the morning of my son's death and brought back waves of grief. I wanted that day back. I wanted a do-over.

I had always thought of my husband as a hardworking man who slaved away to provide a great life for his family. In that moment, everything changed for me and I saw him as a selfish bastard looking to go out of town and get laid by another woman. He wanted to have his fun rather than dealing with the reality of a wife and two children at home. In that moment, I hated Joey so much, I actually wished that Drew could come back and Joey could go away.

Before long, my thoughts shifted and I was reminded that Drew was always present. I only had to think of him and I could feel him touch me and see him in beautiful hues of lavender and blue.

As I held Hope while she slept in her Nyquil induced state, I was reminded of the moment when I was holding Drew in my arms and had the premonition that he wouldn't be with us for long. Then I remembered Drew—in spirit—saying to me after his death, "Mommy, I love you so much, I will never leave you." And he never had. He came to me in colors that turned from soft lavender-blue to bright purple to beautiful vibrant blue.

I am wrong, I realized. *Nothing was ever going to change these circumstances. My son was always going to go before me. I just wish we'd had more time.*

Interestingly, as my perspective about Drew shifted, my rancor toward Joey and Gabby faded. I was still angry but mostly over the ongoing lie about their affair. I was angry that Joey had failed to tell me the truth and thereby robbed me of my power to make choices based upon the truth.

I thought, *How dare he deny me the information about the affair and thereby cast me as the other woman?*

Even as I asked myself the question, the answer presented itself: Joey knew that he would have lost me forever if he had come clean with me, considering everything that Gabby put me through over the years.

I knew that Joey's decision to lie to me had nothing to do with me and I was not about to let this disclosure about the affair change the way I felt about myself. I had been a really good wife and a wonderful mother, every bit the same worthy woman I was when he married me. I didn't change or falter or fail in any way that would warrant the sort of heinous position he had forced me into.

I asked myself, *Rather than focusing on the past, what are you going to do with this information now that you have it?*

I wanted to call upon my highest good and not act out of vengeance or anger or hatred. There had already been enough ugliness and I wanted to act in a way that was dignified and kind. I was really craving a spiritual response to the situation. I wanted to conduct myself with as much love as I could embrace. My children deserved it, I deserved it—and my husband deserved it.

I decided to delay making a decision until I knew with absolute certainty what I wanted to do. I would not make a decision while I was angry and hurt. Any knee-jerk reaction would have brought with it considerable emotional fallout.   Despite my resolve, I questioned whether I was sane and normal to even consider staying with my husband after what he had disclosed.

I would ask myself, *Am I crazy? It is so far beyond societal norms to make such a decision. Am I actually taking the easier road by not running out on my husband and my marriage?*

I had to remind myself that we are all fallible and we all fall short. I was far from perfect, myself, and had done things to hurt my husband and our marriage. My husband was still a man worthy of love. The only thing I had to reconcile was Joey's future role in my life—husband? Friend?

I did what I'd always done, seeking a deeper level of understanding, compassion and love. I listened to my heart and my spirit—what I believed to be the voice of God. Whenever I was the most broken, I would be inspired by something greater than myself. Then I would be reminded that, rather than being the easy way out, the high road was the hardest thing in the world to embrace, and that's why so few people did.

Crazy or not, I decided, *I like this version of myself! I like not being hateful!*

From that day forward, I have never regretted being kind or loving to Joey. After all, he is the father of our children, and our children are the living, breathing iterations of the best parts of ourselves.

Of course, any time I was frustrated or tired, it was tempting to respond from a baser side of myself. But, I considered it a new frontier—this life where I endeavored to offer that higher love not only to Joey but to every person I met. You could say that it was God and, of course that would be true, but for me, God comes through in the form of Drew. God loves me and understands that the fastest way to draw me closer to Him is to have my son Drew guide me back.

Drew was—and is—my little Peter Pan. He would never be an angel for that is too boring. He is a celestial Peter Pan, smudged and dirty as he battles Captain Hook and avoids the crocodile one more time. He is Peter Pan, laughing and doing backflips as he flies through the air. That's how he lives on in my mind and heart—as a free, adventurous, brave and fearless little guy, living every single second, alive. That's my Drew.

Joey must have returned to the house later that night and slept in the guest room. The following morning, he got up with Hope, made breakfast for her and took her to school. He always instinctively seemed to know what I needed. He was caring for me in a way I needed but couldn't ask for at that moment in time.

Before he took Hope to school, he came to where I was sitting on my bed, dropped down beside me and took my hands. "I love you and I'm sorry for everything. I was a fool and I know it but I love you like no other. And I will spend a lifetime, if you'll let me, trying to be worthy of your love."

I really needed to hear him say those words and yet they hurt. "I don't know how to get around this," I said. "I don't know what to do."

"Let's get some help," he suggested. "Not help for us. You need to heal and be happy, no matter what happens."

"Okay, I think you're right," I said. "I am going to need some help."

Joey left the house on that tender note.

Devin came to talk to me before leaving for school. He had come home the previous evening and heard Joey and me arguing and was old enough to put the pieces together.

"Mom, I don't want to talk about it—but I know. And I know you're in pain. What he did was wrong. But I want you to know I'm fine. I also know he's not that man anymore. I believe in you two, even if you don't, and I believe in this family. And I believe in you! I understand you're really angry right now but I don't want to see you stuck in anger. Anger will destroy you and you have so much more to offer. I'm going to pray for you because I know you're angry so you won't turn to God. I believe in this family and when you're done being angry, you'll remember that you do too!"

I was embarrassed and sad that Devin knew what his father had done. I was also dumbstruck. From as young as three years old, Devin had always been wise beyond his years, and he blew me away with these words. He often said things that were so sophisticated and insightful that they had to be divinely inspired. He was the person I wanted to become.

I have always learned a lot from my children. Thanks to open communication in our house, my children truly know me and I know them, warts and all. I don't hide from them and we've always had a beautiful and open closeness.

"I love you, Button," I said. "But I'm very confused right now and I have no idea how this is going to turn out. I can't promise you that this marriage can be saved—I just don't know. But I can promise you that I'll be good to your dad through the process of figuring this out."

"Okay, I've got to go to school now."

"Yes, go," I said. "Don't worry about me. I'll be fine. After all, tomorrow's your birthday!"

He gave me a hug and said something that made me giggle, and then my wiser-than-his-years son was off to school, leaving me alone with my thoughts and feelings.

I was alone in the house when the phone rang. I could see that it was Detective Richardson calling but I wasn't up to answering the call. I didn't want to hear more, if there was more to hear, and I didn't want to talk about the situation. I knew I was going to have to do a lot of talking about it now that the affair was out in the open and that knowledge made me annoyed and frustrated.

As the day wore on, I started connecting more and more dots and this made me angrier and angrier. I thought a lot about Gabby and Hugo, Gabby in particular. And I knew that, regardless of whether or not my husband had feelings for her—and he swore that he didn't—she certainly had feelings for him. This explained, at last, why she had always treated me as if I was in her way. It turns out that I was in her way! I had no idea.

Thief, liar, unstable woman—these were the words she used to try to paint a picture of me that would cause Joey's love for me to die. Joey's interactions with Gabby's police officer husband helped complete the narrative—a narrative that my husband bought into to a certain extent.

As I turned my focus on Hugo, I started to wonder, *Was this a team thing? How much did he know and when did he know it?*

The more dots I connected, the more certain I became that Hugo was very much a part of Gabby's misconduct. I thought of the way they spoke of each other and it was always odd to me. Their union seemed more like an alliance than a marriage—two people working toward a common goal, monetarily driven.

With all of these thoughts swirling in my head, I got into the shower. As I got dressed and put on my workout clothes, I listened to Detective Richardson's message: "I am calling to see how you're doing and I also need to talk to you about the case…"

I called him on my way to the gym.

"How are you?" he asked.

"Not great! I'm pretty upset," I said, "but I'm going to be okay. Listen, I want to talk to you about something. I think Hugo had to know what Gabby was doing."

"Funny you should mention Hugo because that's what I wanted to talk to you about," he said.

Detective Richardson let me know that the local police department had initiated an internal affairs investigation into Hugo's dealings. He asked me several questions related to Hugo and mentioned that there may have been a connection between Hugo and the state audit we'd had to endure at the dental practice. And yet, as I said earlier, the state audit meant for our harm had turned out to be a huge saving grace because it put to bed many of the accusations against us that were anonymously told to the FBI.

"Apparently," he continued, "when Hugo retired from the police department in 2012, the department scrubbed his computer as part of normal protocol. They found some deleted files and, when they did data recovery on the files, they discovered rough drafts of emails he had sent to your attorney. There were enough statements in there to lead us to believe he covered up his wife's crimes."

52

I turned my focus toward Devin. He was about to turn eighteen years old and he deserved his mother's undivided attention. I was determined that, one way or another, my son would have a wonderful birthday. Everything else would have to wait.

Somehow we got through Devin's birthday as a family and he seemed to enjoy his party. I was determined not to let Gabby and Hugo ruin Devin's birthday and I managed to hold it together. But, from time to time, I couldn't help but break down in tears.

Was it easy being at Devin's party with Joey? No. Were we happy, happy, happy? No. But somehow we got through it together and it wasn't terrible.

A couple of weeks after Devin's birthday party, we had to deal with Joey's FBI interview. In advance of the interview, there was a lot of discussion as to what questions might be posed to him. Meanwhile I was in constant discussions with our attorney, Duke, trying to determine whether this new information about Joey and Gabby's affair could chip away at the merits of our case, sink our battleship and somehow allow Gabby (and Hugo if he was involved in a cover-up) to evade prosecution.

Duke said, "The affair is separate from the crime. The crime is the crime. The fact that Gabby and Joey were engaged in an extramarital affair does not negate the fact that Gabby committed a crime. Think of it like this...let's say an individual is committing the crime of driving while intoxicated and happens to hit a privately owned car. The fact that the driver hit a car is a separate offense and wouldn't preclude them from being prosecuted for the crime of driving while intoxicated. In this analogy, hitting the privately owned car would be the equivalent to Joey and Gabby's affair."

"I see. Let me ask you one more question," I said. "Let's say, God forbid, the FBI was unable or unwilling to prosecute Gabby for some reason. Would the fact that I didn't know about the affair when I signed the settlement agreement allow me to have the document set aside so I could proceed with a civil suit against Gabby?"

"Well, if Joey and Gabby and Hugo all knew about the affair during the settlement agreement talks but you didn't, you could claim you were defrauded out of information which might have impacted your desire to prosecute Gabby. You might not have been so conciliatory had you known."

He was right, of course. I should have been given the information about the affair before I was given the settlement agreement to sign. I felt like I'd been manipulated the whole way through.

"Don't worry," Duke said, "there is no way the FBI is going to walk away from this case. We've got all this documentation as well as her confessions and discussions about how she went about stealing the money. The case against her is solid."

Duke accompanied Joey to his interview with the FBI. Duke was a former judge and had a criminal defense practice, so he was better suited than our attorney Jack to be the counsel by Joey's side during this interview.

Special Agent Smith came forward and confirmed that, after reviewing the state audit report, he had concluded that no insurance fraud had been committed. Then he asked Joey which of our dental companies Gabby had a vested interest in and why she had been given such ownership interest. There were also many questions about the specifics of the way the business was run during the time we employed Gabby.

The fact that Joey had turned full control of the office over to Gabby made it difficult for him to answer some of the questions.

Only Gabby would have known the answers. I am sure Joey may have seemed to the FBI to be evasive during his interview but the truth was that he wasn't detail oriented in that way, which was why he'd hired Gabby in the first place.

Meanwhile on the home front, we were trying to recover from the bombshell about the affair. One minute, I'd be angry. The next minute, I'd think, *Okay, he really loves me.* It was hard to stay in an *Okay, he really loves me* state of mind when I had to constantly discuss the affair with the police, the FBI and our attorney. I didn't appreciate having my pain on display. Every conversation about the affair made me feel like my privacy was being violated.

Throughout all this, my husband kept right on loving me and, at some point, this thought dawned on me: *You can't really ask someone to feel any worse about something than they already feel—especially when they already feel terrible.*

This caused a shift in my perspective. I looked back and acknowledged that Joey really had dedicated himself to me and the kids over the previous five years since he had stopped sleeping with Gabby. He was changing and becoming a better man and I was a strange combination of grateful for that change and pissed off over everything that had happened with Gabby. I wasn't about to pitch a tent in either the gratitude or anger camp and I spent my time vacillating between the two.

Not long after Joey's FBI interview, we got some interesting news related to Hugo. The police department had legal counsel consulting on Hugo's internal affairs investigation and, in the course of the investigation, several police officers and former police officers were interviewed.

Somehow Hugo got wind of the fact that these interviews were taking place and he made an all-out attempt to reach Detective Richardson. Hugo started by calling the detective's father, who happened to be the principal of the private school attended by Hugo and Gabby's children. When Hugo was unable to persuade Detective Richardson's father to give him Detective Richardson's cell phone number, he left his own cell phone number so that

Detective Richardson could call him. Then Hugo left messages for Detective Richardson at the police department, asking that he contact him immediately.

Detective Richardson called me. "I wanted you to be aware that Hugo knows he's being investigated. You and Joey need to exercise extreme caution. Hugo has already threatened your family's lives and he may get desperate now that he knows he's under investigation. If you see him parked outside your house or even driving past your house, I want you to notify us immediately."

This information made me feel like I was standing in quicksand. I was terrified that Hugo would come after our family. Detective Richardson had not given me any reason to think that Hugo wouldn't. The police department wasn't providing protection for us but Detective Richardson encouraged me to seek a restraining order against Hugo.

The detective offered to accompany me to the courthouse. When we got in front of a judge, Detective Richardson testified that it was the police department's considered opinion that Hugo was a dangerous man with the potential to harm us. The police department agreed that an order of protection should be granted in order to keep Hugo from making any contact with us now that he was aware of the investigation.

The judge granted the order but warned, "You could be kicking a snake here. This might make him more aggressive. You should keep in mind that a piece of paper will not keep you safe. You should get a firearm and learn to use it. Carry it at all times and be vigilant."

I became not only vigilant but hypervigilant and the constant adrenaline pumping through my body (which was already sensitive to adrenaline due to a medical condition involving my adrenal glands) began to erode my ability to function. I had become quite adept at living under stressful conditions but it really rattled my cage when I thought that my children or Joey or I could be harmed. That was too much for me to handle.

By this point in time, I was clear that I needed some support. I was not in a good place—until I found Mike. He was extremely personable and approachable and not your typical therapist. He had not had an easy childhood, himself, so he was able to relate to my childhood. He helped me see how my extremely dysfunctional childhood had primed me to marry a man like Joey.

What Mike was getting at was my tolerance for a certain level of emotional remoteness. This tolerance was instilled in me by my remote father. Mike also helped me identify what I was getting out of our marriage. He pointed out how Joey's tendency to do his own thing felt familiar and suited me in many respects. Joey would be so busy doing his own thing that it would free me to do my own thing.

I started identifying my own behavior patterns and began to see how I had contributed to the consequences with which I now had to contend. He also helped me see how long I had struggled with profound depression.

53

*I*n early February of 2015, Special Agent Smith called to inform me that he had concluded his investigation and the FBI would not be continuing on with the case. Apparently, by the time Special Agent Smith had concluded his interview with my husband, he had come to the conclusion that this was a matter better handled at the state level.

Had there been insurance fraud, the FBI absolutely would have continued their investigation. Since it was primarily a crime of embezzlement, and since there seemed to be evidence that Hugo, a former police officer, had covered up his wife's crimes, this needed to be handled at the state level.

I felt completely defeated. "What about the wire fraud aspect of the case? Isn't that a federal crime?" I knew that, by taking money from our business account and transferring it into her bank account via the internet, Gabby was committing wire fraud.

"Even though that's a federal crime, the state still has jurisdiction," he explained.

I discussed this with my attorney. He explained that, in these types of embezzlement cases, there simply isn't enough money at stake for the federal government to consider it worth their while.

This made me angry—and I found it shocking. I said, "This is why people get away with this sort of thing! It sounds like the likelihood of prosecution is pretty low."

My anger over the situation always led me back to anger toward Joey. By failing to stop Gabby, he had allowed this situation to mushroom until it was out of control. I started replaying various moments throughout our marriage and suddenly the puzzle pieces fit together in a whole new way. Hugo's threats made more sense, for example, when seen in the light of Joey and Gabby's affair.

I asked Joey, "Did Hugo threaten to expose your affair unless you agreed to let Gabby and Hugo walk?"

Joey said, "No."

"Well, do you think that Hugo knew about you and Gabby?"

"He did used to comment that I shared his bed with him," Joey said.

"Oh, really? That sure sounds like he might have known! That's a big piece of information, Joey! I certainly never would have made the comment that Gabby shared my bed. I said she was a third wheel in our marriage but I never felt like she was actually in bed with us."

I pointed out to Joey that, if Hugo knew about the affair, and if he knew about the money his wife was embezzling, he may have figured that the affair gave Gabby leverage and immunity against Joey pursuing legal remedies.

"Maybe Hugo didn't mind you sleeping with his wife as long as they were getting millions out of the deal," I said. "It's pretty perverse to think of him pimping out his wife, but you never know. And I wouldn't be surprised if he was helping guide Gabby and keeping her from getting caught," I said. "After all, investigating fraud and embezzlement did used to be his job at the police department!"

Once the FBI had determined that investigating Gabby's crimes was a matter for the state to pursue, the investigation was initially turned over to our local police department. Due to Hugo's long-standing employment with them, however, they felt that there was a conflict of interest and passed it along to the county attorney's office. And they decided to reach out to the state attorney general's office.

The state attorney general's office was very interested in the case, in light of the involvement of the current chief of police of the local police department, who had admitted to the FBI that he had accepted gifts from Hugo during the time when he was Hugo's direct superior, and the fact that Hugo and perhaps other former officers may have helped cover up a major crime.

It was interesting to me that Hugo seemed to be the focus of this investigation now. The fact that, oh, by the way, his wife stole over a million dollars from our dental practice seemed to be a footnote. I was encouraged, not discouraged, by this turn of events. I knew that the involvement of the local police department raised the stakes of the investigation.

This all seemed quite positive and I was very optimistic that justice might finally be served. Both of our attorneys, Jack and Duke, were also optimistic. Everyone agreed that this case seemed to finally be ready to take off, and we couldn't wait to see what was going to happen.

We arranged the date of March 17th of 2015 and Joey and I traveled independently to the interview with the state attorney general. I would be meeting Devin the following day to fly to Texas and tour a university he was considering for college.

Joey left in the morning and I took my own car and met him at Duke's office, which was located a few blocks from the state attorney general's office. Once we got to the state attorney general's office, Joey and I were immediately separated and Joey was taken into an interview room.

I was told that I wouldn't be needed for hours. I had left my vehicle at Duke's office so I was stuck. After what seemed like an endless amount of time had elapsed, I called Detective Richardson. "Is it normal to be kept waiting this long?"

"It's pretty normal," he said. "Everything's going to be okay. Go get a sandwich or something." So I found a food truck and bought a beverage and an apple and sat outside for a while.

Two and a half hours later, a female agent, Special Agent Dakota came and took me into an interview room where Joey and Duke were already present. My husband looked like somebody had hit him with a Mack truck. He was disheveled and seemed emotionally undone. Somebody had clearly dismantled him.

I didn't know what to make of this. My FBI interview hadn't been necessarily easy but it was friendly and cordial. And, as I said,

Joey's FBI interview went pretty smoothly as well. This, on the other hand, had clearly been an interrogation. Something had changed.

I sat down with Joey, Duke, Special Agent Dakota and a man called Special Agent Hartman. They closed the door and turned on the tape recorder.

They began to ask me basic questions about myself, listening closely to my answers. It was easy to see that they were trying to determine whether or not I was credible. Once they seemed satisfied with the veracity of what I was saying, they dropped the first bomb on me.

"How is it that this joint checking account for which you provided bank statements could have been opened without your husband's full knowledge and consent?"

Oh, my God! I thought to myself. I see where this is going! They're trying to make this all about the affair!

"That's a very fair question," I said. "You live in a big city. But I do not live in a place where things are conducted in a businesslike fashion. It is a very small town where, for the most part, everything is done with a handshake and a smile. I've had bank signature cards brought to me in the hospital because I was giving birth and couldn't make it to the bank. I have taken loan documents out of the bank and signed them at home. Everything is very casual. So it's very possible that the account was opened without my husband ever even seeing the signature card, much less signing it. Or, Gabby may have presented the signature card to Joey under false pretenses, had him sign it, and then added her name as a secondary signer on the account. Absent the actual signature card, you will never know and neither will I. The bank should have the card on file."

During this entire interview, one thing was clear to me—they were sizing me up to try to determine whether I had any intelligence or whether they could dismiss me as a dumb blonde. I spoke in a manner which was very professional and detailed, using phrases like, "If you'll look in this section, you'll notice...and this is substantiated over here..." By being so professional, I was making it known that I was not about to let them dismiss me as a bimbo.

When I asked, "What other questions do you have for me?" the line of questioning zigzagged all over the place and included inquiries about Hugo's use of bullying and intimidation tactics with me. I had to recall and recount what Hugo had said to me after Drew's death when he said, "If not for Joey, you'd be in prison right now for child endangerment, neglect and manslaughter!"

I explained that I had spent years afraid that, if I angered Hugo, he would find a way to get me sent to prison. Out of fear, I avoided our own dental practice.

When they questioned why I took Hugo's threats seriously, I started to crack, tears streaming down my face. "You seem to have forgotten that I had lost a child and I was grieving during all of this. I was overwhelmed and terrified, and feeling like I was responsible for my son's death. You'll never know what that is like unless you have the unfortunate circumstance of burying a child of your own. I hope that never happens to you. But until and unless it does, you can't tell me you understand what I was going through psychologically! Whether or not it makes sense to you, I did the best I could under abnormal and stressful circumstances."

Special Agent Hartman followed up with questions about whether or not I was satisfied with my lifestyle and implied that I had turned the other cheek in the face of everything going on because I was determined to hang onto the lifestyle being provided to me by Joey.

"My lifestyle certainly was not the focus of my world!" I explained. "You forget I had just buried a child and then, a year later, I lost a pregnancy at twenty-two weeks! You have no idea what I was going through. I was heartbroken and trying to care for my remaining son at home who was still very young. I was giving my entire attention to him because he needed me. If you think life was rosy and I chose to turn the other cheek, you're absolutely wrong! I was terrified of being taken from my child if I pissed off Gabby and Hugo and Hugo chose to arrest me. I lived under incredibly stressful conditions and felt that Gabby and Hugo were emotionally torturing me. I felt like they were trying to break me so that I would either divorce my husband or kill myself. No one deserves to be put through something like this!"

I then turned to Joey and said, "I am sorry if you are offended by hearing this but you should have protected me!"

Suddenly, Special Agent Hartman's demeanor changed and he softened toward me a little. It was as if he had been trying to see if I would fall to pieces if he pushed me hard enough.

The line of questioning turned back to the documents. He asked how I had managed to put the puzzle pieces together and wanted to know whether I was absolutely sure I didn't know anything about the money Gabby had embezzled.

I explained that I had no access to any of the financial documents and reiterated that I intentionally avoided the dental office during that time. Often, if I needed something, I called or I sent Devin in to grab it for me.

"If you had a police officer threatening you with 'Don't piss me off or make trouble for my wife or I'll throw your ass in jail,' you would tend to stay away, too!" I said.

It mattered a great deal to them whether or not I knew about the money Gabby was embezzling, and about the affair. They fired questions at me in such a way that I felt they were taking the same tact Gabby's attorneys would take and cross-examining me to find out what I would say. It was impossible to understand what they were getting at with their questions. They seemed to simply be sizing up me and my credibility to see if they could discredit me.

They couldn't discredit me. I showed them the timeline of when I discovered Gabby's crimes and when I found out about the affair and I had the emails to prove it. I had put all the evidence before our attorney and CPA and let them be the ones to form their own conclusions. Everything I put before them was examined under a microscope and I was happy to have that level of scrutiny. After Gabby had expended so much energy trying to convince everyone that I was unstable, I knew I had to earn my credibility as a sane person and I was happy to do so.

The interview—or should I say interrogation!—concluded abruptly.

When I asked our attorney how they thought it went, I was told, "Oh, it went great! You guys did great! Based on everything I heard, there's no way the case will get dropped. You supplied them with more than enough to go forward, and more than enough to go after

Hugo. The documents speak for themselves on Gabby. It may be a few months before you hear anything, though. They still have to subpoena and review additional records and interview more people..."

I told Joey I would drive him to his car, and then I drove to my sister Jennifer's house in Phoenix where I stayed the night. The following morning, Devin and two of his best friends, Sophie and Joey, along with Joey's mom, Christina—a lifelong, close and trusted friend—met us at the Phoenix airport and we all flew to Texas for the college campus tour.

After everything I had been put through during the interrogation, my son was an absolutely welcome breath of fresh air. And it felt great to get out of town for a few days. I needed a change of scenery.

54

$\mathcal{S}$itting on the plane, I looked over at Devin and was overwhelmed with my love for him. I was reminded that it was my deep and abiding love for my kids that has always driven me to keep our family intact, even when it has meant that I had to endure a level of emotional distress most people can't even fathom. I have an indomitable will that has never been broken and it is my will that enables me to safeguard my family, despite the obstacles.

I also knew that Joey had evolved into a different man than he was prior to 2010. When I left him and he realized that I was no longer willing to go along to get along, it was a turning point for him.

The plane landed and we drove from Dallas to Fort Worth. After touring the campus, we went out to dinner and then made our way to the hotel. The kids were in a suite and Christina and I were sharing a room.

"The state attorney general interview was bad, wasn't it? I could tell just by looking at you," Christina said. "I'm sure this brought up a lot of feelings about Joey and his failure to protect you through everything Gabby put you through. I always knew Gabby was a bad seed! And if I hadn't seen Joey transform into this spiritually evolved man who adores you and the kids, I'd tell you to leave him in a heartbeat for cheating with her!"

"So you don't think I'm a fool for not leaving him?"

"Not at all!" she said. "A fool would discount his transformation!"

"Thanks. I really needed to hear that."

"This is not going to break you," she said. "You'll be okay. You're here with Devin and he's getting ready to start his adult life. This is an exciting time—not the time to focus on the past."

The next morning, we woke up and toured another campus. It was an awesome day and I enjoyed the time with my son. I stopped thinking and worrying about Gabby and Hugo and I didn't think too much about where things were going to go with Joey and me. I put everything out of my mind and trusted my instinctive sense that everything would be okay.

Circumstances are what they are, I thought, *but life is a choice.*

I had learned that when Drew died. I chose not to miss the beauty of living in the moment with Devin. I refused to be one of those people who lost a child and then got forever stuck and engrossed in the daily painful experience of reliving the loss over and over again. That is not living! You can breathe in air every day, and wake up and go to bed, but if you're never experiencing joy, that is not living. I did not want that for myself and I certainly did not want it for my family. I forced myself to focus on the now.

I knew that there had been some sort of divine guidance behind the sequence of events as they'd unfolded. I also knew that, had anything happened out of order, the outcome would have been completely different in terms of the tremendous personal growth that has arisen as a result. Knowing this filled me with a sense of peace. It's not that I stopped experiencing pain but I now knew that I didn't have to worry about outcomes. Everything was divinely ordered and it was my job to trust that—and I did.

Devin fell in love with the campus in Texas and the southern charm of the people and the area. Seeing how happy he was going to be there helped to alleviate my fears about my son leaving for college, and we had the time of our lives together. I laughed and had fun with him and didn't worry about any unresolved circumstances at home. Devin lifted me up in a way I couldn't articulate and didn't even realize until later.

As we were driving home from the airport, Devin said to me, "You know, Mom, I love you and I love Dad. I know that, whatever happens between you and Dad, you're strong enough to face everything. And I think you're the best mom any son could ask for. I'm proud to be your son."

His words touched me so much. I let him know how important he was to me and how much I loved him. And I reassured him that I'd always be there for him when he went away to college.

"I know I'm not the perfect mom," I said, "but I've always tried to be perfect for you."

"Mom, you're the best!" he said. Ever since he was three years old, he had been coming to me and saying things that simultaneously melted my heart and lifted my spirit.

"Don't be mad at me if I come and visit you a lot while you're in college!" I said.

"I won't, Mom. It's okay."

We looked at each other and smiled. Then he grabbed my hand and held it for a couple of minutes.

When we got home, Joey and Hope came out to meet us and Hope jumped into my arms. I held Hope and told her how much I missed her, and then I grabbed Joey and hugged him.

"Did you miss me, too?" he asked.

"I did miss you! And it's good to see you," I said.

We had a long road ahead of us and it would be filled with challenges but, for the moment, I was enjoying being together as a family. That had always trumped whatever conflict or adversity we were facing. Regardless of the circumstances, something undeniably special binds us together.

My husband is a great man with deep flaws and his flaws don't make him any less of a great man. I see his humanity and his struggles and I have my own struggles. Miraculously, I have never been tempted to make his struggles all about me. They are not—they are his demons and his burdens to carry. I never felt that I am responsible or the root cause of his issues.

My ability to maintain this perspective goes back to Drew. When I was told that I had absolutely killed my son and I was a horrible mother, I had to start asking myself some really tough questions: *What is true about myself? What do I believe?*

I looked at the things the world had said—and might say— about the fact that my son died while I was asleep and I separated it from the actual truth of who I am. I questioned myself in a deep way and came to a better understanding of myself and what I am—and am not—responsible for in this lifetime.

I came to the conclusion that I was not responsible for Drew's death. I realized that his journey in life was predestined when he arrived here on earth. No matter what emotions I may have experienced during those moments when I questioned whether or not I was responsible for his death, Drew was only going to be here for a brief moment in time. I had no control over how long he was destined to be here on earth and I will never have that control with my other children, either.

I considered myself blessed and lucky to have such insight and I was absolutely certain that this insight was guided by my little Peter Pan. Any time I am tempted to fall into self-loathing, Drew goes to whatever lengths necessary to help me find my way back.

I sometimes write letters to Neverland. Sometimes these letters are on paper and sometimes they are just in my heart. In my letters and in my daily life, I always talk to Drew as if he's still in the room.

For example, I might say, "Hey, Drew, Dad said this about me falling asleep that night and it's making me feel really badly and I don't know what to think. Please tell me I never harmed you or caused that kind of outcome."

And I would feel him respond, "Oh, Mom, don't be silly! Let's go eat some Bif Raviolays!"

Then I would chuckle and, suddenly, everything felt different. Drew was never going to allow me to think such thoughts about myself. With his help, I worked through a lot of the questions, doubts and self-recrimination that followed his death.

When you lose a child, you can't help but entertain every alternative scenario. You ask yourself, *What if...? What if I had done this differently... or what if I had done that differently?* Thanks to my strong connection with Drew's spirit, I didn't get stuck in the *What if...?* questions. I was able to arrive at the conclusion that I loved my son more than life itself and he knew that and loved me too. Unfortunately, he passed on before me.

I can almost hear him saying, "I won the race, Mama! I beat you to the finish line!" That's how I look at it now.

He is such a wonderful little fella and, one day, I will meet him at the finish line. In the meantime, he is with me in spirit.

Anyway, as I returned from my wonderful trip to Texas with Devin, I discovered that, for the first time in my life, I was in limbo and fine with it. I didn't have all the answers and I didn't need to. I was happy to let life unfold in its own time and its own way. I didn't need to have everything figured out then and there.

This state of mind allowed me to enjoy my husband without putting pressure on him or on myself. I accepted that what had already happened with him and Gabby was over and there was no way to rewrite the past. All we could do was move forward. It made no sense to be angry or go back over past events to try to figure out what went wrong. I had no interest in going backwards, hashing things out, or beating up Joey or myself with an endless string of pointless questions. I wanted to stay focused on what was to come.

Naturally, in the course of running the household and raising our children, little flare-ups and misunderstandings occurred between us. It was during those momentary setbacks that I was triggered and tempted to rehash the past.

Then I would remind myself that I didn't have anything figured out and I didn't need to. There was no set rulebook or manual to govern our particular set of circumstances. Knowing I could write my own manual left a whole lot of room for a myriad of possibilities. Now that I no longer had to look at my husband as a jerk, I was free to get to know him for the person he had become and open my heart and mind to the possibilities.

I had no idea what the future would hold for us. Maybe we would stay together as husband and wife—and maybe we would move on from each other romantically but continue to be co-parents and wonderful friends who love each other. As long as my heart is open, that kind of loving friendship is possible.

I plan to continue to live my life intentionally and to live every day putting forth my best self for both me and my children. I have learned not to expect myself to be further along the road or have definitive answers. I believe that when I have the answers, I will know and be able to utilize that information to move forward in my life.

55

*A*round noontime on a late April day in 2015, I was standing in line at Taco Bell, waiting to order Hope her favorite lemonade. I heard my phone ring.

"I just wanted to let you know…" It was Special Agent Dakota from the state attorney general's office, and her tone was all business. "We have spent several weeks going over all the financials, and I brought all the evidence to my superiors for review. I am sorry, but there simply isn't a strong enough likelihood of conviction. So we have decided to stop the investigation and pass it back to the county attorney's office."

I thought, *What? She can't be serious!*

"Stop the investigation?" I said. "I'm shocked! This doesn't make any sense. Gabby verbally confessed to both our attorney and our accountant by phone. Did you interview the suspects? And what about the witnesses? Gabby even showed our accountant how she had been covering up the embezzlement!"

Special Agent Dakota never said whether they did or did not interview Hugo and Gabby. They interview victims first and interview suspects and witnesses last. That way, they are fully armed with evidence, making it much harder for the suspects and witnesses to get away with lies.

"I'm sorry," she said, "I know this is disappointing but unfortunately it is not my call. My supervisors told me they're going to stop the investigation."

"But I don't understand how this could happen. It doesn't make sense!"

"I know this is not what you want to hear and I'm sorry." There was just a hint of empathy beneath her professional demeanor. "We are not able to move forward. You could, however, pursue a civil case. It seems that the evidence you have gathered more than meets the criteria to initiate a civil suit and I encourage you to do so. Or, you might be able to pursue it through local law enforcement. In any case, we won't be involved."

"So that's it?" I asked. "It just doesn't seem right that the suspects have never been questioned!"

"I am very sorry. Have a good day." She had said what she called to say and that was the end of that.

I was still waiting in the Taco Bell line as I hung up the phone, and I needed to get away from people. I took my daughter outside and we got in the car, and went through the drive-through for her lemonade. As I was pulling out onto the street, I started to cry.

Special Agent Dakota's recommendation that I pursue a civil suit against Gabby and Hugo made me wonder. Was the unspoken subtext that they didn't want to spend the money to investigate and litigate when I could simply sue Gabby in a civil suit? I was incredibly frustrated and that frustration was bringing me to tears.

Hope said to me, "It's okay, Mama. Something good will happen. Please don't be sad." She was ten years old, knew the basics of what had transpired with the crime and watched the aftermath and its effects on our family.

"Mama, when people do bad things to other people," she said, "even if they don't go to prison, they will pay a price. God knows their soul."

Those were pretty wise words coming from a ten year old. Her words were right in line with the principles my husband and I had always tried to impart to our children, and I could hear my own words coming back to me through my daughter.

Hope had been wholeheartedly influenced by attending Catholic School and mass, where she was inundated with messages about morality and God and forgiveness. I, myself, wasn't a Catholic and my husband Joey only became a Catholic later in life. But when it was time for Devin to begin school, we decided without hesitation that we would send our kids to Catholic School.

As we pulled out of the Taco Bell parking lot, I was still crying and Hope was still being her wise little self, and suddenly I thought, *You know what? She's right! I need to let this go.*

I had done everything I could do in order that justice might prevail, and if those in charge of meting out that justice could not or would not enforce it, what could I do? I had no choice but to let it go—or no healthy choice, anyway. It would have been very bad for my physical, emotional and mental health to continue to obsess over the situation.

I decided that I would call Detective Richardson, who had proven himself to be one of the good guys. As it turned out, he had just gotten off the phone with Special Agent Dakota and she had been more forthcoming with him.

Detective Richardson explained to me several things...that the state attorney general's office had never interviewed Gabby and Hugo...that the affair complicated everything...that the fact that Joey couldn't recall enough of the specifics of what he authorized Gabby to do was an exacerbating factor...that the defense could claim that Joey gave the money to Gabby to "try to keep his mistress happy."

"...in short," the detective said, "all of these things make taking it to trial impossible—in their eyes, anyway. Another agency might have a different take on it."

"But she confessed!" I shouted into the phone, unable to contain myself. "I understand the affair could complicate things but..." I continued to throw reasons at Detective Richardson as to why I believed the investigation should not have been abandoned.

"Don't we have any victims' rights in this state?" I asked.

"Yes, you do, and you can file a complaint with the victims' rights advocacy group. And I'll make some phone calls and see if there's anything else that can be done locally. Don't give up hope!"

I thanked him for his time and then I called my attorney, Jack.

Jack was furious and momentarily speechless. "But she confessed to me!" he said. "She confessed! This makes no sense. There must be something bigger going on. If it's political, I can see it. But just saying it's a complicated matter because of the affair…issues of complexity are not grounds for abandoning an investigation! An investigation requires that you interview everyone—the victims, the witnesses and the suspects. That's the definition of an investigation. You don't just interview the victims and stop there. With all the financial documents you brought to them, and her confession, and the emails between her and the accountants where she confessed…it's asinine for them to decide there's not a strong enough likelihood of conviction! This makes no sense."

When all was said and done, the consensus was that there had to be some kind of political motivation behind the decision to end the investigation. Maybe the state attorney general's office was afraid that, with Hugo implicated in the lawsuit, it could lead to the reopening of cases he'd worked on before he retired from the police department. Then there was the fact that it appeared that several different officers on the force had covered up things for Hugo, hiding complaints against him and purging them from his personnel file.

In summation, it would have been a huge tangled mess. We had the police chief on record admitting that he had accepted bribes, gifts and trips from Hugo. We also had him on record admitting that he knew the money to purchase those items came from us. Then there was the fact that Hugo's career advanced each time the police chief accepted a gift or a bribe.

Proceeding with the investigation into Gabby's and Hugo's crimes against us could have potentially meant the overturning of many convictions as well as the end of many careers. There was a lot more at stake than just our personal and professional losses.

Jack said, "Believe me, Melissa, I don't like it and I don't think this is right by any means. But I just don't know at this point what else we can do on the criminal front. We can sue them civilly and maybe that's what we should do!"

I knew the potential problem with a civil suit: it raises questions in the minds of the jurors. They ask themselves, "Why was this not criminally prosecuted? If the defendants really did all these heinous things, why aren't they in jail?" That could raise credibility questions and give jurors reasonable doubt.

In closing, Jack promised to appeal the decision to drop the investigation. "Don't get your hopes up. This has all the earmarks of a political decision that has been made for the so-called greater good."

The news that the state attorney general's office was discontinuing the investigation was such a letdown and I was very upset. It was mind blowing to me that we had what seemed like such an open-and-shut case and yet they were declining to proceed.

No wonder there's so much crime in the world, I thought to myself. *It takes an awful lot for the criminals to get prosecuted!*

The Friday that I got the call from Special Agent Dakota, I returned home from Taco Bell with Hope and decided to wait to mention the phone call to Joey. I was angry but I knew that no good would come from picking a fight. I needed to vent everything to my therapist first and have him help me process my feelings. I also wanted to go to the gym and work off some of my frustrations.

I didn't want to argue with Joey and I didn't want to make him feel badly. When he's in pain, the whole household is in pain. And I knew he already felt badly. Asking someone to feel worse than they already do about an offense they've committed is abusive.   My husband had spent a lot of time trying to redeem himself and I didn't want to take that from him.

The reality was, the state attorney general's decision not to proceed with the case was undoubtedly a complex decision and not entirely Joey's fault. Sure, his actions related to the affair with Gabby played into it, but I also knew that there were probably many other factors that influenced their decision.

After the gym, I went straight to my therapist's office. "I just wanted to talk everything through with you before I did any harm to Joey or to our already injured marriage," I explained to Mike.

"That's probably a good decision."

"Throwing one more stone at Joey isn't going to lead me any closer to knowing the ultimate outcome of my marriage. All I know right now is that I feel so cheated out of this moment of justice!" I said. "And it makes me so mad that Joey's affair with Gabby called his credibility into question and made the state attorney general's office decide not to proceed with the investigation! What makes it even worse is that I've often felt during our marriage that Joey gave his loyalty to Gabby rather than me. So, I wouldn't be surprised if he was breathing a sigh of relief knowing that Gabby won't be tried for her crimes. This will spare both of them the public humiliation! Why does everything always happen like this? It seems like I'm always coming out on the bottom."

Mike allowed me to express what I was thinking and feeling and be upset over it. Then he started challenging me.

"Really, Melissa? Everything always happens like this? *Everything?* You're always coming out on the bottom? Maybe you're winning and you just don't know it!"

"Oh, come on, Mike," I said. "The last thing I want to hear right now is how the sun's going to come up tomorrow! I can't take the sunshine and rainbows talk right now. For today, I need to feel this and be upset about it!"

"Sorry, Melissa. I am not here to help someone feel bad about life. I am here to help you make sense of the challenges. You are choosing to feel your feelings right now and that's fine. But you know that tomorrow will be better and this isn't the end of the world. Life will be fine and you'll be okay. You'll see."

56

*W*hen I got home from my therapy session, I did have a conversation with Joey—a conversation, not an argument. Instead of blaming and shaming him, I kept my words focused on my feelings.

"My heart is heavy," I told my husband, "because I really feel like they should have been held accountable. I am saddened and hurt that it's not going to happen. And yes, your actions with Gabby complicated the investigation. But I also know you did your best in that interview and, if they can't make a case with what we presented to them, I'll let it go."

Joey was honest with me about the fact that he was indeed relieved. He said that he didn't want to upset me by admitting this but the truth was that he didn't want to go through a public trial. Nevertheless, he was willing to pursue a civil suit if that's what I needed to do.

"Melissa, if you really need to continue trying to hold them accountable, we can sue them. At least we'd be forcing them to deal with what they've done. Hiring an attorney will be very expensive but we can out-resource them and tie them up in court."

I realized that, over the previous five years, Gabby had taken up an immense amount of my mental and emotional energy and caused great discord. Knowing that a person has gotten away with this kind of offense against you gnaws away at you. You find that you're angry and you don't even realize it. You have a sharp edge and impatience for the whole human race.

I didn't want to live like that. I knew that to go the route of filing a civil lawsuit would have been to invite another year or two of dealing with Gabby and her husband mentally and emotionally. I would have constantly been thinking about and having feelings about her, her husband, the case, and what they got away with doing to us.

I prefer to enjoy my life, my home and my family, I thought to myself, *and to expend my mental and emotional resources thinking about what my loved ones and I are doing—not Gabby and Hugo.*

Dragging this situation around with me for the previous several years had worn me down to the point where I decided I would rather deal with my disappointment and the pain that resulted from that than deal with Gabby and Hugo for one more minute. I knew that would lead to personal growth as I learned from what Gabby and Hugo did to me and my family.

I made the decision to move out of the mental territory that centers around thoughts of *I'm gonna get her...and she'll be held accountable...and justice will be served.*

I was perfectly prepared to move on and put the whole mess behind me. From time to time, however, I would get wind of some new avenue that might bring us the satisfaction we so longed for and deserved, and I'd get my hopes up all over again.

Within a few days of that distressing phone call from Special Agent Dakota, I had a dream in which bright lights began to appear on a black background like little dots of color on a canvas. As the lights danced around, some began to spiral off into different directions. I began to identify these segments of light against this black backdrop as being my soul. I had the dawning awareness that the light—my soul—is illuminated by divine love.

I posed questions to this light source, aware that I was essentially talking to myself. *Why do you struggle?* I asked myself.

As if in response, the lights rearranged into a pattern that felt like physical trembling. The answer came to me: *Because I'm still afraid.*

Go deeper. There's something beneath the fear that you're not quite seeing.

Then it came to me. I remembered being a very young girl, crying in pain, and holding my hands up. I was fearful of my environment and reaching my hands up to someone, hoping they would pick me up and hold me. I was afraid, in pain and wailing at the top of my lungs because I needed someone to pick me up.

The light jumped across the black background and spiraled into the shape of a conch shell. As I followed its path, I noticed that it touched the sides of this shell-like pattern, and each time it touched, it caused a bright illumination. I recognized in that moment that I was moving through time, being carried through childhood, through the pain of my mother being very sick and the uncertainty of whether or not she would ever get well.

Then the pattern shifted and I recognized the pain and mourning associated with my difficult relationship with my father and my longing for closeness with him.

Am I dying? I wondered in the dream. *Is that why I can see my soul and my life in front of me?*

"No, Mama!" It was Drew, talking to me. "It's so you will heal and you won't cry anymore. I love you so much, I always want to be with you and you can't feel me when you're sad."

When I awoke from the dream, I understood that I had to stop running from the pain. I had spent a lifetime avoiding painful outcomes and, as a result, I had created a painful existence! I knew that I had to embrace whatever pain I had not yet faced and welcome it.

As I fully awoke from the dream, I realized I had been given a tremendous gift and the knowledge that I could finally help myself truly live instead of merely existing. I had been craving a full, robust life for as long as I could remember—but pain had become my constant companion and it was familiar to me.

My constant companion had become my jailer but I now had everything I needed to get out. Until I had that dream, I didn't know how to unlock the door of my proverbial cell. Now I knew that embracing the pain would allow me to move to wherever I needed to be. I would grow and learn and evolve.

Perhaps it is my evolution that I've longed for the most—to be different, better, happy, *present.* To stop looking back at the things that hurt me. To resolve things and settle them once and for all so I can live my life *now*. And to feel the love that lives within me but has been so overshadowed by all this pain.

One day, my attorney, Jack, called and said, "A political decision like this often leaves the victims in a very unsatisfied position. But I still believe there will be a way for you to see Gabby and Hugo interviewed, at the very least. Victims are entitled to have any crime investigated fully, and full investigation requires interviewing not only the victims but the suspects. That's what I am going to continue to push for—a full investigation by the county attorney's office. And it's up to them if they conclude at the end of it that there was no crime and they are not going to move forward with prosecution. At least Gabby and Hugo will have to go in and talk about it. Their testimony will then be on record and you can use that in a civil matter."

As of the date of this writing, the case remains with the county attorney's office. I have sent to them eight to ten banker's boxes filled with financial documents and related documents. Once they review the financial documents, they will issue a report and, from that point, the next step will be to interview the witnesses—the people Gabby confessed to, including my attorney and accountants. That should give them enough corroborating statements to warrant interviewing Gabby and Hugo.

As I wait to see how this is going to unfold, I am starting this whole new chapter of my life. There are so many aspects of my life over which I have lost control, including, to name a few, the FBI, the state attorney general's investigation, the ongoing county attorney's investigation and whether or not Gabby and Hugo are ever prosecuted for their crimes against our family.

I have often imagined myself as a woman riding on horseback down a long stretch of beach, holding tightly to the reins because I didn't trust that, if I let go, I would be okay. Now, I am galloping down a beach toward the horizon as soft, picturesque waves are crashing against the sand and a breeze is blowing in my hair. The horse is steady and sure beneath me and I am ready to embrace my destiny. It is possible that one of the horse's hooves will hit a pebble in the sand and he'll stumble but, for this moment, I am liberated, free and light as air. The heaviness has been lifted and I love this feeling—it's transformative. I have left all possibilities open and closed the door on nothing and it's the best feeling in the world.

Growing up with so much trauma and dysfunction, my sense of normalcy was skewed. I took that off kilter sense of what is and is not normal into my adult life and made decisions based upon it. As the years passed during my marriage, and as I became a mother to my children and they grew and I grew, I slowly became healthier.

Along with that improved mental and emotional health, I began to look differently at certain elements in my marriage that I had considered normal and tolerable. And I started to question what was truly normal and acceptable. I looked around at the relationships of others, many of which seemed healthier than mine, and I asked myself what I really needed, and truly felt, and was really willing to accept and tolerate.

This process of redefining what I want, feel, think, and am willing to accept, as well as what I need to thrive, has been very difficult. Joey and I have both had to dig deeper than we ever have before and ask ourselves and ask each other what we need and are willing to give to each other, where our boundaries lie, and what we are unable and unwilling to give. It is a difficult and painful and challenging process to redefine our relationship and it is anyone's guess where we will find ourselves.

I don't know whether Joey and I will remain married or I will end up as a single mother. What I do know for sure as I stand at this crossroads is that the journey is the important thing. I look at the forks in the road and ask myself which direction I will take as an individual and we will take as a couple, and I know that this honest and authentic and heartfelt process will serve both of us well, regardless of where we end up.

Will we remain husband and wife, within newer, healthier parameters, and find a new beginning for ourselves and our marriage? Or will we discover that we can't meet each other's deepest and most authentic and healthiest needs and decide to part as the best of friends?

Only God knows the answers.

Afterword

*A*fter Drew was gone, there was one particular moment when I was sitting on the sofa in the living room, feeling blue. I wasn't thinking of anything in particular. I was just staring into space, daydreaming. Suddenly, I felt my son very close to me.

"Hey, Drew," I said. "How are you? Gosh, I miss you and love you…"

A beautiful image of a tree came forward and strung from the tree was a tire swing—with Drew sitting on it. I walked toward him and he saw me and hopped off the swing. He ran toward me with his arms outstretched and we hugged. I was crying. I could physically feel him in my arms. My arms were crossed like he was inside them in an embrace and I was rocking him back and forth.

"Please don't be sad, Mommy. Let's go get burgers and fries!"

It reminded me of the day of Drew's preschool birdhouse project, and the car ride on the way home, when he said, "Mama? Jesus wants us to get burgers and fries. He likes families to eat burgers and fries!"

As he walked away from me, I watched him walk and then run toward a big tubular slide.

"Okay," I said. "I'll meet you there!"

I don't doubt for a minute that he was there too. It was real and I felt the weight of him. The words weren't audible but he was speaking to my spirit and I knew he was okay.

This vision or encounter reminded me that Drew's soul was very much alive. Of course, this didn't make me stop missing him or mourning him, but I didn't ache quite as much over wondering whether or not he was okay. In that moment, I knew that he knew that I loved him and thought of him.

For a very long time, I struggled with the feeling that I had fallen short of my potential in life and failed to accomplish much. Since Drew's passing, I often get the feeling he is trying to tell me, "Mommy, you can do anything!"

I often see an image of myself hugging people and connecting and talking with them in a loving way. At those times, it's as if my darling son is sitting on my shoulder saying, "See, Mommy? See how loving you are?"

As much as I thought I was Drew's mother and teacher, I have come to wonder if he was given to me to help me learn to love myself so that I could in turn love others. The immense childhood trauma I endured caused me to be very closed off and reluctant to let anyone close enough to hurt me. But, with my little angel on my shoulder, I have been able to see myself through different eyes.

When I woke up on the morning of Drew's death, I began looking for him. As the minutes passed with me unable to find him, I became more and more frantic and I panicked. I just couldn't find him. That's when I got the sensation that he grabbed hold of my hand and whispered, "Mommy, I'm right here!"

"No, no! I'm going to find you!" I said.

"But, Mommy, I'm RIGHT HERE!"

I couldn't find him because I was looking for him in his physical form. My son is no longer in physical form but he is very much alive. He is now a little traveler, a spiritual Peter Pan, on a grand adventure that will go on forever. And someday I will join him in Neverland.

In the moment we make our transition from this life, we are beckoned by joy and wonderment and it is those things that allow us to transition joyfully into the next life. If an ominous, blinding white light was shone into our eyes, it wouldn't be very inviting. I think of it like being at a surprise party, and suddenly someone whips your blindfold off and everyone jumps out and says "Surprise!" They were there the whole time—you just couldn't see them.

Pondering life and the meaning of life after life, I have always felt guided by my grandmother—my no-nonsense grandmother who paid for my first semester at college. I always picture her sitting at her celestial coffee table in her nightgown, with a cigarette in one hand and a cup of perfectly brewed coffee in the other. I know she'll be one of the first people I will see when I make my transition. And I know that, when we're reunited, the feeling will be a return to love, reminiscent of being gathered around the Thanksgiving dinner table as a child.

Author's Note

*I*t is my greatest hope that you, the reader, will pause and consider that life is a series of moments and contained within those moments are actions that lead to consequences we can't always anticipate in advance.

There is a certain sense of responsibility I will always feel over my son's death. I cannot change that. I fell asleep and I lost my child. I would give anything if I could go back to those pre-dawn hours on the day Drew died, and keep from falling asleep during the fifteen or twenty minutes it took him to make his way out of the house and down to the irrigation canal. Those fifteen or twenty critical minutes changed my life forever.

I have wished, prayed and begged God for a do-over. Sadly, there are times in life when a do-over is beyond our reach. Eventually I came to realize that I had to make the choice to live again. In order to live again, I had to stop turning away from my pain. I had to embrace it. In so doing, it became my greatest teacher and ultimately my liberator.

I welcomed the heaviness of my sorrow. I opened myself up to feel the full effect of its crippling grip around my heart, and I became aware of how it kept me from finding the joy I so desperately desired. That awareness gave me hope and my hope led to the discovery that I was blessed beyond anything that I could have ever imagined.

I discovered the depths of my compassion and empathy for others as well as myself. I began to see myself through kinder eyes. I came to understand that my life is a series of moments and contained within those moments are actions with sometimes unintended and tragic consequences. But the final outcome is mine to choose.

I choose love. I choose forgiveness. I choose to live.

About the Author

*M*elissa Hull Gallemore is an intuitive and healing arts practitioner and inspirational speaker who shares her message worldwide. She uses her own life experiences to coach and mentor others through the bereavement process.

The author believes that every person is given a life filled with varying degrees of pain or trauma. "That pain or trauma can either be embraced or rejected," she says. "And this is what I know to be true: the choice to embrace and learn from your pain is the harder choice but it is also where the wisdom of life takes hold."

Melissa is a proud mother of five wonderful children, one of whom now lives in Neverland. When she isn't socializing with friends and loved ones, she enjoys working out and painting.

And now, a few words from Devin...

When I think of my big brother, Drew, I remember being about three and a half years old, standing on the bank of the irrigation canal, looking for him. The next memory I have of him is when everyone was huddled around the interment site and we were placing him inside the tomb. I remember my mom crying and I remember feeling confused.

Because I was so little when Drew passed on, I have very few memories of him, but the memories I do have are very clear. I remember going to Burger King with Drew and Mom, and while Drew and I were playing in the play house, he took off his pants and went down the slide. When Mom realized he had his pants off, she had to climb into the play house and get his pants. These were crazy shenanigans typical of Drew and they made me laugh.

From what I remember and what I've been told, my brother was such a little character. And he could be ornery. We had a chicken coop inside our house with a little latch on top and it had been turned into a piece of furniture—a table. Drew liked to lock me in there. I couldn't figure out how to get out and Drew would let me sit in there until Mom heard me screaming and came and got me out. For me, it was upsetting but, to Drew, it was the funniest thing ever.

I also heard the story of how Drew and I decided we wanted to repaint the house and started painting part of a brick wall—and each other.

It took me a long time to process my brother's death. The fact that I had lost my big brother didn't really sink in until my junior year of high school. That's when it hit me, *Wow...if he had lived, Drew would have been a senior and we would have been in school together.*

I have always been real quiet about what I'm going through. I don't like people to know I'm upset. I prefer to internalize my emotions and deal with them on my own. And I like to process my emotions by writing. Here are some poems I've written about my brother. I wrote these poems from the perspective of different family members...

A Living Hope
No one told us how long we had,
To live a life with our child.
His life was short and ended bad,
With his beautiful face defiled.

I never said my last goodbye,
To my son who wandered away.
He walked beneath the morning sky,
'Til sacred wings swept him away.

Here's his tale told by us all,
From Daddy, Mommy, Your brother and sister.
But you will come and answer the call,
And renew to this family a sacred hope.

Mom

My son, he was born today.
I can see him now.
My beautiful son whom I waited to see,
Is here with me now.

"Bless this day, bless this day!
Bless this family ever more!"
A handsome boy I am blessed to have
With brown hair and brown eyes.
He resembles his father
Much more than me.

Time passed, and then we could leave,
So I took my son in my arms and left that room.
I took my son home today,
To our house in the desert.
A place where he can make memories
A place for him to call home.

When he grows he can explore,
And go on adventures and more.
But at the end of each day,
He will come back ready for bed.

I'll tuck him in every night,
When it's time for him to sleep.
I'll make sure he is nestled in his crib,
Near his parents who hold him so close, so dear.

"I love you, my beautiful son.
You are my angel, my precious joy."

I can't wait to watch him grow,
And see him turn into a good man.
He will grow up and be strong,
But still a sweet boy like he is now.

The years will fly, I know,
But my boy will never go too far.
My son will be the boy,
That I always dreamed him to be.
He will come home and see his mom,
And remember all the great memories.
For I will be the best mom for my son,
My beautiful baby boy.

Dad
The son I love, my boy of one,
Now has a brother, my new son.
He was born early this night,
But he's ok, he is healthy, he is fine.

So much like me he looks,
Except his nose, that's his mom's.
This new boy of ours will be
The best brother for our oldest son.

"Welcome to the world,
Welcome to life, welcome to your family!
Come home to your brother now,
Come home and go play!"

We took him home
We watched him grow.
And watched him play
All day with his brother.
We watch them play,
for hours on end.
They play all day,
They play all night.

But when the sun
Finally fades away,
My boys know
It's time for goodnight.
I tuck them in
Nice and tight.
So they can sleep
Sleep all night.
I check on them as they sleep,
To make sure they are always there.

New days will come,
And things will change.
Our time in this home,
Is coming to an end.
Soon we must leave this house,
To a new one across town.
A new place where we can live,
A place where we will thrive.

This new oasis in the fields,
Is a home away from it all.
A place for us to feel safe,
A place for us to play.
But despite all the things to see,
It means little to me.
Because my family is what matters,
What means the world to me.

Brother
My brother is mean,
My brother is fun.
My brother locks me up,
In the box with all the bars.
He leaves me there for a long time,
Until Mommy comes and gets me out.

Then she gets mad and yells at him,
And I just laugh and have fun.
We eat ice cream while in underpants,
And play dinosaurs and Power Rangers too.
We run around the hall all the time,
And paint the walls for Mom.
But she gets mad, and then she laughs,
And tells us she loves us so much.

Daddy lets us ride Tony the Pony,
Until one of us is scared and cries.
He lets us play outside,
And lets us roll around in the mud.

He is my brother,
And he's really mean.
He's also my best friend,
And we laugh a lot.
I love him so much because
He is the best big brother for me.
I love my big brother,
I love him very much.

Mom

I woke up this morning,
And went to your bed.
But when I peeked in,
There was no seeing you.
I looked by the TV and the kitchen,
Your usual spots.
But I couldn't find you,
You were gone.

"My God, My God, where is he,
where is my son?"

I woke up your father,
Your brother too.
And we looked all over,
Searching for you.
Inside and outside we looked,
Still no sign of you.

We called the police,
We said you were gone.
They sent officers, dogs, and more,
Just to find my sweet boy.

We searched and searched,
We searched the whole day away.
Hours seemed to pass,
And still we couldn't find you.
We cried and we prayed,
We looked for an answer but we knew,
The worst was happening,
The worst had come.

"Please Jesus, help us find our son!
It's too soon, too soon for his life to be done!"

Minutes later they found a sign,
Of a boy lying in the levee.
Our cry was heard,
Our prayer was answered.

But not all the prayers,
You pray are answered.
In the way you hope,
The way you want.

They found you lying there,
Swollen and blue.
From the moment we heard,
We couldn't believe it, but we knew.
The worst had happened,
The worst had come.

Brother
Where is my brother?
Why won't he come home?
I want to play with my brother,
I want to have some fun.

I looked all over for you,
All around the house.
We even went outside,
And looked in the desert for you.
Why won't you come home?
I just want to play with you.

But Mommy and Daddy tell me
That you've gone somewhere far away.
They tell me that I will be alone,
Because you won't be coming home.

I cried, I cried a lot
Because I want you here.
Want you by my side
So we can play today.

Mommy and Daddy took me to a place,
And we saw you asleep in a bed.
"Look! Look! There he is!
He's asleep over in that bed!"

Daddy said "Shh! Don't wake him up!
He's asleep, let him sleep for a while."

All of our family is here,
Here to watch you sleep.
People said things about you,
And a lot of people cried.

"Why are they crying, mommy?
They'll wake him up!"

"Because he's going away
And he's not coming back."

We carried you outside,
And walked along the path.
I held you in the bed,
And you still were asleep.

We walked you really far,
Until my feet began to hurt.
We went by a wall with names,
Hey, I see your name too!

We put you down,
By that spot.
By that wall,
Where your name was.
A man in dark clothes spoke for minute,
He spoke about you.

Then Daddy told me that it was time,
Time for me to say goodbye.
He said one day I will see you again,
But I don't understand.

"Why won't I see him?
Where is he going?"
Mommy said, "He is leaving,
Going to a new land."

They put you in the wall,
And shut it with a big rock.
Then we stood there,
Stood there for a while.

We walked away,
And it was silent.
This was it,
My last goodbye.

Sister
I like talking to you,
You make me laugh a lot.
It's fun to listen to you talk
About your adventures and more.

Momma saw me
Sitting on the carpet.
She saw me talking
But she didn't see you.

She asked me,
"Who are you talking to, sweetie?"
And then I pointed
Right at you.

"I'm talking to him, mommy,
To my older brother!"

Then she looked funny,
And her eyes got wide.
"Who, sweetie?
No one is there."

"Yes, mommy, look!
He's sitting right there!"

She looked where you sat,
And then she smiled.
"Tell him I miss him
And that I love him."
Then she walked away,
And left us alone again.

I like talking to you,
You make me laugh.
I wish you could stay
For a little bit longer.
But if it's time to go
Then it's time to go.
But maybe next time,
You can talk to Mommy?
Instead of only me.

Dad
My son, my boy of four,
Was gone, not living anymore.
"WHY, WHY MY SON?
WHY MUST HIS LIFE BE DONE?"

We cried,
We prayed,
Asking and praying for God,
To grant us a miracle, and save our son.
But he consumed too much of the wave,
And angelic wings swept him away.

We went to see him,
But they wouldn't let us near.
They told us there was nothing,
Nothing they could do to save him.

They took him away,
Took him to the morgue.
When they finally finished,
We were let in to see our son.
So still, so calm
He seemed to be.

I didn't want to believe
That he wasn't with us.
He looked so calm,
I thought he was asleep.

With one last attempt,
I called upon your name.
"Son, please come back,
come back to your dad.
Mom, your brother, and I miss you,
We want you home."

We waited for his reply,
We waited for him to move.
We waited for a while,
As long as we could.
We stayed longer
Longer than we should.

I wish I could have saved you,
I wish it were me.
Because no parent has the right,
To bury a child.

I wish that you were still here,
I wish this wasn't the last goodbye.
But all things serve a purpose,
All things are meant to be.
Even things as terrible as this,
Serve some kind of purpose.

You will always be in my heart,
You won't ever be far.
Son, we all love you,
We all miss you.
"I love you,
My beautiful son."

Mom

It's been four years,
Four years since that day.
Four years since he was washed away,
Swept to Holy shores.

But despite the pain that we have felt,
The pain I feel I have dealt.
New life has found its way
Into our life, on this blessed day.

My daughter is born,
A sister to my boys.
She's the answer to our prayers,
The answer we have needed.
She brought us hope,
For a better future.

We will always remember,
And keep you in our hearts.
This girl will never know you,
But she will learn about you.
She will care about you,
Just like we all do.
We love you.

CPSIA information can be obtained
at www.ICGtesting.com
Printed in the USA
LVOW10*2314240817
546259LV00001B/1/P